grab
a
pencil nº 3

by Harold H. Hart

AN A&W VISUAL LIBRARY BOOK
PUBLISHED BY
A&W PUBLISHERS, INC.
95 MADISON AVENUE
NEW YORK, NY 10016

MANUFACTURED IN THE UNITED STATES OF AMERICA

1 2 3 4 5 6 7 8 9 10

LIBRARY OF CONGRESS CARD NO. 81-69524

ISBN 0-89104-282-2

CONTENTS

WORD GAMES

MAZES

BLANKIES

HILARIOUS HEADLINES

THREEZIES

HUMOROUS POETRY

FUNNY STORIES

PUZZLES AND CONUNDRUMS

QUIZZES

ALFABITS

CRYPTOGRAMS

ACROSS-TICS

TEST YOUR PERSONALITY

CROSSWORD PUZZLES

FUNNY ADS

DIAMONDS

GRAB A PENCIL NO. 3

THE SILVER GAME

Below, you will find 25 expressions, phrases, or names. Each one of these should suggest to you another expression which contains the word SILVER. For example: A *small shiny insect which damages books* is a SILVER*fish*.

A score of 13 is average; 15 is good; 17 is excellent; and 21 is brilliant.

Answers on page 328

1. Born to exceptionally rich parents _____
2. Suburb of Washington, D.C. _____
3. Cry of the Lone Ranger _____
4. Treasure Island buccaneer _____
5. Proverbial sign of hope _____
6. What Wm. Jennings Bryan advocated in his "Cross of Gold" speech _____
7. Eloquent _____
8. Famous children's novel by M. M. Dodge _____
9. Tear-jerker song bemoaning old age _____
10. Play by Sidney Howard about mother-fixation _____
11. Motion pictures _____
12. Knives, forks, and spoons _____
13. Well-known comedian _____
14. Metalworker _____
15. Anti-war play by Sean O'Casey _____
16. Not Sterling _____
17. Galsworthy play about social injustice _____
18. An artificial fly used in fishing _____
19. Top of a round of beef _____
20. Congressional award for gallantry in action in any war _____
21. Nickname for Colorado _____
22. Mercury _____
23. Aphorism about the merits of silence _____
24. One of the flowers in Mistress Mary's garden _____
25. T. B. Costain's biblical novel _____

NAME THE BEAST

Each of the 24 phrases below should suggest a common expression which characterizes a human in terms of something in the animal world. For example: *A modern-music fan* has been dubbed *a jazz*-HOUND; and *a diligent worker* is called *a busy* BEE.

A score of 16 is good; 19 is excellent; and 22 is extraordinary.

Answers on page 328

1. A solo adventurer _____
2. A saloon habitué _____
3. An enthusiastic doer _____
4. An usurious money lender _____
5. A ne'er-do-well easy-chair frequenter _____
6. A bon vivant _____
7. A chronically unpleasant visage _____
8. An inconsiderate driver _____
9. A dawn-rising go-getter _____
10. Sacrosanct person immune to criticism _____
11. A jazz-dancing addict _____
12. A rejected legislator _____
13. An undersized individual _____
14. A betrayer of criminals _____
15. A shapely young miss _____
16. A family disgracer _____
17. An incessant laborer _____
18. A dolt; a dope _____
19. A nocturnal reveler _____
20. One who hasn't a chance _____
21. A reporter _____
22. An auto mechanic _____
23. A drawing room bigwig _____
24. An abnormally timorous individual _____

FAMOUS PAIRS

Following, you will find a list of 97 names or words, each of which is but half the story. You've met these couples on television, in the movies, on the stage, on the radio, in literature, in conversation.

Your job is to supply the name or word which is invariably linked with the half presented here. The number of letters in the missing word is the same as the number of dashes opposite the given word.

A score of 60 is average: 66 is good; 77 is very good; 84 is excellent; and 92 entitles you to a brown derby.

Answers on page 328

1. ADAM and _ _ _
2. ROMEO and _ _ _ _ _ _
3. MUTT and _ _ _ _
4. PUNCH and _ _ _ _
5. JACK and _ _ _ _
6. ASSAULT and _ _ _ _ _ _ _
7. CAIN and _ _ _ _
8. OZZIE and _ _ _ _ _ _ _
9. CURDS and _ _ _ _
10. DAMON and _ _ _ _ _ _
11. BURNS and _ _ _ _ _
12. LAUREL and _ _ _ _ _
13. TROILUS and _ _ _ _ _ _ _
14. ALPHA and _ _ _ _ _
15. PROCTOR and _ _ _ _ _ _
16. LUCY and _ _ _ _
17. WARP and _ _ _ _
18. JUDGE and _ _ _ _
19. HEARTS and _ _ _ _ _ _
20. SAMSON and _ _ _ _ _ _
21. BALL and _ _ _ _ _
22. HALF and _ _ _ _ _
23. JOHN SMITH and _ _ _ _ _ _ _ _ _
24. WILLIAM and _ _ _ _
25. LANCELOT and _ _ _ _ _ _ _ _

14

26. SACCO   and _ _ _ _ _ _ _ _

27. BOW   and _ _ _ _ _

28. TWEEDLEDUM   and _ _ _ _ _ _ _ _ _ _

29. AMOS   and _ _ _ _

30. FLORA   and _ _ _ _ _

31. POPEYE   and _ _ _ _ _ _ _ _ _

32. LOCK   and _ _ _

33. ANTONY   and _ _ _ _ _ _ _

34. PIERROT   and _ _ _ _ _ _ _ _

35. ALPHONSE   and _ _ _ _ _ _

36. SOUND   and _ _ _ _

37. FERDINAND   and _ _ _ _ _ _ _

38. RODGERS   and _ _ _ _ _ _ _ _ _ _ _

39. FLOTSAM   and _ _ _ _ _ _

40. CUPID   and _ _ _ _ _

41. SIMON   and _ _ _ _ _ _ _

42. TOM   and _ _ _ _ _

43. GILBERT   and _ _ _ _ _ _ _

44. VENUS   and _ _ _ _ _ _

45. FISH   and _ _ _ _ _

46. HÉLOÏSE   and _ _ _ _ _ _ _

47. DAEDALUS   and _ _ _ _ _ _

48. HAIL   and _ _ _ _ _ _ _

49. ROMULUS   and _ _ _ _ _

50. LIGGETT   and _ _ _ _ _ _

51. JONATHAN   and _ _ _ _ _

52. HUE   and _ _ _

53. EVANGELINE   and _ _ _ _ _ _ _

54. HANSEL   and _ _ _ _ _ _

55. BERGEN   and _ _ _ _ _ _ _ _

56. CASTOR   and _ _ _ _ _ _

57. STRESS   and _ _ _ _ _

58. JOHN ALDEN   and _ _ _ _ _ _ _ _ _

59. ORPHEUS   and _ _ _ _ _ _ _

60. HILL   and _ _ _ _

61. BEAUMONT   and _ _ _ _ _ _ _

62. LUNT   and _ _ _ _ _ _ _ _

63. BED   and _ _ _ _ _

64. AUCASSIN   and _ _ _ _ _ _ _ _ _

65. JACOB   and _ _ _ _ _ _

66. MASON   and _ _ _ _ _ _

67. HARLEQUIN   and _ _ _ _ _ _ _ _

68. BIB   and _ _ _ _ _ _

69. KISS   and _ _ _ _

70. DANTE   and _ _ _ _ _ _ _ _

71. STORM   and _ _ _ _ _ _

72. PELLEAS   and _ _ _ _ _ _ _ _ _

73. FRANKIE   and _ _ _ _ _ _

74. ABBOTT   and _ _ _ _ _ _ _

75. STOCKS   and _ _ _ _ _ _

76. CHECKS   and _ _ _ _ _ _ _

77. JOHNSON   and _ _ _ _ _ _ _

78. TRISTAN   and _ _ _ _ _

79. PYRAMUS   and _ _ _ _ _ _

80. SOHRAB   and _ _ _ _ _ _

81. BENCH   and _ _ _

82. SCOTCH   and _ _ _ _

83. CHAPTER   and _ _ _ _ _

84. DAPHNIS   and _ _ _ _ _

85. CALM   and _ _ _ _ _ _ _ _

86. LEWIS   and _ _ _ _ _

87. PAOLO   and _ _ _ _ _ _ _ _

88. EBB   and _ _ _ _ _

89. PETRARCH   and _ _ _ _ _

90. SCYLLA   and _ _ _ _ _ _ _ _

91. NIP   and _ _ _ _

92. WILL   and _ _ _ _ _ _ _

93. ARCHY   and _ _ _ _ _ _ _

94. MARQUETTE   and _ _ _ _ _ _

95. POMP   and _ _ _ _ _ _ _ _ _ _

96. ROOT   and _ _ _ _ _ _

97. PYGMALION   and _ _ _ _ _ _

TWO OF A KIND

The English language is positively cruel when it comes to spelling its plurals. Even words that rhyme are often pluralized differently without any reason. Here is a list of 46 singular nouns. You score 2 points for each correct plural.

A score of 62 is passing; 78 puts you near the head of the class; and 86 is really exceptional.

Answers on page 328

1. MOUSE _____

2. OX _____

3. ECHO _____

4. MARY _____

5. CHATEAU _____

6. ALTO _____

7. EMBRYO _____

8. TALISMAN _____

9. MOSQUITO _____

10. TAXI _____

11. IT _____

12. SHEAF _____

13. EMPHASIS _____

14. VETO _____

15. EMBARGO _____

16. AXIS _____

17. GENUS _____

18. OWL _____

19. BISON _____

20. MADAME _____

21. OPUS _____

22. MYSELF _____

23. LARVA _____

24. ALIBI _____

25. DATUM _____

26. DIAGNOSIS _____

27. GALLOWS _____

28. RESIDUUM _____

29. BATTLE ROYAL _____

30. TESTATRIX _____

31. INSPECTOR GENERAL _____

32. SERGEANT MAJOR _____

33. NOTARY PUBLIC _____

34. OTTOMAN _____

35. IMPETUS _____

36. SPECIES _____

37. VALLEY _____

38. ARMFUL _____

39. LULLABY _____

40. GROSS _____

41. TITMOUSE _____

42. MAN-OF-WAR _____

43. REINDEER _____

44. MONGOOSE _____

45. STIMULUS _____

46. CRITERION _____

THE LITERARY ZOO

The richness of the English language and its genius for particularization are no better demonstrated than in this quiz. It's all about animals and the words we use to talk and write about them. What is required, in each instance, is the *exact* word. There *is* an exact word. Don't let the stiffness of the requirement frighten you, or make you doubt your answer merely because it's too simple.

A score of 60 is good, 76 is excellent, and 87 exceptional. If you score over 94, you can tell the world. If you get 100, don't tell anybody. Nobody will believe you!

Answers on page 329

MALE, PLEASE!

1. Cow _____
2. Hen _____
3. Goose _____
4. Doe _____
5. Duck _____
6. Sow _____

That was fairly easy, but FANCY THE FEMALE!

7. Tiger _____
8. Ram _____
9. Stallion _____
10. Stag _____
11. Fox _____

And now let us CONSIDER THE YOUNG!

12. Bear _____
13. Sheep _____
14. Duck _____
15. Frog _____
16. Swan _____
17. Chicken _____
18. Hen _____
19. Horse _____
20. Mare _____
21. Swine _____
22. Deer _____
23. Elephant _____
24. Cat _____
25. Oyster _____

26. Seal   _____

27. Goose   _____

28. Bull   _____

29. Cow   _____

30. Cod   _____

31. Lion   _____

And what do you call THE SOUNDS THEY MAKE?

32. Cats   _____

33. Lions   _____

34. Pigs   _____

35. Hogs   _____

36. Sheep   _____

37. Stags   _____

38. Bulls   _____

39. Cows   _____

40. Pheasants   _____

41. Ducks   _____

42. Wolves   _____

43. Crows   _____

44. Snakes   _____

45. Eagles   _____

46. Bitterns   _____

47. Donkeys   _____

48. Geese   _____

49. Wild geese   _____

50. Hens   _____

51. Cocks   _____

52. Magpies   _____

53. Frogs   _____

54. Doves   _____

55. Sparrows   _____

56. Goats   _____

57. Elephants   _____

58. Turkeys   _____

59. Wild turkeys   _____

60. Owls   _____

61. Bees   _____

62. Beetles   _____

63. Mice   _____

64. Horses   _____

65. Blackbirds   _____

66. Snipe   _____

67. Monkeys   _____

And now, can you tell what we call CERTAIN GROUPS OF ANIMALS?

68. A _____ of sheep.

69. A _____ of cattle.

70. A _____ of grouse.

71. A _____ of lions.

72. A _____ of wolves.

73. A _____ of pheasants.

74. A _____ of snipe.

75. A _____ of fish.

76. A _____ of ants.

77. A _____ of quail.

78. A _____ of partridge.

79. A _____ of geese.

80. A _____ of bears.

81. A _____ of bees.

82. A _____ of whales.

83. A _____ of roes.

84. A _____ of elephants.

85. A _____ of peacocks.

And to shelter them, WE BUILD:

86. A _____ for dogs.

87. A _____ for chickens.

88. A _____ for sheep.

89. A _____ for rabbits.

90. A _____ for cows.

91. A _____ for pigeons.

92. A _____ for pigs.

93. A _____ for fish.

While we call THEIR NATURAL HOMES:

94. A lion's _____

95. A beaver's _____

96. An eagle's _____

97. A rabbit's _____

98. A penguin's _____

99. A rat's _____

100. A bee's _____

20

THAT FOREIGN FLAVOR

Following, you'll find a potpourri of foreign phrases that are a la mode in English. You have met each of these 58 well-known terms and expressions in conversation or in literature. Can you translate them?

A score of 25 is fair; 32 is good; 40 is excellent; and 47 is exceptional.

Answers on page 329

1. Sang-froid _____

2. Ex libris _____

3. Eureka _____

4. Cum laude _____

5. Mal de mer _____

6. Persona non grata _____

7. Weltschmerz _____

8. Caveat emptor _____

9. Amour-propre _____

10. Coup de grâce _____

11. Skoal _____

12. Andante _____

13. Mirabile dictu _____

14. Ultra vires _____

15. Demi-monde _____

16. Ipso facto _____

17. Lèse-majesté _____

18. Kibitzer _____

19. Tête-à-tête _____

20. Non compos mentis _____

21. Hoi polloi _____

22. Chile con carne _____

23. Noblesse oblige _____

24. Alter ego _____

25. Cause célèbre _____

26. Intermezzo _____

27. Cherchez la femme _____

28. Sine qua non _____

29. Casus belli _____

30. Requiescat in pace _____

31. Enfant terrible _____

32. De rigueur _____

33. Schlemiel _____

34. Mutatis mutandis _____

35. Hors de combat _____

36. Deus ex machina _____

37. Ex post facto _____

38. Bête noire _____

39. O tempora! O mores! _____

40. Laissez-faire _____

41. Honi soit qui mal y pense _____

42. E pluribus unum _____

43. Table d'hôte _____

44. Demi-tasse _____

45. Gesundheit _____

46. Tovarisch _____

47. Wanderlust _____

48. Savoir-faire _____

49. Per se _____

50. Prosit _____

51. Décolleté _____

52. Répondez, s'il vous plaît _____

53. Quid pro quo _____

54. Objet d'art _____

55. Faux pas _____

56. Fortissimo _____

57. Hara-kiri _____

58. De gustibus non est disputandum _____

PLACE NAMES

All of the persons described below have one thing in common: each of them has a name that contains the name of a city, state, or country. For example: *Noted American playwright* would be TENNESSEE *Williams.* How many of them can you locate?

A score of 7 is good; 11 is really going places.

Answers on page 338

1. American popular songwriter ("God Bless America")
   _____

2. The first child born of Colonial parents in the New World
   _____

3. Depression-era nightclub comedi-enne, known for the saying, "Hello, suckers."
   _____

4. American author (*Real Lace, Our Crowd*)
   _____

5. American writer (*Call of the Wild*)
   _____

6. Ashley Wilkes' sister in *Gone with the Wind*
   _____

7. Big gambler in *Guys and Dolls*
   _____

8. American woman painter (1887–), often uses Southwestern motifs
   _____

9. French author (*Thaïs*)
   _____

10. American sculptor, best-known for "LOVE" statue
    _____

11. Name by which plainsman William F. Cody is better known
    _____

12. Noted British author, name used in an Edward Albee title
    _____

13. American actor and comedian (*The Dick Van Dyke Show*)
    _____

14. American writer (*Rip Van Winkle*)
    _____

15. American actor, 1920–1966 (*A Place in the Sun, From Here to Eternity*)
    _____

BONING UP

All 45 definitions below identify words, names or phrases that contain the letters BON. For example: *Household cleaner* would be BON *Ami*. How many of them can you fill in?

A score of 25 is good; 32 is excellent; 39 proves you're no BONehead.

Answers on page 330

1. Link, connector; type of negotiable instruments
   _____

2. Charcoal; element number 6
   _____

3. Extra dividend
   _____

4. Slavery
   _____

5. Ex-husband of Cher
   _____

6. Strip of cloth used for tying things attractively
   _____

7. Type of lady's hat; in England, a car's hood
   _____

8. Suave; dashing; cultured
   _____

9. Capital of West Germany
   _____

10. Agent 007 created by Ian Fleming
    _____

11. Japanese dwarf tree
    _____

12. Sliding member of a band's brass section
    _____

13. Kentucky corn whiskey
    _____

14. Symbol of piracy, or of poison
    _____

15. Annual football game in Houston
    _____

16. Goof; error
    _____

17. Type of ape
    _____

18. Long-running TV Western starring Lorne Greene
    _____

19. Wanderer; rover; itinerant
    _____

20. Admit freely
    _____

21. Jet-black wood
    _____

22. Disease which ravaged Europe in 14th century

_____

23. Conflagration for celebration

_____

24. Western film starring John Wayne and Joanne Dru

_____

25. Type of African antelope, or drum

_____

26. Early 19th-century ruler of France and conqueror of Europe

_____

27. Legitimate; on the level; for real

_____

28. Candy with cream filling

_____

29. A song of the Confederacy

_____

30. Legal phrase meaning "for the common good"

_____

31. Author of *The Decline and Fall of the Roman Empire*

_____

32. Ship commanded by John Paul Jones

_____

33. West African nation, capital Libreville

_____

34. Much-parodied song about a faraway lover

_____

35. Tuna-like fish

_____

36. A witticism (Fr.)

_____

37. An innkeeper

_____

38. University of Paris

_____

39. Slang term for a surgeon

_____

40. Subject of disagreement

_____

41. French painter, noted for her pictures of animals, 1822–1899

_____

42. Farewell wish for someone taking a trip

_____

43. An apéritif wine

_____

44. Porterhouse or club steak

_____

45. Family name of Giotto, famous Florentine painter and architect

_____

MOVING VAN

Each of the 35 definitions below refers to a word, name, or expression containing the letters VAN. For example: *Transient, ephemeral* would be *evANescent.* How many of them can you come up with?

A score of 17 is good; 23 is excellent; 30 or more means you're really advANced!

Answers on page 330

1. Disappear into thin air _____

2. State in the eastern U.S. _____

3. Destructive hoodlum; originally, a marauding ancient people of Europe _____

4. Germane or pertinent; what some students think school isn't _____

5. Jimmy Carter's Secretary of State _____

6. Device, often shaped like an animal, indicating wind direction _____

7. Head start; superiority; term used in tennis _____

8. TV comedian; star, with Mary Tyler Moore, of landmark 60's sitcom _____

9. U.S. President, 1837–1841 _____

10. Major city in British Columbia, Canada _____

11. Move forward; money paid in anticipation _____

12. Element number 23 _____

13. Billy Graham, Billy Sunday, and Oral Roberts, e.g. _____

14. Actress who played Lucille Ball's sidekick _____

15. Organized train of cars, trucks, or pack animals _____

16. Ice cream flavor _____

17. Film starring Jack Lemmon and Juliet Mills

_____

18. Roman god of forests and untilled land

_____

19. Novel by William Makepeace Thackeray

_____

20. Flemish painter, 1599–1641; beard bearing his name

_____

21. Capital of Soviet Armenia

_____

22. Invention or mechanical device; deceitful practice

_____

23. Forefront; first line of an army; type of U.S. missile

_____

24. American millionaire; Nashville university bearing his name

_____

25. British actress (1888–1976); star of *Tom Jones* and *The Whisperers*

_____

26. Conquer or defeat utterly

_____

27. Huge American electronics manufacturer

_____

28. Narrative poem by Henry Wadsworth Longfellow

_____

29. European region straddling the Romanian-Hungarian border; famous as setting of *Dracula* and other horror stories

_____

30. British actress, Oscar-winner for *Julia*

_____

31. Movie actor, starred in *Brigadoon, Wives and Lovers*

_____

32. Wooded; of the forest

_____

33. Large, low couch or sofa

_____

34. Cruel Russian Czar, 1530–1584

_____

35. Author of *Don Quixote*

_____

FOOT BY FOOT

Below, you will find 24 expressions, phrases, or names. Each one of these should suggest to you another expression which contains the word FOOT. For example: *A secure position* is a FOOT*hold.*

A score of 17 is good; 19 is excellent; and 21 is extraordinary.

Answers on page 330

1. Front of stage _____

2. An American Indian _____

3. To put best appearance in evidence _____

4. Tennis term _____

5. A reference _____

6. Western newcomer _____

7. Free and untrammeled _____

8. To insist _____

9. Highwayman _____

10. To make an inauspicious start _____

11. Disease of cloven-hoofed animals _____

12. Unit of energy _____

13. Matchstick prank _____

14. Carriage attendant _____

15. Impression in earth or snow _____

16. Small mountain or elevation _____

17. To be near death _____

18. Rose Bowl game _____

19. Indicating lasting impression _____

20. Boxing term _____

21. Verbal blunder _____

22. To pay an account _____

23. Foundation _____

24. Trodden down _____

RAINBOW RIDDLE

All 28 of the terms defined below contain within them, as you can see, the names of colors. The dashes indicate the missing letters. Can you fill in the blanks?

A score of 15 is good; 20 is excellent; 24 wins you a blue ribbon.

Answers on page 330

1. SCARLET __ __'__ __ __ __   Heroine of *Gone with the Wind*

2. YELLOW

   __ __ __ __ __ __ __ __   Animated film starring the Beatles

3. ORANGE __ __ __ __   Miami football stadium

4. __ __ __ __ __ RED   In debt; losing money

5. "__ __ __ __ __ __

   GRAY __ __ __ __"   American folk song

6. BROWN __ __ __   Partial reduction of electrical power

7. PURPLE __ __ __ __ __   San Francisco nightclub

8. YELLOW __ __ __ __ __   Jingoist's term for Oriental immigration

9. __ __ __ LAVENDER

   __ __ __ __ __ __ __   1952 film starring Sir Alec Guinness

10. __ __ __ __ __ __ __ __ __

    __ __ __ __ __ __ __

    BROWN __ __ __   British poetess (1806–1861), *Sonnets from the Portuguese*

11. YELLOW __ __ __ __ __   Oldest and largest U.S. National park

12. PINK __ __ __ __ __   Cocktail of gin, brandy, and grenadine

13. BROWN __ __ __ __ __ __   Reverie, meditation

14. __ __ __ __ __ __ __

    __ __ __ __ __ __ __ __

    BROWN   America's first novelist (1771–1810)

15. CRIMSON _ _ _ _   Football team at Harvard, or
                            U. of Alabama

16. _ _. PINK _ _ _ _ _ _   Treacherous American lover
                            in *Madame Butterfly*

17. _ _ _ _ _ _ _ _   Arthur Conan Doyle novel
    SCARLET

18. YELLOW _ _ _ _ _   Capital of the Northwest
                            Territories, Canada

19. "_ _ _ _ _ _ PURPLE   Nonsense rock song of the 1950's

    _ _ _ _ _ _ _ - _ _ _ _ _"

20. _ _ _ _ GRAY   Satiric epithet for *The New York
                            Times*

    _ _ _ _

21. "_ _ _ YELLOW   Folk song about the Lone Star
                            State

    _ _ _ _ _ _

    _ _ _ _"

22. PINK _ _ _   Contagious opthalmic disorder

23. "PURPLE _ _ _ _"   Best-known song of Jimi
                            Hendrix

24. GREEN _ _ _ _ _ _ _   Play by Lynn Riggs, basis for
    LILACS   *Oklahoma!*

25. _ _ _ SCARLET   1905 novel by Baroness Orczy

    _ _ _ _ _ _ _ _ _

26. _ _ _ _ _ _ _   Father of Dutch independence

    _ _ ORANGE

27. _ _ _ _ _ _ _ _   Western starring John Wayne
    YELLOW _ _ _ _ _ _ _   and Joanne Dru

28. BROWN _ _ _ _ _   Famous Los Angeles restaurant;
                            kind of hat

FOWL PLAY

Do you have a brain for the birds? Below are 24 names or expressions containing the names of specific fowl. How many blanks can you fill in?

A score of 13 gets you off the ground; 17 and you're off and winging; 21 and you're in the stratosphere.

Answers on page 331

1. The _____ and the pussycat

2. Florence _____

3. Hark, hark, the _____

4. Christopher _____

5. Quoth the _____, "Nevermore"

6. Bye, bye _____

7. Who killed Cock _____

8. "Special providence in the fall of a _____"

9. Baltimore _____

10. _____ Islands

11. As the _____ flies

12. When the _____ come back to Capistrano

13. _____ clock

14. Watches like a _____

15. Philadelphia _____

16. Graceful as a _____

17. Donald _____

18. _____ of Peace

19. Buries his head in the sand like an _____

20. The _____ hangs high

21. Poll _____

22. Atlanta _____

23. Tom _____

24. _____ Little

AN ALPHABET OF T'S

Each of the 26 words defined below is seven letters long. In every case, the middle letter of the word is T. The words are in succession from A to Z, each one beginning with the next letter of the alphabet. Can you use the clues to fill in the blanks?

A score of 13 is good; 18 is better; 22 is the besTest!

Answers on page 331

1. A __ __ T __ __ __   Harsh; stern; severe
2. B __ __ T __ __ __   Male sibling
3. C __ __ T __ __ __   A type of lens
4. D __ __ T __ __ __   The female side
5. E __ __ T __ __ __   Statement on a tombstone
6. F __ __ T __ __ __   Opposite of fact
7. G __ __ T __ __ __   Meaningful hand motion
8. H __ __ T __ __ __   Record of the past
9. I __ __ T __ __ __   Emulate; ape
10. J __ __ T __ __ __   Fairness; equity
11. K __ __ T __ __ __   Kinky, as a rope; gnarled, as a tree
12. L __ __ T __ __ __   Instruct; scold
13. M __ __ T __ __ __   Large breed of dog
14. N __ __ T __ __ __   Nourish; care for
15. O __ __ T __ __ __   Enthusiastic tribute
16. P __ __ T __ __ __   Simulate; make-believe
17. Q __ __ T __ __ __   Central American bird; Guatemalan currency
18. R __ __ T __ __ __   Break apart; burst
19. S __ __ T __ __ __   Support; bring through a difficult period
20. T __ __ T __ __ __   Inflict severe pain
21. U __ __ T __ __ __   Person who has suddenly risen in the world
22. V __ __ T __ __ __   A risky undertaking
23. W __ __ T __ __ __   Pensive; melancholy; yearning
24. X __ __ T __ __ __   River of Troy, mentioned often by Homer
25. Y __ __ T __ __ __   Talks idly; jabbers
26. Z __ __ T __ __ __   Marked by keen enjoyment

ALL IN ALL

Each of the 44 terms defined below contains the letters ALL. For example: *A season of the year* would be *f*ALL. How many of them can you get?

A score of 21 is good; 28 is excellent; 34 or more wins you ALL the marbles!

Answers on page 331

1. Four quarts _____

2. October 31 holiday _____

3. The great American pastime _____

4. Delay; obfuscate; a place for a horse _____

5. Ravine; gully _____

6. Best Picture of 1950, starring Bette Davis and Anne Baxter _____

7. Ashen or pasty-white complexion _____

8. Jack London's best-known novel, made into film with Clark Gable _____

9. A relative of the kangaroo _____

10. Muse of epic poetry; hand organ with whistles _____

11. Gather in support of a cause _____

12. Major city in Texas _____

13. Long-running TV series about the Bunkers _____

14. Sport played by Maravich, Irving, Jabbar, etc. _____

15. Fast trot _____

16. Comedy by Shakespeare _____

17. Sacred; consecrated _____

18. Capital of Florida _____

19. Famous fan-dancer _____

20. Place for exhibition and sale of art _____

21. One of the Beatles' very first hits   _____

22. Historic Philadelphia building   _____

23. Vote; poll   _____

24. Male horse   _____

25. Vice-president for FDR's third term   _____

26. Bewitched; enchanted   _____

27. Distinctive sign; giant greeting-card manufacturer   _____

28. Greek-American soprano, one of the century's greatest singers   _____

29. God of Islam   _____

30. Radio comic   _____

31. Anti-war film based on Remarque novel, Best Picture of 1930   _____

32. Mistake in reasoning; illogic   _____

33. Capital of Malta   _____

34. Flexible; pliable   _____

35. Sport of Unitas, Namath, Tarkenton, etc.   _____

36. Uncultivated; unplanted   _____

37. What makes Jack a dull boy   _____

38. Flirtation; brief affair   _____

39. Congressman from Arizona, unsuccessful '76 Presidential aspirant   _____

40. Green and pungent relative of the onion   _____

41. 1976 film made from book by Woodward and Bernstein   _____

42. Repetitively named city near the Washington-Oregon border   _____

43. Author of "The Raven"   _____

44. Simple poem or song, usually narrative in nature   _____

HIM AND HER

Each of the 38 terms defined below contains either the letters HER or the letters HIM. The blanks tell you the number of missing letters. For example: *Female parent* would be *mot*HER.

A score of 19 is good; 25 is excellent; 31 makes you the Person of the Year!

Answers on page 331

1. __ HIM __ __ __ __   Santa Claus' means of entry

2. __ HER __ __ __ __   Curative treatment

3. __ HIM   Arbitrary notion; yen

4. __ HER __ __ __ __   County law-enforcement officer

5. __ __ __ HIM __   Japanese delicacy of raw fish

6. __ __ HER   Anesthetic first used by Crawford W. Long

7. __ HIM __ __ __ __ __ __   Small variety of ape

8. __ HER __ __ __ __   Container for keeping liquids hot or cold

9. __ HIM __   Bell; ring out

10. __ HER __ __ __ __ __ __ __ __ __ __ __   Robin Hood's sylvan retreat

11. "__ __ __ __ __ __ __ __ HIM"   Male chauvinist song from *My Fair Lady*

12. __ HER __ __ __ __   Cucumber variety often used for pickles

13. __ HIM __ __ __ __   Finger-shielding device used in sewing

14. __ __ __ __ __ __ __ __ __ __ __ __ HER __ __ __   Morris West novel about a Russian pope

15. HIM __ __ __ __ __ __ __   Vast mountain range in Asia

16. __ HER __ __ __ __   Love; appreciate; be grateful for

17. __ HIM __ __ __ __ __ __   Mythical; visionary; imaginary

18. __ HER __ __ __ __ __   French seaport on the English Channel

19. __ __ __ HIM __ __ __ __   Greek physicist and inventor (275–212 B.C.)

20. __ __ __ __ HER   Climatic conditions

21. __ HIM __ __ __   Whine; mournful cry

22. __ __ HER __ __ __   Innate, characteristic

23. __ __ __ __ __ HIM __   City devastated by atomic attack August 6, 1945

24. __ __ __ __ __ __ __ __ HER   Patron saint for travelers

25. __ HIM __ __ __   Gleam faintly

26. __ HER __ __ __   Union general who burned Atlanta during his march to the sea

27. __ __ __ HIM __   Japanese writer Yukio _____, a famous suicide and author of *The Sailor Who Fell from Grace with the Sea*

28. __ __ __ __ HER   Jungle cat

29. HER __ __ __ __ __   Greek hero noted for his strength

30. __ HER __ __   Type of angel; adorable child

31. __ HIM __ __   Quaintness; fanciful notion

32. __ __ __ HER   Dry up

33. HIM __ __ __ __   Head of the Gestapo in Nazi Germany

34. __ HER __ __ __ __   English designer of fine furniture, 1751–1806

35. __ HIM __ __   A jazz dance

36. __ __ __ __ __ __ HER __   Physical, mental, or moral environment

37. __ __ __ HIM   Hebrew name for God

38. __ HER   Popular singer, ex-wife of Sonny Bono

THE LONG AND SHORT OF IT

Each of the 44 terms defined below contains either the word LONG or the word SHORT. For example: *Cash or folding money* would be LONG *green*. How many of them can you get?

A score of 25 is good; 30 is excellent; 36 indicated you can't be SHORTchanged.

Answers on page 331

1. Lack or dearth   _____

2. Possessions or property   _____

3. Hotly debated 1977 rock song by Randy Newman   _____

4. Dessert of pastry, fruit and whipped cream   _____

5. Ubiquitous police or other peace-keeping officers   _____

6. Understaffed, with too few assistants   _____

7. American poet ("The Song of Hiawatha")   _____

8. Baseball infield position   _____

9. Character in *Treasure Island*   _____

10. Existing only briefly   _____

11. Popular World War I song   _____

12. Literary form invented by American authors   _____

13. Little Richard song later recorded by the Beatles   _____

14. Chef in a fast-food diner   _____

15. Distance east or west of Greenwich   _____

16. Summertime wear named after an island resort   _____

17. Georgia doctor, first to use ether   _____

18. Type of radio favored by "ham" operators   _____

19. An eighth of a mile   _____

20. Faults; limitations   _____

21. Louisiana demagogue   _____

22. Breathless; lacking lung power   _____

23. Extend the duration of   _____

24. To relate concisely; to summarize   _____

25. Propaganda song sung by Nazis in *Cabaret*   _____

26. A native of Milan   _____

27. Electrical malfunction   _____

28. Infamous Northern Ireland detention camp for political prisoners   _____

29. Fat used in pastry-making   _____

30. A great risk or unlikely winner   _____

31. Type of men's underwear named after horsemen   _____

32. Well-known watch manufacturer   _____

33. Cut of meat used in "soul food"   _____

34. Weapon used in archery   _____

35. Stenography   _____

36. Very late Beatles song   _____

37. Miguel Pinero play and film set in prison   _____

38. Slang term for classical music   _____

39. Easier way or less-lengthy way   _____

40. Eugene O'Neill's masterpiece   _____

41. Defeat easily and quickly   _____

42. Stevedore   _____

43. Myopic; without regard to future consequences   _____

44. Cornelius Ryan World War II novel, made into 1962 film   _____

ART SMARTS

All of the following terms have within them the word ART. The dashes correspond to the letters which are missing. A definition for each item is given. For example: *A graph* would be *ch*ART.

If you get 12, you're sm*ART*; 15 puts you f*ART*her out front; and 18 means that you are p*ART*iculary bright.

Answers on page 332

1. __ ART — Trade Center

2. __ ART __ __ — Kilt cloth

3. __ __ __ __ __ ART — *You Can't Take It with You*

4. __ __ __ ART __ __ __ __ — Seeing both sides

5. __ ART __ __ __ '__ — Gem of a place

6. __ __ __ __ ART — Parvenu

7. __'ART __ __ __ __ __ — One of the famous Musketeers

8. __ ART __ __ __ — Sharer—for better or worse

9. ART __ __ __ __ __ __ __ __ __ — *Death of a Salesman*

10. __ ART __ — English pub game

11. __ __ __ __ __ __ __ __ — French existentialist

    __ ART __ __ —

12. __ ART __ __ — Snake; hose holder

13. __ ART __ __ __ __ '__ — You can quote me

14. __ __ __ __ __ ART __ — American short story writer

15. __ ART __ __ __ __ __ — Greek temple

16. __ ART __ __ __ __ ART __ — Judo, Karate, etc.

17. __ __ ART __ __ — Disciplined Greek

18. __ ART __ __ __ __ __ — Ivy League college

19. __ __ __ __ __ __ __ __ — Artist who painted George Washington

    __ __ __ ART —

20. __ ART __ __ __ — Cocktail with a twist

FILTHY LUCRE

The missing element of each of the 23 phrases below is a coin or a unit of currency. For example: _____*back* would be QUARTER*back*. How many of the blanks can you fill in?

A score of 12 is good; 15 is excellent; 20 or better means you're worth your weight in gold.

Answers on page 332

1. "Brother, Can You Spare a _____?"

2. "_____ from Heaven"

3. _____ _____Legs

4. "Shave and a haircut, _____ _____"

5. Not worth a plugged _____

6. A _____ of flesh

7. Baby _____ piano

8. _____ Rogers

9. "I've Got _____, Jolly, Jolly _____"

10. The March of _____

11. _____ wise and _____ foolish

12. 100 per _____

13. "Don't take any wooden _____"

14. A _____ for your thoughts

15. "What this country needs is a good _____ _____ cigar"

16. _____ master

17. The almighty _____

18. _____ dreadful

19. "I Found a _____ - _____ Baby in the _____ -and- _____ _____ Store"

20. _____ novel

21. "Why, for _____ _____ I'd . . ."

22. *The Remarkable Mr. _____ packer*

23. I'll bet you _____ to doughnuts

WE'LL GIVE YOU A CUE

Using the 23 definitions below, fill in the blanks with the proper synonym. Each answer begins with the letter Q and contains only five letters.

If you correctly fill in 10 answers, you're doing fine; 13 is particularly good; 17 is excellent; and 20 rates you tops.

Answers on page 332

1. Jokes   Q _ _ _ _

2. Feminine ruler   Q _ _ _ _

3. Peculiarity in manner or behavior   Q _ _ _ _

4. Swift; rapid   Q _ _ _ _

5. Tranquil; still   Q _ _ _ _

6. Search, seek   Q _ _ _ _

7. Completely; entirely   Q _ _ _ _

8. Seemingly; as if; almost   Q _ _ _ _

9. To drink freely   Q _ _ _ _

10. Strange; eccentric   Q _ _ _ _

11. A game bird   Q _ _ _ _

12. To cite; adduce; repeat   Q _ _ _ _

13. Proportional part or share   Q _ _ _ _

14. Two pints   Q _ _ _ _

15. Feather   Q _ _ _ _

16. Said; spoke   Q _ _ _ _

17. A question   Q _ _ _ _

18. Misgiving; apprehension   Q _ _ _ _

19. Coverlet   Q _ _ _ _

20. Overpower; suppress; soothe   Q _ _ _ _

21. To annul; make void   Q _ _ _ _

22. Shiver   Q _ _ _ _

23. Pigtail; waiting line   Q _ _ _ _

ALL IN SEASON

On these three pages, there are 50 definitions for names, words, or phrases which contain one of the seasons. The dashes indicate the number of letters in each answer.

Fill in the correct answer. For example: *The particles in the atmosphere after a nuclear explosion* are FALLout.

If you score 25, that's fine; 30 is very good; 35 is excellent; 40 is outstanding; and 45 is extraordinary.

Answers on page 338

1. ＿＿＿＿SPRING — A coil supporting a mattress.

2. ＿＿＿＿＿＿＿ SUMMER — A period of warm, mild weather in late autumn.

3. WINTER-＿＿＿＿＿＿ — To render a car's engine safe for use in freezing weather.

4. ＿＿＿＿FALL — Dangerous area, situation, or snare.

5. ＿＿＿＿＿＿＿ SPRING — Famous book by Rachel Carson about the environment.

6. WINTER＿＿＿＿ — Play by Maxwell Anderson.

7. ＿＿＿＿＿SPRING — The coiled drive of a watch.

8. SUMMER ＿＿＿＿＿＿＿ — Where one makes up credits lost through absence or failure.

9. WINTER＿＿＿＿＿＿ — Herbal plant with aromatic leaves which yields a useful oil.

10. ＿＿＿＿＿＿＿ FALL＿ — Famous honeymoon spot.

11. ＿＿＿＿SPRING — One's children.

12. WINTER ＿＿＿＿＿＿ — Fruit with a smooth rind and a sweet flesh.

13. ＿＿＿＿＿SPRING — Common tumbling feat.

14. SUMMER ＿＿＿＿＿＿ — Repertory company playing in a resort area.

15. ＿＿＿＿ WINTER ＿＿ ＿＿＿ ＿＿＿＿＿＿＿＿＿ — Novel by John Steinbeck.

16. ＿＿＿＿＿＿FALL — The close of day; dusk.

17. WINTER'＿ ＿＿＿＿＿＿ — Story collection by Isak Dinesen.

18. _____
WINTER__   Popular comedian, originator of Maude Frickett

19. FALL____ _____   Meteor

20. SUMMER_____   Gershwin's hit song in *Porgy and Bess*

21. ____ SPRING ____
____ _____   Shelley's question: "O, wind, if Winter comes . . ."

22. FALL _____   To be unable to keep pace with.

23. _____
_____ SUMMER   Tennessee Williams' play

24. _____ FALL__   City in South Dakota

25. _____SPRING   A source of continual supply

26. WINTER
_____   Song popular during Christmas season

27. _____ ____ FALL   Play by Arthur Miller

28. ____SUMMER
_____'_ _____   Comedy by William Shakespeare

29. ____ FALL ___ ____
_____ __
_____   Short story by Edgar Allan Poe

30. SPRING_____
_____   Breech-loading gun used in Spanish-American War.

31. FALL ___!   An order to line up

32. _____ SPRINGS   A Maryland suburb of Washington, D.C.

33. SUMMER ____
_____   A Tennessee Williams' play

34. _____FALL   Destruction; descent

35. SPRING____   African gazelle noted for graceful leaps

36. ____ WINTER'__
_____   Shakespearean play

37. ____ _____ FALL
_____   Novel by Rebecca West

38. SPRING _____ H_2O from a natural source

39. SPRING___
_____   Medium-sized sporting dog

40. _ _ _ _ _ _ _ _ _ FALL   Novel by William Shirer about
     _ _ _ _ _ _ _ _ _ _   Germany
     _ _ _ _ _ _

41. _ _ FALL _ _   To fail so completely as to appear
     _ _ _ _ _ ,_ _ _ _ _ _   ridiculous

42. SPRING _ _ _ _ _ _ _ _ _ _   Yearly extended household chore

43. _ _ _ _ _ _ _ _ _   Hit song of the early 1900's pro-
     _ _ _ SUMMER _ _ _ _ _   claiming seasonal joy

44. FALL _ _ _ _ _ _ _   Have a quarrel; clash

45. SPRING _ _ _ _ _ _ _ _ _ _   Early baseball games

46. _ _ _ _ _ _ _ _ _ _   Movie adaptation from Faulkner's
     SUMMER   novel *The Hamlet*

47. _ _ _ _ WINTER   Famous playhouse in New York
     _ _ _ _ _ _   City

48. _ _ FALL _ _ _ _ _ _ _   To have recourse to another source
       for money or help

49. _ _ _ _ ',_ _ _ _ SPRING   Unkind remark about another
     _ _ _ _ _ _ _ _   woman's loss of youth

50. _ _ _ _ _ _ _ _ _ WINTER   Movie about Henry II, starring
       Katharine Hepburn and Peter
       O'Toole

PIN YOUR HOPES

Below, you will find 50 expressions, phrases, or names which should suggest to you another expression which contains the word PIN. For example: *A fastener that has a guarded point* is a *safety* PIN.

If you get 25, that's fine; 33 is excellent; and 42 is outstanding.

Answers on page 332

1. Cheesecake photo. _____

2. Sports equipment on an alley. _____

3. Describing intense quiet. _____

4. Highest point of development or achievement. _____

5. Support; prop. _____

6. Contemporary English playwright. _____

7. Military term describing an enveloping tactic. _____

8. Design in fabric of men's suits. _____

9. Fastener for infant's equipment. _____

10. To woo in a collegiate fraternity manner. _____

11. Perilous curve on a road. _____

12. Popular birthday party game. _____

13. Assign responsibility for; accuse. _____

14. Penny arcade amusement device. _____

15. Juvenile hero created by Gepetto _____

16. Leather made from young aquatic mammal. _____

17. To administer a sound scolding. _____

18. The No. 5 pin in bowling; the big boss. _____

19. Famous Russian basso. _____

20. Card game using special 48-card pack. _____

21. In a very nervous or jumpy state. _____

22. A utensil for flatting dough or an errant husband. _____

23. A variety of web-footed bird. _____

24. An apron; a wraparound. _____

25. A millinery fastener, sometimes used as a weapon. _____

26. Animals sometimes envisioned after heavy drinking.

27. Spectacles without ear pieces.

28. To force someone to be specific.

29. Table tennis.

30. One of Columbus's ships.

31. Cash for minor expenses.

32. A toy that is maneuvered by the wind.

33. The little finger.

34. A stand-in for someone in baseball.

35. English playwright, author of *The Second Mrs. Tanqueray.*

36. Scissors with saw-toothed inner edges.

37. A spotted or calico horse or pony.

38. Mechanical device in bowling alley for spotting the pins simultaneously.

39. Locate with great precision or accuracy.

40. Slang expression for Communist.

41. Private detective; originally last name of famous American detective.

42. In the best of health.

43. To practice strict economy.

44. With reservations; to be regarded somewhat suspiciously.

45. Smooth coil of hair secured by a clip.

46. Small stuffed object used by seamstress to hold pins.

47. Wing of a bird; flight feathers.

48. Cocktail consisting of gin, brandy, lemon juice, grenadine, and egg white.

49. Male singer, starred in "South Pacific."

50. Decorated pottery jar filled with candies, toys, etc., which blindfolded children try to break. Part of traditional Mexican Christmas festivity.

PULLING YOUR LEG

Each of the 17 clues below should lead you to a term which contains the letters LEG. How many of them can you fill in?

A score of 8 is good; 12 is excellent; 15 gets you into the LEGion of Honor!

Answers on page 332

1. Institution of higher education   _____

2. Artificial limb, as worn by Long John Silver   _____

3. In accordance with law   _____

4. Readable   _____

5. Musical direction meaning "bright" or "cheery"; a Rodgers and Hammerstein musical comedy   _____

6. U.S. veterans' organization   _____

7. Myth; tale; story   _____

8. Assign to an undesirable location or inferior position   _____

9. Opposite of knock-kneed   _____

10. Proper; duly appointed; born within wedlock   _____

11. Taking an untenable or indefensible position (slang)   _____

12. Modern French artists, did murals at United Nations   _____

13. Implied; hinted at; so-called   _____

14. Person stricken with paralysis of lower half of body   _____

15. Appointed representative or ambassador (e.g. to the UN)   _____

16. Thick substance secreted by mucous membranes   _____

17. Vegetable; e.g., peas, beans   _____

A FAR CRY

Each of the 35 clues below should elicit from you a word, name, or expression that contains the word FAR. For example: *Extending over a large distance* would be FAR-*flung*. How many can you fill in?

A score of 17 is good; 22 is excellent; 29 places you FAR above average.

Answers on page 333

1. What Old McDonald had   _____

2. Creator of Studs Lonigan   _____

3. Western stagecoach company, now a major bank and security firm   _____

4. Union admiral, famous for "Damn the torpedoes!"   _____

5. Hyperopic; planning ahead; forward-looking   _____

6. Shirley Temple film based on novel by Kate D. Wiggin   _____

7. Type of flour or meal, popular as breakfast food   _____

8. Safety; security; government assistance for needy   _____

9. Actor who plays B.J. Hunnicutt on TV's *M*A*S*H*   _____

10. Comedy; parody; mockery   _____

11. Poignant Hemingway novel about World War I   _____

12. Chairman of Democratic National Committee and postmaster general under F.D.R.   _____

13. Country-Western singer   _____

14. Agribusinessman's handbook   _____

15. Mixture; medley, potpourri   _____

16. Up until now   _____

17. Blond bombshell, an ex-Angel _____

18. Sinister, brooding character in
    A Tale of Two Cities _____

19. Wicked; unspeakable _____

20. Cornelius Ryan novel and 1977 film _____

21. Major street, avenue or boulevard _____

22. Political satire by George Orwell _____

23. 19th century physicist, pioneer in
    electromagnetics _____

24. Thomas Hardy novel, made into
    film starring Julie Christie _____

25. Old British coin worth next to
    nothing _____

26. Strained; forced; extraneous _____

27. Expression meaning the joy of
    idleness (Italian) _____

28. Leader of Boston School of Cooking _____

29. Sidney Carton's guillotine statement _____

30. Famous line from Tennyson's
    In Memoriam _____

31. Rare _____

32. Arthur Mizener's work about
    F. Scott Fitzgerald _____

33. A hooped skirt worn by women in
    the 16th and 17th centuries _____

34. Ram's horn blown in Jewish temples
    on Yom Kippur _____

35. American social worker and
    reformer, matron at Sing Sing
    prison _____

CALCULATED RISK

Each of the 47 clues below defines a term that contains the letters CAL. For example: A kind of cotton is CALico.

A score of 22 is good; 30 is excellent; 35 or better is doing fantastiCALly well!

Answers on page 333

1. Units of heat; something dieters count _____

2. Nearby; close to home; slow train _____

3. Most populous of the 50 states _____

4. Of government; the kind of animal man is _____

5. Kind of organ; the Muse of epic poetry _____

6. Campus in Pasadena _____

7. Placid, serene _____

8. A Broadway show with song and dance _____

9. Widow of Humphrey Bogart, star of *Murder on the Orient Express* _____

10. Picture or design transferred from paper _____

11. Mad Roman emperor (37–41 A.D.) _____

12. Type of onion _____

13. Young cow; part of the leg _____

14. Site of the crucifixion _____

15. Moving staircase _____

16. Element number 20, found in bones and teeth _____

17. 30th United States President _____

18. Cord connecting fetus to mother _____

19. Important; vital; censorious _____

20. Cotton fabric often used in bed linens _____

21. A chart or register that shows dates _____

22. Catastrophic; disastrous _____

23. Unruly; defiant _____

24. Burn, especially with steam _____

25. Old name for Scotland _____

26. Sensible; reasonable; predictable _____

27. Name for collaborationist Southerners during Reconstruction _____

28. Alfalfa, Spanky *et al.* _____

29. Site of the University of Alabama _____

30. Heckler's noise _____

31. Long, long word popularized by Mary Poppins _____

32. Hair-covered part of the head _____

33. Slander; disgrace; invective _____

34. Existing only in legend or fiction _____

35. Surgeon's knife _____

36. Exercises; work-outs _____

37. Hallucinogenic drug made from peyote _____

38. Type of higher mathematics _____

39. Father of Presbyterianism _____

40. Type of shellfish; term used in cooking _____

41. Beautiful handwriting _____

42. Relating to sight, often used with "illusion" _____

43. Bachelor's degree _____

44. Cold; unfeeling; unsympathetic _____

45. Opposite; in total contrast _____

46. Character in Shakespeare's *The Tempest* _____

47. Poison ivy remedy _____

THE LOW-DOWN

All 40 of the following clues should suggest to you words, names, or expressions that contain the letters LOW. How many of them can you fill in?

A score of 20 is good; 27 is excellent; 34 should leave you with a warm GLOW!

Answers on page 333

1. Underneath   _____

2. Canary-colored   _____

3. Buffoon; circus comic   _____

4. Move smoothly like water   _____

5. Permit; tolerate   _____

6. Cushion   _____

7. Member of a fraternal society, originated in 18th-century England   _____

8. Blossom; bloom   _____

9. Frown; scowl   _____

10. Work action just short of a strike   _____

11. Ingest orally; type of bird   _____

12. American poet (1807–1882)   _____

13. With little depth or personality   _____

14. Idiom meaning person of least importance in a hierarchy   _____

15. Red-baiting term of the McCarthy era   _____

16. Tree with drooping, almost vine-like leaves   _____

17. Collective term for Holland, Belgium, and Luxembourg   _____

18. Fat by-product used in candle-making   _____

19. What Isaiah would have us turn our swords into   _____

20. Ship which landed at Plymouth Rock _____

21. Softened by experience; mature _____

22. Pursue; come after _____

23. Early Hollywood sex symbol _____

24. 60's term for hippies _____

25. Moving below normal speed _____

26. Confection toasted at campfires _____

27. Blacksmith's instrument for forcing air into forge _____

28. Clifford Odets play about Noah and the ark _____

29. Empty, superficial _____

30. Nobel Prize-winning American novelist _____

31. Founder of the Girl Scouts _____

32. Bob Dylan song made popular by Peter, Paul, and Mary _____

33. 1959 film starring Doris Day _____

34. Structure for execution by hanging _____

35. English dramatist and poet, 1564-1593 _____

36. Negro spiritual _____

37. Person lacking cultivated intellectual tastes _____

38. American poet, *Patterns*, e.g. _____

39. Forgive because of mitigating circumstances _____

40. Novelist, author of *Under the Volcano* _____

ARE YOU A PRO?

Below you will find 24 expressions, phrases, or names, Each one of these should suggest to you another expression which contains the word PRO. For example: *A description of the evening's entertainment* is *a* PRO*gram.*

A score of 10 is fair; 12 is good; 14 is exceptional; and 18 is worthy of applause.

Answers on page 333

1. Hoover's noble experiment. _____

2. Schmaltzy song sung at weddings. _____

3. Famous work by Paul Bunyan. _____

4. Not poetic. _____

5. Flat; still, motionless. _____

6. Melon and ham, Italian style _____

7. Introductory comments. _____

8. Axiom; adage; maxim. _____

9. Advancement. _____

10. On time. _____

11. A question proposed for solution. _____

12. To act for another, especially in voting. _____

13. German toast. _____

14. As a matter of form; type of invoice in which customer pays in advance. _____

15. To lengthen; extend. _____

16. Grain, peas, alfalfa, etc. _____

17. Protracted, tiresome, diffuse. _____

18. Constitutional concern. _____

19. I.O.U. _____

20. The first of the trilogy by Aeschylus. _____

21. Spendthrift; wayward child. _____

22. To transmit; to carry; to multiply. _____

23. Kahlil Gibran's masterpiece. _____

24. Cape Cod resort town. _____

PLACE YOUR BETS

Each of the 19 terms defined below contains the letters BET. For example: *To help and encourage* would be *to aid and a*BET. How many of them can you get the BETter of?

A score of 13 is fair; 15 is BETter than average;.and 17 is terrific!

Answers on page 334

1. ABC's _____

2. State of lethargy; obtuseness _____

3. In the middle position; neither here nor there _____

4. Frozen dessert made with fruit and water _____

5. Mountainous Asian country, part of China since 1951 _____

6. American actress (*All about Eve*, *Jezebel*) _____

7. Second letter of the Greek alphabet _____

8. Much-hated object, pet peeve (French for "black beast") _____

9. Birthplace of Jesus Christ _____

10. Type of nut grown in the tropics _____

11. To promise in marriage _____

12. Queen of England 1558–1603 _____

13. Slang term for spouse _____

14. 1978 film from a Harold Robbins novel _____

15. Washington suburb, site of a tremendous naval hospital _____

16. Cartoon character created by Max Fleischer _____

17. Commit treason, deceive _____

18. National honor fraternity _____

19. Play by Shakespeare _____

THE SKIN GAME

Below, you will find 25 expressions, phrases, or names. Each should suggest an expression which contains the word SKIN. For example: *A bruin's hide* would be a *bear* SKIN.

A score of 12 is average; 15 is good; 18, excellent; 20, super; and 22 is positively brilliant!

Answers on page 334

1. To flay. _____
2. Stingy man. _____
3. To be terribly frightened. _____
4. Famous behavioral psychologist. _____
5. Pornographic movie. _____
6. Just barely. _____
7. As much as the stomach can hold. _____
8. Shallow; superficial. _____
9. To be of no significant personal concern. _____
10. Song about love addiction. _____
11. To be immune to criticism. _____
12. To emerge unscathed. _____
13. Famous actor of early 20th century. _____
14. Actress daughter of No. 13. _____
15. Thin; underweight. _____
16. Artist-sculptor who creates figures which seem to be decaying. _____
17. 19th-century English essayist and reformer. _____
18. To irritate. _____
19. To be very sensitive. _____
20. Skeleton-thin. _____
21. A nose job. _____
22. The way teenagers wear blue jeans. _____
23. Asserting that multiple solutions are available. _____
24. Old-fashioned, high-laced boots. _____
25. To bathe nude. _____

STONE UPON STONE

Below, you will find 24 expressions, phrases, or names. Each one of these should suggest to you another expression which contains the word STONE. For example: A *nativity gem* is a *birth*STONE.

A score of 15 is good; 19 is excellent; and a score of 22 is exceptional.

Answers on page 334

1. Graveyard _____

2. Abdominal impediment _____

3. Confederate general _____

4. Femininist _____

5. First period of human culture _____

6. To work unceasingly _____

7. Aphoristic injunction not to hop around _____

8. Fashionable pelt _____

9. Old Faithful _____

10. Without any hearing _____

11. What fell on Sodom _____

12. Franconia Range, New Hampshire _____

13. Very near _____

14. Justice of Supreme Court _____

15. To exhaust all possible action _____

16. Polarized magnetite _____

17. Oft-kissed Irish monument _____

18. Penniless _____

19. To extract money from a skinflint _____

20. Notable Greek and hieroglyphic inscription _____

21. English neolithic monuments _____

22. Semi-precious gem _____

23. Nineteenth century urban dwelling _____

24. Inaugural foundation piece _____

HAPPY LANDINGS

Each of the 42 answers in this quiz contains the letters LAND. With the definitions provided, how many of these terms can you identify?

A score of 20 is good; 27 is excellent; 33 is a real LANDmark!

Answers on page 334

1. Famous line from John Donne _____

2. Home of the shamrock _____

3. TV actor (*Bonanza, Little House on the Prairie*) _____

4. Strainer used in the kitchen _____

5. Plain; mild; undistinguished _____

6. Novel by Virginia Woolf _____

7. Epithet of USA; official nickname of Arkansas _____

8. False or harmful statements _____

9. Victor Herbert musical _____

10. Former immigration center in New York Harbor, now a museum of immigration _____

11. Name of major cities in Oregon and Maine _____

12. TV actor (*Mission: Impossible, Space: 1999*) _____

13. European nation, capital Bern _____

14. Notorious French penal colony off South American coast _____

15. Line that follows "My country, 'tis of thee" _____

16. To whom you pay rent _____

17. Official nickname for New Mexico _____

18. Bodily organ secreting blood components _____

19. Hawaiian's term for the 48 _____

20. A wreath of flowers _____

21. Adventure novel by Robert Louis
    Stevenson _____

22. Asian nation, capital Bangkok _____

23. Posthumously published Hemingway
    novel, made into film _____

24. Smallest of the 50 _____

25. World-famous California
    amusement park _____

26. Flattery; coaxing; persuasion _____

27. Eastern European nation, capital
    Warsaw _____

28. Peter Pan's home _____

29. Stephen Spielberg film starring
    Goldie Hawn _____

30. 22nd and 24th President _____

31. Region straddling French-Belgian
    border, World War I site _____

32. Phrase paired with "home of the
    brave" _____

33. American actor, Oscar-winner for
    The Lost Weekend _____

34. Country of peace and rest, from
    Bunyan's *Pilgrims's Progress* _____

35. Mayor of Chicago (1976-1979) _____

36. Overwhelming electoral victory _____

37. Feathered character in "Pogo" _____

38. Stealthy; furtive; secret _____

39. One's country of birth _____

40. Home of windmills and wooden
    shoes _____

41. Well-known folksong by Woody
    Guthrie _____

42. African nation east of South Africa _____

FOR OLD TIMES' SAKE

Every one of the 43 clues below should suggest to you a name, word, or expression that contains the letters OLD. For example: *Pleat* would be *f*OLD. How many of them can you get?

A score of 23 is good; 30 is excellent; 36 means you've got it COLD!

Answers on page 334

1. Delay; rob   _____

2. Supporting structure   _____

3. Nickname for the U.S. flag   _____

4. Deduct; keep (money, e.g.) from   _____

5. American actor (*Network, Bridge on the River Kwai*)   _____

6. Double; twice as much   _____

7. Traditional; antique; a cocktail   _____

8. Warrior   _____

9. Important name in the history of the automobile   _____

10. The first half of the Bible   _____

11. Berate   _____

12. Early James Bond adventure   _____

13. Israeli stateswoman   _____

14. Spinster   _____

15. Collection of stories by Nathaniel Hawthorne   _____

16. Brave; daring   _____

17. Ernest Hemingway novella   _____

18. Foolishness; frivolity   _____

19. Joseph Kesselring play, made into film starring Cary Grant   _____

20. Melancholy; unhappiness; "the dumps"   _____

21. Look! goes with lo   _____

22. Wildflower in disfavor with hay fever victims _____

23. Nickname for Andrew Jackson _____

24. Title character in *The Music Man* _____

25. Vended; convinced; persuaded _____

26. British actress (*Gigi, A Little Night Music*) _____

27. Indebted to _____

28. Espionage novel by John LeCarré, made into film starring Richard Burton _____

29. Well-known Stephen Foster song, mistakenly called "Swanee River" _____

30. Nostalgic term for times past _____

31. Cash; paper currency _____

32. Aphorism about an aging canine _____

33. Best-known song from *Show Boat* _____

34. A Soviet Socialist Republic _____

35. California historical period; 1925 Chaplin film _____

36. Soft metal used for sealing electrical connections _____

37. Nursery rhyme character, a merry soul _____

38. First opera in Wagner's *Ring* cycle _____

39. American actress and comedienne (*Cactus Flower, Butterflies Are Free*) _____

40. Nickname for the Bank of England _____

41. American Zionist, founder of Hadassah _____

42. Region in England, site of Banbury cross _____

43. Furry type of fungus (on bread, e.g.) _____

ON THE ROCKS

Each of the 37 definitions below should lead you to a name, word, or expression containing the letters ROCK. For example: *The capital of Arkansas* would be *Little*ROCK.

A score of 18 is good; 24 is excellent; 30 means you're leaving no stone unturned!

Answers on page 335

1. American frontiersman, a hero of the Alamo _____

2. A dress _____

3. Seat which moves on two curved pieces _____

4. Modern musical form born in the 50's _____

5. Protestant hymn _____

6. American actor (*Giant, Send Me No Flowers*) _____

7. Jet-propelled vehicle _____

8. TV series starring James Garner _____

9. Popular ice cream flavor with nuts and marshmallows _____

10. Nickname for CBS's New York headquarters _____

11. 1976 film starring Sylvester Stallone _____

12. American Indian monument in central Georgia _____

13. Symbol of strength and reliability _____

14. Folk song made popular by Burl Ives _____

15. Earthenware container or vessel _____

16. 1956 classic by Bill Haley and the Comets _____

17. One of America's richest families _____

18. Solid basis; geological stratum; Fred Flintstone's hometown _____

19. Cartoon character, friend of Bullwinkle the Moose _____

20. Caper film with Robert Redford and George Segal _____

21. America's first novelist (1771–1810) _____

22. Famous office complex in New York City with ice-skating rink _____

23. Cog; ratchet _____

24. Irish landmark _____

25. Simon and Garfunkel hit _____

26. Chorus line at Radio City Music Hall _____

27. Remove from the priesthood _____

28. Boxer portrayed by Paul Newman in *Somebody Up There Likes Me* _____

29. Western starring Spencer Tracy _____

30. Idiom meaning "in a tight spot" or "caught between two opposing sides" _____

31. Notre Dame football coach _____

32. Novel by James Stephens _____

33. Acute infectious disease transmitted by ticks _____

34. Ruined; whiskey without a mix _____

35. Type of cooking without a stove _____

36. The very lowest price _____

37. City near Boston, shoe-manufacturing center _____

UP IN ARMS

All 40 of the names, words, or phrases defined below contain the letters ARM in the positions indicated. The dashes indicate the missing letters needed to complete the term. Using the clues provided, can you come up with the right answers?

A score of 18 is good; 24 is excellent; 30 should really give you a WARM feeling inside!

Answers on page 335

1.	_ _ A R M _ _ _ _ _	Bedside timepiece
2.	_ A R M _ _ _ _	Agriculture
3.	_ _ A R M	Gathering of bees
4.	_ _ _ _ _ A R M _	Policeman in Paris
5.	_ _ A R M	Winning quality; kind of bracelet
6.	_ A R M _ _ _ _	Mischievous person or animal
7.	_ _ _ A R M _ _ _ _ _ _ _ _	Nothing ventured, nothing gained philosophy
8.	_ A R M _ _	Opera by Georges Bizet
9.	_ _ _ _ _ _ _ _ A R M	Prairie teacher
10.	_ A R M _ _ _	Runway surface
11.	A R M _ _ _ _ _ _ _ _ _ _ _ _ _ _	Book by Norman Mailer
12.	_ A R M _ _ _ _ _ _	Pertaining to marble
13.	A R M _ _ _ _ _ _ _	Treaty; truce
14.	_ _ A R M _ _ _ _	Drugstore
15.	_ A R M _ _ _ _	Lady pub-keeper
16.	A R M _ _ _ _	Spanish fleet
17.	_ A R M _ _ _ _ _ _	Preserves usually made of orange rinds
18.	_ _ A R M _ _ _ _	Piece of clothing
19.	_ A R M _ _	Artists' colony in California

20. _ A R M _ _ _ _   Accord; musical term

21. _ A R M   _ _ _ _ _ _ _   Roosevelt's retreat in Georgia

22. _ _ _ _ _ A R M   Tepid; indifferent

23. _ _ _ _   _ A R M _ _ '_
      _ _ _ _ _ _ _ _   1947 film, an Oscar-winner for Loretta Young

24. A R M _ _ _ _ _ _ _   Desert repile

25. _ A R M _ _ _ _   Shade of scarlet

26. _   _ _ _ _ _ _ _ _ _ _
      _ _ A R M _   Hemingway novel, made into a film with Rock Hudson

27. _ _ A R M _   Unctuously ingratiating

28. _ _ _   _ _ _
      _ _ _ _   _ _ _
      _ _ _ _ _ _   A R M   1955 film with Frank Sinatra

29. _ A R M _ _ _ _   Italian cheese, usually served grated

30. A R M _   _ _ _ _ _ _ _ _   Hollywood columnist

31. _ A R M _ _ _ _ _   Tropical monkey

32. A R M _   _ _ _   _ _ _
      _ _ _   G.B Shaw play; noted quote from Vergil

33. _ A R M _ _ _ _   Innocuous

34. _ A R M _   Destiny, to a Buddhist

35. A R M _ _ _ _ _ _ _   Ultimate or decisive battle

36. _ _ _ _ _ _ _   _ A R M   Satirical work by George Orwell

37. A R M _ _ _ _ _   Caucasus region, where Saroyan came from

38. _ A R M _ _ _ _ _ _   Confederate general, later governor of Missouri

39. _ _ _ _ _ _ _ _ _
      _ _ - A R M _   Ceremonial official

40. _ _ _ A R M _ _ _ _ _ _   Agreement to curtail war weaponry

HERE AND NOW

Each of the 21 definitions below should suggest to you a term containing the letters NOW. For example: *Frozen precipitation* would be sNOW. How many of them can you recognize?

A score of 11 is good; 15 is excellent; 19 means you kNOW your stuff!

Answers on page 335

1. Beginning of a bedtime prayer   _____

2. Symbolic grave in Washington, D.C.   _____

3. Not anywhere   _____

4. Tiny fish used for bait   _____

5. 1942 film starring Bette Davis   _____

6. Companion of the Seven Dwarfs   _____

7. Fame; celebrity; reputation   _____

8. Sub-human creature said to live in the Himalayas   _____

9. Early song by the Beatles   _____

10. Slogan used as typing exercise   _____

11. Every once in a while   _____

12. Short story by Hemingway   _____

13. Popular sport vehicle in wintry climates   _____

14. Dionne Warwick hit   _____

15. White bunting; a cocaine addict   _____

16. Play by Peter Ustinov   _____

17. Dictum by Francis Bacon   _____

18. Elocution exercise   _____

19. Opening line of Shakespeare's *Richard III*   _____

20. 1957 film starring Deborah Kerr   _____

21. Late 60's Broadway musical about the stock market   _____

BELLRINGERS

Each of the 39 words or expressions defined below contains the letters
BELL. For example: *Colloquial term for stomach* would be BELLy. How
many can you identify?

A score of 20 is good; 26 is excellent; 32 really rings the BELL.

Answers on page 336

1. Nursery rhyme _____

2. Well-known soup manufacturer _____

3. Waging war, or likely to do so _____

4. Famous Philadelphia tourist
   attraction _____

5. Jimmy Carter's Attorney General _____

6. The hit of the party, the loveliest
   lady present _____

7. Roar in anger or pain _____

8. Author of Utopian novel *Looking
   Backward* _____

9. Clown on TV's *The Howdy Doody
   Show* _____

10. Hemingway novel made into 1943
    film starring Gary Cooper _____

11. Another name for deadly nightshade _____

12. Adjective for many beautiful
    Southern mansions (Latin for
    "pre-war") _____

13. Risible dive in which stomach hits
    the water first _____

14. Family of Venetian Renaissance
    painters _____

15. Leader or leading indicator _____

16. Robert Redford's character in *The
    Way We Were* _____

17. To decorate or exaggerate _____

18. Warlike; hostile; bullying   _____

19. Nickname for the phone company   _____

20. John Hersey novel made into 1945 film   _____

21. Little Egypt, e.g.   _____

22. Turn-of-the-century xenophobic movement in China   _____

23. Flamboyant ex-Congresswoman from New York City   _____

24. In Greek mythology, tamer of Pegasus and slayer of the Chimaera   _____

25. Canadian-American novelist, winner of the 1976 Nobel Prize   _____

26. Kind-hearted madam in *Gone with the Wind* (played by Ona Munson in film)   _____

27. Weights used in body-building   _____

28. Colloquial for the navel   _____

29. Film starring Jimmy Stewart and Kim Novak (as a modern witch)   _____

30. Mild expletive   _____

31. 1794 Pennsylvania uprising against Federal excise taxes   _____

32. 1960 film about Franklin Delano Roosevelt   _____

33. Star of #32   _____

34. 1945 film starring Bing Crosby and Ingrid Bergman   _____

35. American novelist, author of *Jurgen*   _____

36. Italian composer of *Norma* and *I Puritani*   _____

37. Novel by the late Sylvia Plath   _____

38. Trousers worn by sailors   _____

39. Eye make-up manufacturer   _____

GET ON THE BANDWAGON

All of the 44 definitions below refer to a term which contains the letters BAN. How many of them can you identify?

A score of 19 is good; 27 is excellent; 35—strike up the BAND!

Answers on page 336

1. Where you deposit your money   _____

2. To condemn to exile   _____

3. American national anthem   _____

4. Headdress worn chiefly in Asia   _____

5. Adjective meaning "of a large city"   _____

6. Forbidden goods   _____

7. Popular yellow fruit   _____

8. Cloth applied to a wound   _____

9. Major city in Alaska; Hollywood star Douglas   _____

10. Character in Shakespeare's *The Tempest*   _____

11. To break up an organization   _____

12. To leave behind or leave stranded   _____

13. University town in Illinois   _____

14. Jewels—partner of baubles and beads   _____

15. Handrail found on stairways   _____

16. Broadway musical starring Phil Silvers   _____

17. Cause of trouble or woe   _____

18. Kind of tent found at the beach or pool   _____

19. Israeli statesman and former UN ambassador   _____

20. Four-stringed instrument resembling a guitar   _____

21. Middle Eastern nation   _____

22. Greek reveler _____

23. Capital of Thailand _____

24. Brightly colored handkerchief _____

25. Witty, sophisticated _____

26. Rallying cry heard in many 60's peace
    marches _____

27. Capital of New York State _____

28. Humdrum, mundane _____

29. Sensual Cuban dance; an aria from
    Carmen _____

30. Woody Allen film lampooning Latin
    American politics _____

31. Small variety of chicken; class in
    boxing _____

32. Thief, highwayman _____

33. Durable dance program hosted by
    Dick Clark _____

34. Actor who played Schultz on *Hogan's
    Heroes* _____

35. The whole affair (slang); the works _____

36. Locks of hair hanging over the
    forehead _____

37. Mythical creature found in Carroll's
    "Jabberwocky," characterized as
    "frumious" _____

38. Balkan nation, capital Tirana _____

39. Sumptuous meal, feast _____

40. Large South African city _____

41. Jest, repartee, drollery _____

42. Alabama-born actress (*The Little
    Foxes*) _____

43. Wailing spirit of death (Irish and
    Scottish legend) _____

44. Asian nation, formerly East Pakistan _____

BOTTOMS UP

Below, you will find 20 words, phrases, or expressions. Each should suggest an expression or word which contains the word UP. For example: *To honor or support* is to UP*hold.*

A score of 11 is fair; 14 is above average; and 18 is outstanding.

Answers on page 336

1. A junior or senior in college _____

2. Evening meal _____

3. Vehement expression meaning "Go to Hell!" _____

4. Violent social commotion or agitation _____

5. Good times and bad times _____

6. Surrender _____

7. The Uncola _____

8. Famous Mae West expression _____

9. To stuff furniture and cover with decorative fabric _____

10. Author of *The Centaur* and *Marry Me* _____

11. Pep pill _____

12. Rounded roof or dome _____

13. Big Bird and Kermit the Frog _____

14. Author of *The Jungle* _____

15. Conspiracy or plot to incriminate someone on false evidence _____

16. Famous 1960s Fifth Dimension song _____

17. Enjoy greatly; have a good time _____

18. Snobbish; fresh _____

19. Television takeoff on "The Princess and the Pea," starring Carol Burnett _____

20. Mentally distressed or perturbed _____

CAT GOT YOUR TONGUE?

Below are 18 definitions. Each should suggest a word, name, or phrase which contains the letters CAT. For example: *A division or genre* is a CAT*egory*.

A score of 10 is good; 13 is even better; and 16 is the CAT's pajamas.

Answers on page 336

1. List: complete enumeration of items _____

2. Eye disorder; part of a waterfall _____

3. Old European coin _____

4. Kurt Vonnegut novel _____

5. Important church _____

6. To Parisians, la sauce americaine; hamburger staple _____

7. American suffragist _____

8. Character in *Alice in Wonderland*, known for his grin _____

9. Underground cemetery, used by Roman Christians _____

10. Heckler's cry _____

11. Disseminate _____

12. Olympic competition of ten events _____

13. Book about Yossarian, Nately, et. al. _____

14. "Borscht Belt" area of New York State _____

15. State of total inactivity brought on by mental disorder _____

16. Roman poet _____

17. Mechanical device for hurling rocks, arrows, etc. _____

18. Type of whip, sung of in "HMS Pinafore" _____

IN THE CAN

Each one of the 41 clues below should suggest to you a term that contains the letters CAN. For example: *Ravine or gully* would be CAN*yon*. How many of them can you come up with?

A score of 22 is good; 29 is excellent; 35 or better is unCANny!

Answers on page 336

1. North American nation, capital Ottawa _____

2. Nut grown throughout the southern United States _____

3. Man-eating man _____

4. Chant; hex; magical formula _____

5. Heavy cloth; artist's painting surface _____

6. Opening line of *The Star-Spangled Banner* _____

7. Person under consideration for job or election _____

8. Holy See of the Roman Catholic Church _____

9. Large gun; howitzer _____

10. Hidden; secret; recondite _____

11. Controversial work by Henry Miller _____

12. Moss Hart play made into Best Picture of 1938 _____

13. Pejorative statement about teachers _____

14. Beggar _____

15. Cloth awning for bed, throne, doorway, etc. _____

16. Empty; unoccupied _____

17. Of or relating to a dog _____

18. One who engages in trade or commerce _____

73

19. Political division of Switzerland; major city in China _____

20. Brightly colored tropical bird with tremendous beak _____

21. Waterway (Panama or Erie, e.g.) _____

22. Spun-sugar confection found at fairs and circuses _____

23. French Riviera resort, famous for film festival _____

24. Ornamental container for wine or liquor _____

25. Injunction to be independent _____

26. Tropical storms afflicting the Caribbean and U.S. Gulf Coast _____

27. Spanish island group off Africa _____

28. Famous American dancer and innovator with controversial life style _____

29. Political novel by William Lederer and Eugene Burdick _____

30. Fraud; deception; double-dealing _____

31. Party sandwiches _____

32. Dried beef, often spicy _____

33. Beatles song from *A Hard Day's Night* _____

34. Region of Italy which includes Florence _____

35. Melon with orange flesh _____

36. Autobiography of Sammy Davis, Jr. _____

37. San Francisco baseball stadium _____

38. Glowing whitely or brightly _____

39. Geoffrey Chaucer's masterpiece _____

40. Fish-eating bird with capacious bill _____

41. Operatic singing style _____

SALLY FORTH

All 43 of the terms to be identified in this quiz contain the letters SAL. For example: *Pay for employment* would be SALary. Using the clues given, how many of them can you come up with?

A score of 23 is good; 30 is excellent; 38 earns you a 21-gun SALute.

Answers on page 337

1. Fresh-water food fish   _____

2. Pertaining to the nose   _____

3. The capital of Oregon;
   Massachusetts city famed for
   witch trials   _____

4. Common spice; NaCl   _____

5. Time of youthful inexperience   _____

6. Practice session   _____

7. Spittle   _____

8. Discoverer of anti-polio vaccine   _____

9. American actor who was murdered
   (*Rebel Without Cause, Exodus*)   _____

10. Germane; pertinent; outstanding   _____

11. Bar, "gin mill"   _____

12. Biblical poem   _____

13. Capital of Utah   _____

14. Novel by Gustave Flaubert set in
    ancient Carthage   _____

15. Newt   _____

16. Book of prayers   _____

17. Regarding something with a
    measure of skepticism or suspicion   _____

18. Heroine of *Cabaret*   _____

19. American actress (*Auntie Mame,
    Mourning Becomes Electra*),
    1911–1976   _____

20. Italian garlic sausage _____

21. The capital of Rhodesia _____

22. Barrage of rockets, shells, etc. _____

23. World-famous Spanish cellist
    (1876–1973) _____

24. Waldorf or Caesar, e.g. _____

25. Dark igneous rock, often forming
    natural columns _____

26. Formal greeting _____

27. Type of food poisoning _____

28. Pulitzer-winning play by Arthur
    Miller _____

29. Region of ancient Greece _____

30. Feudal servant _____

31. Nation of Central America _____

32. Idiom for person(s) with sterling
    qualities _____

33. Doomed son of King David _____

34. Arabian breed of dog _____

35. Capital of Tanzania _____

36. Biblical dancer who asked for the
    head of John the Baptist _____

37. Famous fan-dancer _____

38. Anti-Caesar epic by Roman poet
    Lucan _____

39. Tray, especially of gold or silver _____

40. Early French explorer of North
    America _____

41. Italian dish of veal and ham (the
    name means literally "jumps in
    the mouth") _____

42. Dictator of Portugal from 1932 to
    1968 _____

43. French literary drawing room _____

MONTH BY MONTH

The 39 definitions below should lead you to names and expressions which contain in them a month of the year. For example: *Surprise or discouragement* would be *dis*MAY. How many of them can you get?

A score of 19 is good; 26 is excellent; 33 earns you a month's vacation!

Answers on page 337

1. Highly developed Indian civilization in Mexico and Central America _____

2. Date fatal to Julius Caesar _____

3. Austrian site of tragic romance _____

4. Florida city, oldest in the U.S. _____

5. Laurel and Hardy film about nursery-rhyme characters _____

6. 1978 film with a title that marks the death of James Dean _____

7. Bolshevik insurrection in 1917 _____

8. Ship which brought the Pilgrims to America _____

9. Opening line of T.S. Eliot's *The Waste Land* _____

10. Perhaps _____

11. Song about a warm feeling on a cold day _____

12. First emperor of Rome _____

13. Early 60's TV series starring Spring Byington _____

14. Book by Ron Kovic, a disabled Vietnam veteran _____

15. Hit song and movie starring Pat Boone _____

16. TV actress (*Lassie, Lost in Space*) _____

17. Famous clinic in Minnesota _____

18. Victory song of Sherman's army _____

19. Play by John Patrick, made into film   _____

20. Nickname for John Philip Sousa   _____

21. Capital of Alaska   _____

22. Cole Porter hit   _____

23. Popular sandwich spread and dressing   _____

24. Barbara Tuchman work on World War I   _____

25. Love relationship between two persons of widely separated ages   _____

26. 1969 film with Jack Lemmon and Catherine Deneuve   _____

27. Oft-quoted line from poem by James Russell Lowell   _____

28. Lively song from *Camelot* by Lerner and Loewe   _____

29. The capital of Maine   _____

30. Beatnik character on *Dobie Gillis*   _____

31. Dull; unsatisfying   _____

32. Chief official of a city   _____

33. Knebel-Bailey novel, later a film, about an attempted military coup in the U.S.   _____

34. Big production number from *Carousel* by Rodgers and Hammerstein   _____

35. Mythical North Carolina setting for *The Andy Griffith Show*   _____

36. Actor, starred in *Death of a Salesman, Inherit the Wind*   _____

37. Crime of mutilation   _____

38. International holiday honoring workers   _____

39. Political drama about the Supreme Court starring Henry Fonda   _____

TEACHER'S PET

Below, you will find 20 expressions, phrases, or names. Each one of these should suggest to you another expression which begins with the word PET. For example: *Unimportant* is PET*ty*.

A score of 11 is fine; 14 is above average; and 18 is excellent.

Answers on page 337

1. Part of a flower   _____

2. Little boy who wouldn't grow up   _____

3. Sulking   _____

4. *Sine qua non* of British motorist   _____

5. Leslie Howard, Humphrey Bogart
   movie   _____

6. Favorite gripe   _____

7. Elaborate little pastry   _____

8. Small-time theft   _____

9. Stravinsky ballet   _____

10. Female underpinning   _____

11. Primitive or prehistoric drawing
    or carving on rock   _____

12. Garden flower   _____

13. Request; supplication   _____

14. Fourteenth century Italian poet   _____

15. Epileptic seizure   _____

16. Last Dutch governor of New York   _____

17. Small is beautiful   _____

18. Legal chicanery   _____

19. Fund for minor expenditures   _____

20. Caught in one's own trap   _____

GETTING MAD

The 33 words, names and expressions defined below have one common feature—each contains the letters MAD. For example: *Created by human beings* is man-MADe. How many of these terms can you identify?

A score of 18 is good; 25 is excellent; and 30 means you and this quiz were MADe for each other!

Answers on page 337

1. The capital of Spain _____

2. Well-known New York
   thoroughfare, synonymous with
   the advertising industry _____

3. Bedouin; wanderer _____

4. Mountain range in southern
   Wyoming _____

5. Artistic representation of the Virgin
   Mary _____

6. Drama by French playwright,
   Jean Giraudoux _____

7. Holy month in the Moslem calendar _____

8. Character in *Alice in Wonderland* _____

9. Fourth U.S. President _____

10. Angrier than a doused barnyard
    fowl _____

11. Puccini opera with Japanese heroine _____

12. 1948 Humphrey Bogart film (related to #4) _____

13. American women's magazine (French for "miss") _____

14. Naval fleet destroyed in 1588 by nature and the English _____

15. Island off SE African coast; the Malagasay Republic _____

16. Scented ointment for hair and scalp _____

17. 1963 film comedy, featuring almost every comic in Hollywood _____

18. Major city in India; kind of cloth originally made there _____

19. Segregationist, governor of Georgia 1966-1970 _____

20. Revolutionary War general from Pennsylvania _____

21. Late song by the Beatles _____

22. Noel Coward dictum: "_____ go out in the midday sun" _____

23. Type of poem or harmonic song, popular in the Renaissance _____

24. Large American motel chain _____

25. Principal female singer; temperamental performer _____

26. Portuguese island possession; the wine made there _____

27. Children's story by Bemelmans _____

28. Manager of a brothel _____

29. Well-known London wax museum _____

30. Criticism; censure _____

31. Spanish author and diplomat _____

32. 18th century French writer _____

33. Reckless, impulsive girl _____

BIG MAC

All 38 items defined in this quiz have in common the letters MAC. For example: *Drugstore* would be *pharMACy*. Using the clues below, how many of the words, names or expressions can you supply?

A score of 23 is good; 28 is excellent; and 33 establishes your supreMACy in word games.

Answers on page 338

1. Digestive organ

2. Brightly colored parrot

3. Late American general ("I shall return")

4. Cord knotted in designs

5. Host of *The Original Amateur Hour*

6. Wide-bladed hacking knife sometimes used as weapon

7. Asphalt-like road surfacing material

8. Spotless; pristine; unblemished

9. Type of noodle

10. Kind of shrub, sometimes poisonous

11. H.G. Well's classic science fiction novel

12. Famous New York department store, the largest in the world

13. Kind of fish: "Holy _____!"

14. Facial distortion; look of pain or displeasure

15. Suggestive taste or flavor; slang for kiss or slap

16. Famous drama by Shakespeare

17. Doily for back or arms of chair to prevent soiling

18. Symphonic poem by Saint-Saëns

19. TV series with Rock Hudson and Susan St. James _____

20. British statesman and labor leader; former prime minister _____

21. Confederate ironclad, more correctly known as the *Virginia* _____

22. Starved; reduced to skin and bones _____

23. Diacritical mark signifying a long vowel _____

24. Notorious Italian political theorist (1469–1527) _____

25. Ancient land of Alexander the Great, now part of Yugoslavia _____

26. Kind of nut associated with Hawaii _____

27. Anti-hero of *The Threepenny Opera* _____

28. Portuguese colony in Asia, near Hong Kong _____

29. Slang for "dollar" _____

30. Jewish patriots of the 2nd century B.C. _____

31. New York shop noted for fine housewares _____

32. Small pastry made of coconut and almonds _____

33. Sentimental Irish song _____

34. Son of Penelope and Odysseus _____

35. A kind of raincoat, or apple _____

36. Drama by Racine about Hector's wife _____

37. American poet, author of Pulitzer Prize-winning *Conquistador* _____

38. Character who fulfilled the witches' prophecy that Macbeth would not be overcome by man born of woman, nor until Birnam forest came to Dunsinane _____

FOR THE LITERATI

Here is a list of expression which don't literally mean what they say. You've probably run across all of them as you've turned the pages of literature. If you're up on our literary allusions—both classic and common—most of the 36 phrases should be in the bag!

You score two points for each choice correctly made. However, you lose three points for each incorrect answer. Questions left unanswered do not count. A score of 58 will be a feather in your cap, while an achievement of 64 should transport you to seventh heaven!

Answers on page 338

Answers on page 338

1. Crocodile tears
   False, affected, hypocritical sorrow
   Vulgar lamentation to excite pity
   Loud, sarcastic comment in a compassionate voice

2. To make bricks without straw
   To perform magic   *To perform a task without essential material*
   To make plans for an unlikely enterprise

3. To bury the hatchet
   To stop work   *To compromise*   *To make peace*

4. To carry coals to Newcastle
   To buck competition
   To take things to a place where they already abound
   To do a host of unnecessary acts to carry out a simple job

5. To show the white feather
   To exhibit cowardice   *To betray one's trust*   *To plea for mercy*

6. A Joe Miller
   An unsavory anecdote   *A stale joke*   *A ham comedian*

7. Crossing the Rubicon
   To get married   *To take an irrevocable, decisive step*
   To change one's religious or political affiliation

8. Homeric laughter
   Feigned happiness under pressure   *Cynical agreement*
   Inextinguishable laughter

9. Brown study
   To plan a murderous act
   A mood of serious or perplexed absorption
   An unflinching determination to acquire knowledge

10. The lion's share
    The best or largest part   *The prerogative of noble birth*
                         A conqueror's booty

11. To bell the cat
    To make a scene in public   *To boast vaingloriously*
                         To do a risky deed

12. Achilles' heel
    Concealed weapons   *A vulnerable point*
             Something about which one is inordinately sensitive

13. A skeleton in the closet
    One's unsavory past   *An open secret hypocritically hushed*
               A private, hidden source of shame or grief

14. A Parthian shot
    A cowardly blow   *A parting shot*   *A deadly aim*

15. Hobson's choice
    Accepting a nomination   *A choice without an alternative*
             Accepting a jail sentence rather than paying a fine

16. To speak in lutestring
    To swindle   *To coddle with honeyed words*
                 To use artificial, stilted language

17. The Alpha and Omega
    The waste   *The whole*   *The best*

18. Gilding the lily
    To offer a substitute which must be detected   *To mock*
           To artificially beautify something of supreme loveliness

19. A Job's comforter
    A political adviser who tenders poor counsel   *A priest*
           One who maliciously afflicts while ostensibly comforting

20. To play possum
    To spy for both sides
    To purloin trade secrets from one's employer
    To feign ignorance or illness with intent to deceive

21. A Roman holiday
    A three-day weekend   *A riotous and hilarious good time*
           An entertainment which causes loss to those providing it

22. To eat crow
    To act with utter humility   *To half starve*
               To accept what one has fought against

23. Abraham's bosom
    The abode of bliss in the world to come   *The comfort of religion*
                         A synagogue

24. To catch a tartar
> To swallow a sharp sauce   To discover a disloyal associate
> To encounter an opponent who is unexpectedly strong

25. A Greek gift
> Something given with a treacherous purpose   A bribe
> A present of something received from someone else

26. To kick the bucket
> To defy one's superiors   To flunk out of West Point
> To depart this life

27. Between Scylla and Charybdis
> To be torn between two loves   Loss of both money and honor
> Between two dangers, neither of which can be avoided

28. To turn the cat in the pan
> To accuse one's accuser   To accomplish a miracle
> To cleverly give a dexterous turn to a situation

29. A white elephant
> A burdensome possession
> An institution that exists only through lavish endowments
> A profitless business maintained solely through sentiment

30. To cry wolf
> To frighten by a ruse   To give alarm without occasion
> To claim aggression while one attacks

31. A Barmecide feast
> An easy piece of change   An illusion of plenty
> An orgy of gluttony

32. To talk like a Dutch uncle
> To admonish with severity and directness   To insist
> To make lavish promises

33. Sour grapes
> Cut-throat competition   A secret cause of hidden irritation
> Things affectedly despised because they cannot be possessed

34. To walk in golden slippers
> To be rolling in riches   To belong to a clerical order
> To dream or imagine that one is wealthy

35. Attic salt
> Poignant, delicate wit   Sarcasm   Money used for bribes

36. To cut the Gordian knot
> To act snobbishly
> To break into a society where one has been spurned
> To dispose of a difficulty by prompt, arbitrary action

LYMPHOCYTES

Lymphocytes in our blood help fight disease. But they won't help you find your way through this pesty little puzzler. A solution in 25 minutes is only fair; 20 minutes is bloody good; and 15 minutes or less is tiptop.

Solution on page 339

SHADINGS

The shaded portions of this maze may look interesting, but it's the clear path you're searching for. If it eludes you for more than 15 minutes, you're in the dark; a solution in 12 minutes is a shade better; and 9 minutes or less is a luminous achievement.

Solution on page 340

REVENGE

If you look at this pattern for long enough, you'll begin to see the swastikas repeated. Start at the top and make your way down to the southern front. Victory in 22 minutes isn't bad; 17 minutes is superior; and 14 minutes or less is exceptional.

Solution on page 340

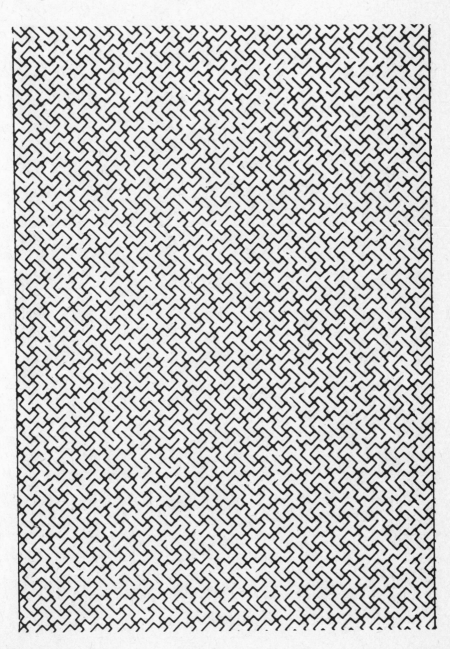

RATTAN RACEWAY

You won't race through this misnamed puzzler. A journey of 20 minutes is no big deal; 16 minutes, rather good; and 13 minutes or less, simply astounding.

Solution on page 341

SIX TRICKS

Start at the top, move from one to six in order, and exit at the bottom. This over-and-under puzzle requires that *no path be followed more than once.* Twenty-two minutes is maximum for this one; 18 minutes is quite good; and a solution in 15 minutes or less adds up to quite a trick.

Solution on page 341

QUADRUPLE WHAMMY

In Dogpatch, a whammy is a hex or a bad-luck sign. Here are four whammies in one. From top to bottom in 20 minutes is good enough; 17 minutes is above par; and 14 minutes or less is first-class.

Solution on page 342

MEDAL OF HONOR

Here's a fancy medal on a ribbon, but what's that mess below it? You'll have to muddle through to find out. Sixteen minutes is a respectable time for this one; 12 minutes is a lot better; and if you can zig-zag through in 10 minutes or less, you deserve a medal.

Solution on page 342

DETOUR

These arrows don't point the way; in fact, they block it. If you can find the road to success in 12 minutes, that's passable; 10 minutes is rather good; and 7 minutes or less is terrific.

Solution on page 343

TIPTOE

There are no tulips to tiptoe through in this garden, but there are leaves and flowers galore. A 15-minute trip is only a garden-variety feat; 11 minutes smells sweeter; and 8 minutes or less shows a fertile mind.

Solution on page 343

SCROLLWORK

This ornamental scrollwork would form an easy labyrinth if it weren't for those pesky one-way arrows. A journey of 15 minutes is an acceptable performance; 12 minutes, a jolly-good show; and 10 minutes or less, a cause for applause.

Solution on page 344

BOXER REBELLION

This maze may look easy, but you'll find yourself boxed in soon enough. If you can untangle this one in 15 minutes, that's fair; 10 minutes is fine; and 7 minutes or less is a knockout!

Solution on page 344

MATH SIGNS

The basic math signs haven't changed, even with the "New Math." Pass through at least one of the signs and out the bottom in 12 minutes and you've passed; in 8 minutes, you've done yourself proud; and a journey of 5 minutes or less earns an honors grade.

Solution on page 345

TAKE FIVE

Here's a maze to rest on. But if you take 5 minutes, you haven't earned your rest. Three minutes is tops for this one.

Solution on page 345

FIVE STRINGS

The ten black dots represent the ends of the five strings that intertwine to form this maze. If you unravel this one in 20 minutes, that's so-so; 15 minutes is good; and 12 minutes or less is superb.

Solution on page 346

REPEAT PATTERN

Template patterns are repeated over and over to form this maze. Enter anywhere you like at the top, but naturally there's only one way to the bottom. Find it in 12 minutes and you're doing well; 8 minutes, even better; and 5 minutes or less, you're an old hand at this game.

Solution on page 346

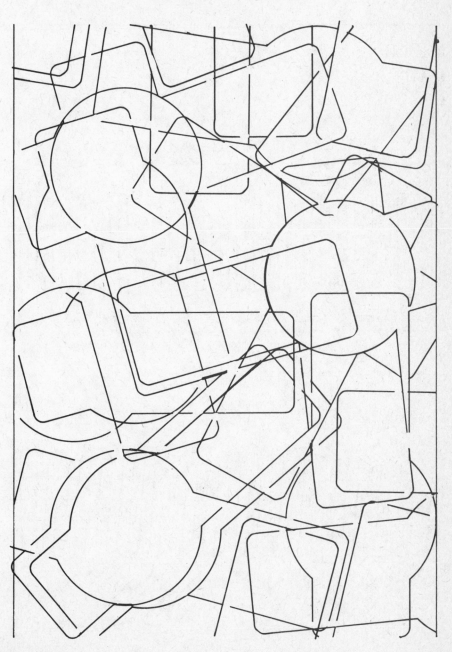

HERRINGBONES

Five strings of herringbones block your path. Then again, they could be radiators. Anyway, a solution in 15 minutes is all right; 10 minutes is much better; 8 minutes or less is magnificent, and there's no bones about it.

Solution on page 347

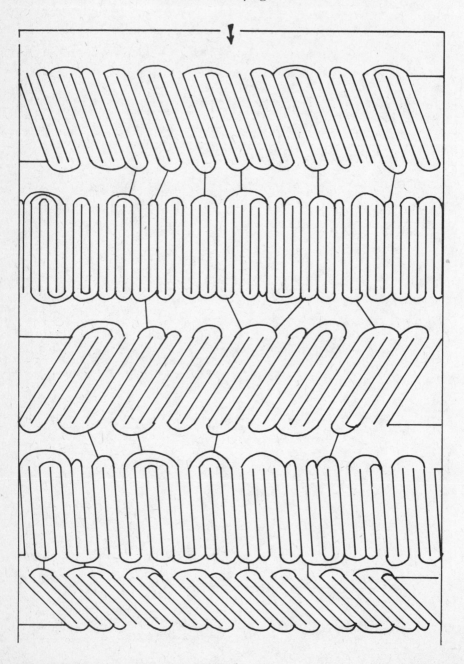

ORBITS

A circle has no beginning and no end. Your troubles start at the top and end at the bottom of this maze. In between, you're in orbit. Spin through in 20 minutes for a passing grade; 15 minutes for hearty congratulations; and 10 minutes or less for resounding cheers.

Solution on page 347

THIRD DIMENSION

The third dimension is depth, and you'll find yourself in deep trouble before you can steer a course through this jumble of objects. If you're home free in 12 minutes, that's mediocre; 10 minutes is good; and 7 minutes or less is sensational.

Solution on page 348

CURVES AND BARS

Start anywhere at the top and find a way to the asterisk. If you can discover the route in 20 minutes, that's nothing to write home about; 15 minutes is fine; and a solution in 10 minutes or less is worthy of note.

Solution on page 348

RIBBON CANDY

This sweet little stumper is sure to lead you astray before you find daylight at the bottom. If you're in the dark for more than 12 minutes, you couldn't have much of a sweet tooth. A solution in 8 minutes is about right, and in less than 5 minutes is extraordinary.

Solution on page 349

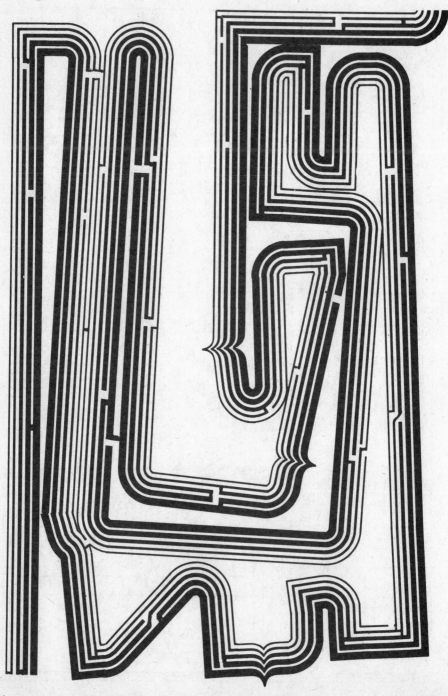

A LITTLE DAB'LL DO YA

Four 3-letter words can be made with the letters A, B, C, and D: BAD, CAB, DAB, and CAD. But you can make only one of those words in this over-and-under maze. Start at the top and visit 3 letters to make that word. A solution in less than 15 minutes is exceptional. *Solution on page 349*

BINGO

Start at the top, find a path to "B," then to "I," and so on, to spell BINGO. Important: *you can't take the same path twice.* After you've made BINGO, exit at the bottom. A solution in 20 minutes or less is something to brag about.

Solution on page 350

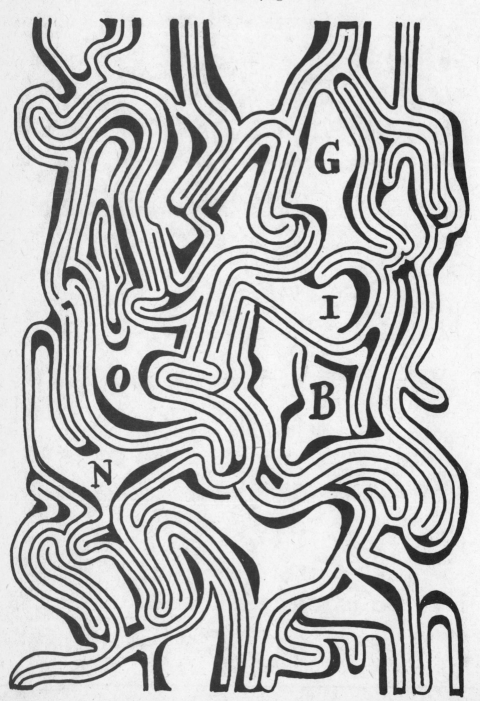

EYES RIGHT

These long columns won't work wonders for your eyes, but the right ones will lead you to the bottom. Success in 12 minutes is all right; 8 minutes is quite good; and a solution in 6 minutes or less is an eye-opening accomplishment.

Solution on page 350

HOW TO SOLVE BLANKIES

The *Blankie* is based on progressive anagrams. Each Blankie is a short story in itself. In each story, a number of words have been omitted. Each omitted word is indicated by a number of dashes. Each dash represents a single letter. For example, a series of three dashes indicates a three-letter word; a series of four dashes, a four-letter word, etc.

In order to start you on your way, the key word in the Blankie is set down in capital letters. In Blankies, every successive word to be found must include each letter contained in the previous word which was found.

For example, if one of the Blankie stories contains four words to be found, with the key word AT, and the second word is represented by three dashes, the third by four dashes, etc., these words might be AT, CAT, TACK, STACK, TRACKS. It will be readily apparent that the word CAT contains all the letters in AT, that the word TACK contains all the letters in CAT, that the word STACK contains all the letters in TACK, etc.

You are respectfully advised to read the entire short story before attempting to fill in any of the words. Inferences drawn from the content as a whole should be of great help in suggesting the connotation of the missing words.

HOW TO HOLD MY OLD MAN

PA is __ __ __ to __ __ __ __ company at any time at a __ __ __ __ __ __. He'll split whenever he thinks things are getting dull.

The only thing that can hold him is good __ __ __ __ __ __

Answers on page 351

GUILTY BUT WHITEWASHED

Now I've had cats, and I've had dogs, and I've had birds, and I've had reptiles, but my little terrier Cutie is the sweetest, dearest, darlingest *P E T* I've ever had. She's so nervy, fresh, vivacious, and _ _ _ _, and particularly so when she does something wrong. I certainly give her enough to eat. She gets all kinds of meat, especially _ _ _ _ _ _.

But she's a born _ _ _ _ _ _ _. She steals. It isn't that she's hungry. It's just that she loves to filch things. When we have _ _ _ _ _ _ _ _ at our house and have prepared platters of cakes and eclairs, she invades the kitchen and, when no one is looking, grabs off a few delectable creampuffs. And then, right before every one else, as if she were innocent as a goldfish, she _ _ _ _ _ _ _ _ _ into the parlor before all the guests, with her face full of whipped cream.

She's small; she's weak; she's no good as a watchdog; the plain fact is she's useless, but one of the most delightful _ _ _ _ _ _ _ _ _ _ alive.

Answers on page 351

IN SHORT ORDER

If I'm desperately hungry, *AN* egg in the _ _ _ is worth two in the refrigerator.

When my innards are crying out for nourishment, the time _ _ _ _ is critical. Never mind the amenities. A rose on the table can be stately, gorgeous, and wildly sensuous, but decor is no boon to a hungry man. A _ _ _ _ _ _ may be beautiful, but you can't eat it.

When I'm ravenous, I want to eat; and you'd better make it _ _ _ _ _ _.

Answers on page 351

GERIATRICS

My *PA* likes to take a _ _ _ after dinner. It relaxes him after a stressful day.

He stretches out for a _ _ _ _ of an hour or so, and the _ _ _ _ _ in his limbs vanish.

If he wakes up suddenly before his hour is up, he _ _ _ _ _ _. He wonders where he is and he thinks his strength has left him. Then he jumps up, runs to the kitchen, and for a restorative, he consumes a full bowl of _ _ _ _ _ _ _.

Answers on page 351

JUST DESSERTS

It was *AT* the _ _ _ Baby, a restaurant of renown where the Black Bottom _ _ _ _ was the _ _ _ _ _ supreme.

We ordered just one portion and nominated Joan to be the first _ _ _ _ _ _. She took one spoonful and howled with delight. We knew the verdict.

So after Joan had served as the _ _ _ _ _ _ _ _, we each ordered one of those unimaginable delights.

Then we followed with two, three, and four apiece. None of us could stop—there were no _ _ _ _ _ _ _ _. Only the price of $2.50 each finally made us surrender.

Answers on page 351

THE LITERATI

There is, *TO* a certain extent, a hierarchy in the world of belles letters. To _ _ _ the writer who currently occupies the pinnacle _ _ _ _ in the field requires nothing less than extraordinary talent.

_ _ _ _ _ _ may be inspired, but their faces hardly ever grace a _ _ _ _ _ _ _. One can't win acclaim in literature through good looks.

Nor, in the literary field, is recognition obtained through a duel of wits. The best _ _ _ _ _ _ _ is a touch of genius.

Answers on page 351

AT THE SHRINK'S

"My ego is blasted and my *ID* is in shambles. I just can't get _ _ _ of the _ _ _ _ fears that inhabit me.

"Tension _ _ _ _ _ _ through my every muscle and hatred and dread _ _ _ _ _ _ _ in my every pore.

"My _ _ _ _ _ _ _ _ are loathsome, and I am ashamed of the concepts that are _ _ _ _ _ _ _ _ _ _ _* of my befouled mind.

"Only fifty-two people in all history had more cares and worries than I. Those men were all _ _ _ _ _ _ _ _ _ _ _."

———
*Add two letters to previous Blankie

Answers on page 351

HILARIOUS HEADLINES

From a Heraldsburg, Cal. paper:

CAR LEAVES ROAD, SUFFERS BROKEN NOSE

From a Burlingame, Cal. paper:

SANTA ROSA MAN DENIES HE COMMITTED SUICIDE IN SAN FRANCISCO

From the Spokane Chronicle:

GRILL SUSPECT OVER BIG BLAZE

From the Boise, Idaho Statesman, announcing birth of triplets:

THREE OF A KIND GIVES PAIR FULL HOUSE

From an Oakland, Cal. paper:

HAMM FAILS TO IDENTIFY YEGGS

From a Dallas paper:

THUGS EAT THEN ROB PROPIETOR

From the Toledo Times:

SCENT FOUL PLAY IN DEATH OF MAN FOUND BOUND AND HANGED

From a San Francisco paper:

DEAD OFFICER ON S.F. FORCE FOR 18 YEARS

From the San Antonio, Tex. Express:

"LEONORE" ONLY OPERA BEETHOVEN WROTE ON MONDAY EVENING

From an Oshkosh, Wis. paper:

PEACE OR WAR DEEMED NEAR

From the La Grange, Ga. News:

REV. KEY RESIGNS; ATTENDANCE DOUBLES

From the Wheeling, W. Va. Intelligencer:

WILD WIFE LEAGUE WILL MEET TO-NIGHT

From a Walla Walla, Wash. paper:

ONION PROSPECTS REPORTED STRONG

From the Springfield Republican:

40 MEN ESCAPE WATERY GRAVES WHEN VESSEL FLOUNDERS IN ALE

From a Los Angeles paper:

COUNTY OFFICIALS TO TALK RUBBISH

From the Greensboro, N.C. News:

SAM M—,80, HELD FOR SHOOTING GRANDMOTHER'S HUSBAND

From the Chicago Tribune:

WIFE GIVES BIRTH TO A BOY; HE ASKS OLD AGE PENSION

From the Halifax, Canada Herald:
JUNE BABIES FLOOD OTTAWA HOSPITAL

From a New York paper, reporting on a rape by a group of soldiers:
COMMISSION TO EXAMINE PRIVATES—WILL LEAVE NO STONE UNTURNED

From the Oakland, Cal. Tribune:
TWO CONVICTS EVADE NOOSE; JURY HUNG

From the New York Journal-American:
STEALS CLOCK, FACES TIME

From an Austin, Tex. paper:
JURY GETS DRUNK DRIVING CASE HERE

From a Texas paper:
NEBRASKA OFFICERS BEST BANK BANDITS

From the Boston Transcript:
HOTEL BURNS; TWO HUNDRED GUESTS ESCAPE HALF GLAD

From the Cleveland Plain Dealer:

GYPSY ROSE HAS A 5½ -POUND STRIPLING

From an Alhambra, Cal. paper:

DRIVER OF DEATH CAR HELD ON NEGLIGIBLE HOMICIDE

From a Los Cruces, N.M. paper:

MAN IS FATALLY SLAIN

From the Lansing State Journal:

SENATE PASSES DEATH PENALTY—Measure Provides for Electrocution for All Persons Over 17.

From a New York paper:

FATHER OF TEN SHOT—MISTAKEN FOR RABBIT

From the Wichita Falls, Tex. Record News:

ENRAGED COW INJURES FARMER WITH AX

From the Redondo Beach, Cal. South Bay Daily Breeze:

MANY ANTIQUES AT D.A.R. MEETING

HOW TO SOLVE THREEZIES

You are given a sequence of three letters. You are to list all the words you can think of which contain these three letters *in exact sequence.*

The sequence may seem quite unlikely. For example, a sequence of letters RRH at first blush might seem completely hopeless, yet with a little thought you may come up with the word *Catarrh* and possibly with the word *Myrrh.* If the given three letters were MBS, you might find that out of this strange sequence you can form the word *Numbskull.*

The rules of the game are very simple. You may use only one form of the word. For example, if the threezie were NDL, a proper answer would be *Fondly.* But then you couldn't count the word *Fondle,* since both these words have the same root. However, where words have a completely different meaning, then they may both be used even though the roots are similar. So, if the threezie were RTH, you could score with the word *Forth* and also with the word *Forthright.*

Proper names are off limits. Hyphenated words are allowed.

LUM

There are at least 32 words which contain the letter sequence L U M. How many can you find? List them below.

If you get 15, that's fine; 22 is excellent; and 25 is superb.

Answers on page 351

1. _____
2. _____
3. _____
4. _____
5. _____
6. _____
7. _____
8. _____
9. _____
10. _____
11. _____
12. _____
13. _____
14. _____
15. _____
16. _____
17. _____
18. _____
19. _____
20. _____
21. _____
22. _____
23. _____
24. _____
25. _____
26. _____
27. _____
28. _____
29. _____
30. _____
31. _____
32. _____

LTI

There are at least 10 words which contain the letter sequence L T I. How many can you find? List them below.

A score of 6 is good; 8 is excellent.

Answers on page 351

1. _____	4. _____	8. _____
2. _____	5. _____	9. _____
3. _____	6. _____	10. _____
	7. _____	

ECH

There are at least 14 words which contain the letter sequence E C H. How many can you find? List them below.

If you can fill in the spaces below with 9 of them, that's swell; 10 is terrific; and 12 is super.

Answers on page 351

1. _____	6. _____	10. _____
2. _____	7. _____	11. _____
3. _____	8. _____	12. _____
4. _____	9. _____	13. _____
5. _____		14. _____

HOU

There are at least 12 words which contain the letter sequence H O U. How many can you find? List them below.

A score of 5 is fair; 8 is excellent; and 10 is really top-notch.

Answers on page 351

1. _____	5. _____	9. _____
2. _____	6. _____	10. _____
3. _____	7. _____	11. _____
4. _____	8. _____	12. _____

CTU

We have listed 34 words that contain the letter sequence CTU. How many can you find?

A score of 17 is creditable; 22 exacts praise; and 28 elects you verbal chieftain.

Answers on page 351

1. _____	12. _____	24. _____
2. _____	13. _____	25. _____
3. _____	14. _____	26. _____
4. _____	15. _____	27. _____
5. _____	16. _____	28. _____
6. _____	17. _____	29. _____
7. _____	18. _____	30. _____
8. _____	19. _____	31. _____
9. _____	20. _____	32. _____
10. _____	21. _____	33. _____
11. _____	22. _____	34. _____
	23. _____	

OPA

We found 19 words with the letter sequences OPA. How many can you list?

A score of 10 is lovely; 15 or more is superior.

Answers on page 352

1. _____	7. _____	14. _____
2. _____	8. _____	15. _____
3. _____	9. _____	16. _____
4. _____	10. _____	17. _____
5. _____	11. _____	18. _____
6. _____	12. _____	19. _____
	13. _____	

MON

There are at least 86 words that contain the letter sequence MON. How many can you list?

A score of 45 is not meager; 60 is most admirable; and 75 is marvelous.

Answers on page 352

1. _____
2. _____
3. _____
4. _____
5. _____
6. _____
7. _____
8. _____
9. _____
10. _____
11. _____
12. _____
13. _____
14. _____
15. _____
16. _____
17. _____
18. _____
19. _____
20. _____
21. _____
22. _____
23. _____
24. _____
25. _____
26. _____
27. _____
28. _____
29. _____

30. _____
31. _____
32. _____
33. _____
34. _____
35. _____
36. _____
37. _____
38. _____
39. _____
40. _____
41. _____
42. _____
43. _____
44. _____
45. _____
46. _____
47. _____
48. _____
49. _____
50. _____
51. _____
52. _____
53. _____
54. _____
55. _____
56. _____
57. _____

58. _____
59. _____
60. _____
61. _____
62. _____
63. _____
64. _____
65. _____
66. _____
67. _____
68. _____
69. _____
70. _____
71. _____
72. _____
73. _____
74. _____
75. _____
76. _____
77. _____
78. _____
79. _____
80. _____
81. _____
82. _____
83. _____
84. _____
85. _____
86. _____

VOR

We have found 14 words that contain the letter sequence VOR. Can you do better?

A score of 8 is very nice; anything over 11 is marvelous.

Answers on page 352

1. _____
2. _____
3. _____
4. _____
5. _____

6. _____
7. _____
8. _____
9. _____

10. _____
11. _____
12. _____
13. _____
14. _____

WED

At least 41 words contain the letter sequence WED. How many can you list?

A score of 20 is worthy; 26 is weighty; and 36 is a winning score.

Answers on page 352

1. _____
2. _____
3. _____
4. _____
5. _____
6. _____
7. _____
8. _____
9. _____
10. _____
11. _____
12. _____
13. _____
14. _____

15. _____
16. _____
17. _____
18. _____
19. _____
20. _____
21. _____
22. _____
23. _____
24. _____
25. _____
26. _____
27. _____

28. _____
29. _____
30. _____
31. _____
32. _____
33. _____
34. _____
35. _____
36. _____
37. _____
38. _____
39. _____
40. _____
41. _____

THU

We list 18 words that contain the letter sequence THU. How many can you find?

A score of 10 is thoughtful; 13 or more is thrilling.

Answers on page 352

1. _____	7. _____	13. _____
2. _____	8. _____	14. _____
3. _____	9. _____	15. _____
4. _____	10. _____	16. _____
5. _____	11. _____	17. _____
6. _____	12. _____	18. _____

FRI

There are at least 36 words with the letter sequence FRI. How many can you list?

A score of 20 is fine; 26 is far better; and 32 is fantastic.

Answers on page 353

1. _____	13. _____	25. _____
2. _____	14. _____	26. _____
3. _____	15. _____	27. _____
4. _____	16. _____	28. _____
5. _____	17. _____	29. _____
6. _____	18. _____	30. _____
7. _____	19. _____	31. _____
8. _____	20. _____	32. _____
9. _____	21. _____	33. _____
10. _____	22. _____	34. _____
11. _____	23. _____	35. _____
12. _____	24. _____	36. _____

SAT

At least 33 words contain the letter sequence SAT. How many can you find?

A score of 17 is all right; 23 is good; and 29 is super.

Answers on page 353

1. _____	12. _____	23. _____
2. _____	13. _____	24. _____
3. _____	14. _____	25. _____
4. _____	15. _____	26. _____
5. _____	16. _____	27. _____
6. _____	17. _____	28. _____
7. _____	18. _____	29. _____
8. _____	19. _____	30. _____
9. _____	20. _____	31. _____
10. _____	21. _____	32. _____
11. _____	22. _____	33. _____

SUN

We list 27 words with the letter sequence SUN. Can you find them?

A score of 15 is bright; 22 or more is brilliant.

Answers on page 353

1. _____	10. _____	19. _____
2. _____	11. _____	20. _____
3. _____	12. _____	21. _____
4. _____	13. _____	22. _____
5. _____	14. _____	23. _____
6. _____	15. _____	24. _____
7. _____	16. _____	25. _____
8. _____	17. _____	26. _____
9. _____	18. _____	27. _____

IDA

We found 28 words that contain the letter sequence IDA. How many can you list?

A score of 14 is fair; 19 is dandy; and 24 is swell.

Answers on page 353

1. _____
2. _____
3. _____
4. _____
5. _____
6. _____
7. _____
8. _____
9. _____

10. _____
11. _____
12. _____
13. _____
14. _____
15. _____
16. _____
17. _____
18. _____
19. _____

20. _____
21. _____
22. _____
23. _____
24. _____
25. _____
26. _____
27. _____
28. _____

RBI

There are at least 27 words that contain the letter sequence RBI. How many can you list?

A score of 14 is not bad; 19 is rather big; and 23 gives you star billing.

Answers on page 353

1. _____
2. _____
3. _____
4. _____
5. _____
6. _____
7. _____
8. _____
9. _____

10. _____
11. _____
12. _____
13. _____
14. _____
15. _____
16. _____
17. _____
18. _____

19. _____
20. _____
21. _____
22. _____
23. _____
24. _____
25. _____
26. _____
27. _____

RDU

We list a mere seven words with the letter sequence RDU. How many can you identify?

Anything over 3 is commendable.

Answers on page 353

1. _____   3. _____   6. _____
2. _____   4. _____   7. _____
                       5. _____

NCI

There are at least 60 words that contain the letter sequence NCI. How many can you list?

A score of 30 is fair; 40 is grand; and 50 is substantial.

Answers on page 353

1. _____   21. _____   41. _____
2. _____   22. _____   42. _____
3. _____   23. _____   43. _____
4. _____   24. _____   44. _____
5. _____   25. _____   45. _____
6. _____   26. _____   46. _____
7. _____   27. _____   47. _____
8. _____   28. _____   48. _____
9. _____   29. _____   49. _____
10. _____   30. _____   50. _____
11. _____   31. _____   51. _____
12. _____   32. _____   52. _____
13. _____   33. _____   53. _____
14. _____   34. _____   54. _____
15. _____   35. _____   55. _____
16. _____   36. _____   56. _____
17. _____   37. _____   57. _____
18. _____   38. _____   58. _____
19. _____   39. _____   59. _____
20. _____   40. _____   60. _____

EMI

There are at least 68 words with the letter sequence EMI. How many can you list?

A score of 35 is to be accepted; 45 is to be praised; and 55 is to be emulated.

Answers on page 354

1. _____	24. _____	46. _____
2. _____	25. _____	47. _____
3. _____	26. _____	48. _____
4. _____	27. _____	49. _____
5. _____	28. _____	50. _____
6. _____	29. _____	51. _____
7. _____	30. _____	52. _____
8. _____	31. _____	53. _____
9. _____	32. _____	54. _____
10. _____	33. _____	55. _____
11. _____	34. _____	56. _____
12. _____	35. _____	57. _____
13. _____	36. _____	58. _____
14. _____	37. _____	59. _____
15. _____	38. _____	60. _____
16. _____	39. _____	61. _____
17. _____	40. _____	62. _____
18. _____	41. _____	63. _____
19. _____	42. _____	64. _____
20. _____	43. _____	65. _____
21. _____	44. _____	66. _____
22. _____	45. _____	67. _____
23. _____		68. _____

NDA

There are at least 23 words which contain the letter sequence N D A. How many can you find? List them below.

If you can fill in the spaces below with 15 of them. that's good; 18 is dandy; and 20 or more is fantastic.

Answers on page 354

1. _____   9. _____   16. _____
2. _____   10. _____   17. _____
3. _____   11. _____   18. _____
4. _____   12. _____   19. _____
5. _____   13. _____   20. _____
6. _____   14. _____   21. _____
7. _____   15. _____   22. _____
8. _____   23. _____

ARD

There are at least 39 words which contain the letter sequence A R D. How many can you find? List them below.

A score of 20 is fine; 25 is terrific; and 30 is splendid.

Answers on page 354

1. _____   14. _____   27. _____
2. _____   15. _____   28. _____
3. _____   16. _____   29. _____
4. _____   17. _____   30. _____
5. _____   18. _____   31. _____
6. _____   19. _____   32. _____
7. _____   20. _____   33. _____
8. _____   21. _____   34. _____
9. _____   22. _____   35. _____
10. _____   23. _____   36. _____
11. _____   24. _____   37 _____
12. _____   25. _____   38. _____
13. _____   26. _____   39. _____

RSI

There are at least 31 words which contain the letter sequence R S I. How many can you find? List them below.

A score of 18 is fairly good; 23 is exceptional; and 26 or more is worthy of a medal!

Answers on page 354

1. _____	11. _____	22. _____
2. _____	12. _____	23. _____
3. _____	13. _____	24. _____
4. _____	14. _____	25. _____
5. _____	15. _____	26. _____
6. _____	16. _____	27. _____
7. _____	17. _____	28. _____
8. _____	18. _____	29. _____
9. _____	19. _____	30. _____
10. _____	20. _____	31. _____
	21. _____	

MPL

There are at least 34 words which contain the letter sequence M P L. How many can you find? List them below.

A score of 20 is very good; 24 is above average; and 28 or over is an outstanding score.

Answers on page 355

1. _____	12. _____	24. _____
2. _____	13. _____	25. _____
3. _____	14. _____	26. _____
4. _____	15. _____	27. _____
5. _____	16. _____	28. _____
6. _____	17. _____	29. _____
7. _____	18. _____	30. _____
8. _____	19. _____	31. _____
9. _____	20. _____	32. _____
10. _____	21. _____	33. _____
11. _____	22. _____	34. _____
	23. _____	

EMO

There are at least 28 words which contain the letter sequence E M O. How many can you find? List them below.

A score of 14 is good; 20 is wonderful; and 23 is magnificent.

Answers on page 355

1. _____	10. _____	20. _____
2. _____	11. _____	21. _____
3. _____	12. _____	22. _____
4. _____	13. _____	23. _____
5. _____	14. _____	24. _____
6. _____	15. _____	25. _____
7. _____	16. _____	26. _____
8. _____	17. _____	27. _____
9. _____	18. _____	28. _____
	19. _____	

EPT

There are at least 28 words which contain the letter sequence E P T. How many can you find? List them below.

A score of 16 is pretty good; 19 is superior; and 22 or more is outstanding.

Answers on page 355

1. _____	10. _____	20. _____
2. _____	11. _____	21. _____
3. _____	12. _____	22. _____
4. _____	13. _____	23 _____
5. _____	14. _____	24. _____
6. _____	15. _____	25. _____
7. _____	16. _____	26. _____
8. _____	17. _____	27. _____
9. _____	18. _____	28. _____
	19. _____	

CLE

There are at least 14 words which contain the letter sequence C L E. How many can you find? List them below.

A score of 8 is fine; 10 is great; and 12 is sensational.

Answers on page 355

1. _____   6. _____   10. _____
2. _____   7. _____   11. _____
3. _____   8. _____   12. _____
4. _____   9. _____   13. _____
5. _____   14. _____

ORS

There are at least 20 words which contain the letter sequence O R S. How many can you find? List them below.

If you get 8, that's pretty good; 12 is excellent; and 18 rates you with the pros.

Answers on page 355

1. _____   8. _____   14. _____
2. _____   9. _____   15. _____
3. _____   10. _____ 16. _____
4. _____   11. _____ 17. _____
5. _____   12. _____ 18. _____
6. _____   13. _____ 19. _____
7. _____   20. _____

OCH

There are at least 12 words which contain the letter sequence O C H. How many can you find? List them below.

A score of 6 is good; 8 is very good; and 10 is excellent.

Solution on page 355

1. _____   5. _____   9. _____
2. _____   6. _____   10. _____
3. _____   7. _____   11. _____
4. _____   8. _____   12. _____

THE OWL-CRITIC

JAMES T. FIELDS

"Who stuffed that white owl?" No one spoke in the shop,
The barber was busy, and he couldn't stop;
The customers, waiting their turns, were all reading
The *Daily*, the *Herald*, the *Post*, little heeding
The young man who blurted out such a blunt question;
Not one raised a head, or even made a suggestion;
    And the barber kept on shaving.

"Don't you see, Mr. Brown,"
Cried the youth, with a frown,
"How wrong the whole thing is,
How preposterous each wing is,
How flattened the head is, how jammed down the neck is—
In short, the whole owl, what an ignorant wreck 'tis.
I make no apology;
I've learned owl-eology.
I've passed days and nights in a hundred collections,
And cannot be blinded to any deflections
Arising from unskillful fingers that fail
To stuff a bird right, from his beak to his tail.
Mister Brown! Mister Brown!
Do take that bird down,
Or you'll soon be the laughing-stock all over town!"
    And the barber kept on shaving.

"I've *studied* owls,
And other night-fowls,
And I tell you
What I know to be true;
An owl cannot roost
With his limbs so unloosed;
No owl in this world
Ever had his claws curled,
Ever had his legs slanted,
Ever had his bill canted,
Ever had his neck screwed
Into that attitude.
He can't *do* it, because
'Tis against all bird-laws.

"Anatomy teaches,
Ornithology preaches,
An owl has a toe
That *can't* turn out so!
I've made the white owl my study for years,
And to see such a job almost moves me to tears!
Mr. Brown, I'm amazed
You should be so gone crazed
As to put up a bird
In that posture absurd!
To *look* at that owl really brings on a dizziness
The man who stuffed *him* don't half know his business!"
    And the barber kept on shaving.

"Examine those eyes.
I'm filled with surprise
Taxidermists should pass
Off on you such poor glass;
So unnatural they seem
They'd make Audubon scream,
And John Burroughs laugh
To encounter such chaff.
Do take that bird down;
Have him stuffed again, Brown!"
    And the barber kept on shaving.

"With some sawdust and bark
I could stuff in the dark
An owl better than that.
I could make an old hat
Look more like an owl
Than that horrid fowl,
Stuck up there so stiff like a side of coarse leather.
In fact, about *him*, there's not one natural feather."

Just then, with a wink and a sly normal lurch,
The owl, very gravely, got down from his perch,
Walked around, and regarded his fault-finding critic
(Who thought he was stuffed) with a glance analytic,
And then fairly hooted, as if he should say:
"Your learning's at fault *this* time, anyway;
Don't waste it again on a live bird, I pray.
I'm an owl; you're another. Sir Critic, good day!"
    And the barber kept on shaving.

SHE WAS POOR, BUT SHE WAS HONEST

She was poor, but she was honest,
    Victim of the squire's whim:
First he loved her, then he left her,
    And she lost her honest name.

Then she ran away to London,
    For to hide her grief and shame;
There she met another squire,
    And lost her name again.

See her riding in her carriage,
    In the Park and all so gay:
All the nibs and nobby persons
    Come to pass the time of day.

See the little old-world village
    Where her aged parents live,
Drinking the champagne she sends them;
    But they never can forgive.

In the rich man's arms she flutters,
    Like a bird with broken wing:
First he loved her, then he left her,
    And she hasn't got a ring.

See him in the splendid mansion,
    Entertaining with the best,
While the victim of his passions
    Trails her way through mud and slime.

Standing on the bridge at midnight,
    She says: "Farewell, blighted Love."
There's a scream, a splash—Good Heavens!
    What is she a-doing of?

Then they drag her from the river,
    Water from her clothes they wrang,
For they thought that she was drowned;
    But the corpse got up and sang:

"It's the same the whole world over,
    It's the poor that gets the blame,
It's the rich that gets the pleasure.
    Isn't it a blooming shame?"

BLOW ME EYES

WALLACE IRWIN

When I was young and full o' pride,
    A-standin' on the grass
And gazin' o'er the water-side,
    I seen a fisher lass.
"O, fisher lass, be kind awhile,"
    I asks 'er quite unbid.
"Please look into me face and smile"—
    And, blow me eyes, she did!"

      O, blow me light and blow me blow,
      I didn't think she'd charm me so—
        But, blow me eyes, she did!

She seemed so young and beautiful
    I *had* to speak perlite,
(The afternoon was long and dull,
    But she was short and bright).
"This ain't no place," I says, "to stand—
    Let's take a walk instid,
Each holdin' of the other's hand"—
    And, blow me eyes, she did!

      O, blow me light and blow me blow,
      I sort o' thunk she wouldn't go—
        But, blow me eyes, she did!

And as we walked along a lane
With no one else to see,
Me heart was filled with sudden pain,
And so I says to she:
"If you would have me actions speak
The words what can't be hid,
You'd sort o' let me kiss yer cheek"—
And, blow me eyes, she did!

O, blow me light and blow me bloe,
How sweet she was I didn't know—
But, blow me eyes, *she* did!

But pretty soon me shipmate Jim
Came strollin' down the beach,
And she began a-oglin' him
As pretty as a peach.
"O, fickle maid o' false intent,"
Impuslively I chid,
"Why don't you go and wed that gent?"
And, blow my eyes, she did!

O, blow me light and blow me blow,
I didn't think she'd treat me so—
But, blow me eyes, she did!

THE YARN OF THE NANCY BELL

W.S. GILBERT

'Twas on the shores that round our coast
 From Deal to Ramsgate span,
That I found alone, on a piece of stone,
 An elderly naval man.

His hair was weedy, his beard was long,
 And weedy and long was he;
And I heard this wight on the shore recite,
 In a singular minor key:—

"Oh, I am a cook and a captain bold,
 And the mate of the Nancy brig,
And a bo'sun tight, and a midshipmite,
 And the crew of the captain's gig."

And he shook his fists and he tore his hair,
 Till I really felt afraid,
For I couldn't help thinking the man had been drinking,
 And so I simply said:—

"Oh, elderly man, it's little I know
 Of the duties of men of the sea,
But I'll eat my hand if I understand
 How ever you can be

"At once a cook and a captain bold,
   And the mate of the Nancy brig,
And a bo'sun tight, and a midshipmite,
   And the crew of the captain's gig!"

Then he gave a hitch to his trousers, which
   Is a trick all seamen larn,
And having got rid of a thumping quid,
   He spun this painful yarn:—

"'Twas in the good ship Nancy Bell
   That we sailed to the Indian Sea,
And there on a reef we come to grief,
   Which has often occurred to me.

"And pretty nigh all o' the crew was drowned
   (There was seventy-seven o' soul);
And only ten of the Nancy's men
   Said 'Here!' to the muster-roll..

"There was me, and the cook, and the captain bold,
   And the mate of the Nancy brig,
And the bo'sun tight and a midshipmite,
   And the crew of the captain's gig.

"For a month we'd neither vittles nor drink
   Till a-hungry we did feel,
So we drawed a lot, and accordin', shot
   The captain for our meal.

"The next lot fell to the Nancy's mate,
    And a delicate dish he made;
Then our appetite with the midshipmite
    We seven survivors stayed.

"And then we murdered the bo'sun tight,
    And he much resembled pig;
Then we whittled free, did the cook and me,
    On the crew of the captain's gig.

"Then only the cook and me was left,
    And the delicate question, 'Which
Of us two goes to the kettle?' arose,
    And we argued it out as sich.

"For I loved that cook as a brother, I did,
    And the cook he worshipped me;
But we'd both be blowed if we'd either be stowed
    In the other chap's hold, you see.

"'I'll be eat if you dines off me,' says Tom.
    'Yes, that,' says I, 'you'll be.
I'm boiled if I die, my friend,' quoth I;
    And 'Exactly so,' quoth he.

"Says he: 'Dear James, to murder me
    Were a foolish thing to do,
For don't you see that you can't cook *me*,
    While I can—and will—cook *you*?'

"So he boils the water, and takes the salt
    And the pepper in portions true,
Which he never forgot, and some chopped shallot,
    And some sage and parsley, too.

"'Come here,' says he, with a proper pride,
    Which his smiling features tell;
'Twill soothing be if I let you see
    How extremely nice you'll smell.'

"And he stirred it round and round and round,
    And he sniffed at the foaming froth;
When I ups with his heels, and smothers his squeals
    In the scum of the boiling broth.

"And I eat that cook in a week or less,
    And as I eating be
The last of his chops, why I almost drops,
    For a vessel in sight I see.—

"And I never larf, and I never smile,
    And I never lark nor play;
But sit and croak, and a single joke
    I have—which is to say:

"Oh, I am a cook and a captain bold,
    And the mate of the Nancy brig,
And a bo'sun tight, and a midshipmite,
    And the crew of the captain's gig!"

FUNNY STORIES

THE PRESIDENT of the congregation had to undergo surgery. The board met to decide how to show their concern. Finally, it was agreed that the secretary of the congregation would visit the president in the hospital.

Two days after the operation, the secretary visited the sickroom. "I bring you the good wishes of our board," he said. "We hope you get well and live to be 120 years old!"

The president smiled back weakly.

"And that's an official resolution," continued the secretary, "passed by a vote of twelve to nine."

A HENPECKED HUSBAND was suffering a torrent of abuse. His wife went on and on, becoming more and more furious until in a fit of frenzy she threatened to hit him on the head with a rolling pin.

Whereupon the cowed man slid under the bed and refused to reappear.

"Come out! You bum! Come out!" yelled the angry woman.

"I will *not*!" shouted the man from under the bed. "I'll show you who's boss in this house!"

THE NEW NEIGHBOR joined the mah johngg group for the first time, and all the ladies gaped at the huge diamond she wore.

"It's the third most famous diamond in the world," she told the women confidentially. "First is the Hope diamond, then the Kohinoor diamond, and then this one—the Rabinowitz diamond."

"It's beautiful!" admired one woman enviously. "You're so lucky!"

"Not so lucky," the newcomer maintained. "Unfortunately, with the famous Rabinowitz diamond, I have received the famous Rabinowitz curse."

"And what is that?" wondered the women.

The woman heaved an enormous sigh. "Mr. Rabinowitz," she said.

SAM BROMBERG HAD BEEN a cutter for some 20-odd years. All his life he had dreamed of owning a Cadillac.

But when Sam got to the point where he had actually saved up enough money to buy such a sumptuous car, he suddenly collapsed at his table and died.

His friends conferred about his burial. One of them spoke up and said, "You know, all his life Sam dreamed about owning a Cadillac. I think it would be fitting and proper if we took the money that he saved up and purchased the best Cadillac on the market and buried him in it." The other friends agreed.

On the day of the funeral, all Sam's friends gathered around the burial plot, which was about ten times as large as an ordinary grave. Six workmen had been employed to dig the grave. While the service was being intoned, the huge Cadillac was lowered from a crane into the grave.

One of the workmen lifted his head and marvelled at this brand new shining monster of a car coming down into the grave. In the front seat sat Sam all dressed up in white coat and tails. The workman nudged the man next to him and exclaimed, "Oh boy! That's the way to live!"

TWO OLD FRIENDS met, after not having seen each other for years. "Rosie! You look marvelous!" exclaimed Gussie.

"Yeh," said Rosie, "I'm feeling great. I'll tell you a secret. I'm having an affair."

Gussie smiled broadly. "Oh, that's marvelous! Who's catering?"

A RUSSIAN JEW had become successful. He was allowed to travel outside the country as a member of the Russian embassy. In England, he met up with some young Jewish Socialists, and found himself subject to many questions.

"Comrade," said one of the Britishers, "I understand you are a Jew; I understand you are a man of integrity. Now it would be of great interest to me to have your opinion of the Soviet attitude toward the Arab-Israeli conflict. Why do the Russians support the Egyptian fascists against the democratic Israelis?"

The Russian said nothing.

But the questioners continued. "I know your country has an official policy, and so does your party. But as a Jew you must have your own view of justice. Who do you think is right?"

The Russian maintained his silence.

But the young Englishmen persisted. "Surely you have some opinion?" they demanded.

Finally the Russian, up against the wall, replied, "Yes, I do have an opinion, but I do not agree with it."

THREE OLD MEN were sitting around drinking tea and philosophizing about life. One said, "You know, it is my opinion that the best thing there is in life is good health. Without good health, life isn't worth a darn."

The second took exception. "Well," he said, "I've known plenty of rich men who were sick, terribly sick. But they had lots and lots of money and they went to the best specialists. They went through all kinds of treatments and operations and they came out almost as good as new. The fact is that without money life isn't worth much. You can be as robust as a lion and still be miserable if you don't have a red cent. On the other hand, with money you can buy practically anything. In my opinion, the best thing in life is to have money."

The third one had listened patiently. And now he demurred, saying, "Yes, health is good, and money is good, but I've seen people with plenty of money who are utterly miserable, and I've seen people in good health who were miserable. The fact is that rich or poor, healthy or sick, life in itself is an enormous overwhelming misery. In my opinion, the best thing in life really is not to be born at all."

The other two responded to this remark by plunging themselves into deep contemplation. Finally, one broke the silence. "Yes, Danny, you're right. The best thing in life, as you say, is not to be born at all. But, tell me, who can be so lucky, one out of a million?"

MRS. MELTZER INVITED her new neighbor in for a cup of coffee, and to show her around the house.

"What a beautiful lamp!" admired the neighbor.

"Yes," said Mrs. Meltzer modestly, "I got it with Bleach-o detergent coupons."

"And I like that painting on the wall!" the neighbor went on.

"I got that with Bleach-o coupons, too."

"Oh, a piano! I've always wanted a piano."

"Well, as a matter of fact, I got that piano from Bleach-o coupons, too."

Then the neighbor tried one door handle that wouldn't budge. "What's in that room?" she asked full of curiosity.

"Bleach-o detergent! What else?"

Mo AND BECK went to City Hall to apply for a wedding license. They were directed to the third floor where they had to fill out forms. When that was done, they were to take the forms to the sixth floor, pay a fee, and then they'd get their license.

They obediently filled out the forms, went up to the sixth floor and waited on a line. Eventually, they came to the front of the line, where the man looked over the forms.

"Beck?" he said. "Your legal name isn't Beck, is it? Go back to the third floor and fill out a new form with your real name, Rebecca."

So the couple went back downstairs, filled out another form, returned to the sixth floor, waited on line, and arrived before the man again.

This time the man got up to the part with Mo's name on it. He frowned, "Mo? That doesn't sound like an English name to me."

"Well, my real name is Michael," said Mo, "but I've always been called Mo—"

"Go back down to the third floor," interrupted the man, "and fill these forms out in full English!"

So the couple went down again, filled out another form, came back up to the sixth floor, waited again on line, and eventually arrived at the window. The names were okay this time, but this time the man found the address unacceptable. They had written 'Williamsburg, New York.' "Williamsburg is just a section of Brooklyn," said the man. "Go downstairs and rewrite the forms, and this time write 'Brooklyn, New York' instead of 'Williamsburg, New York.'"

Mo and Beck went through the whole procedure yet another time and returned to the sixth floor. Finally, after several hours at City Hall, everything seemed in order.

Mo sighed and turned to Beck. "It's worth it, sweetheart. Now our little boy will know that everything is legal."

The official glared at them. "Did I hear you say you have a little boy?" Mo admitted they did.

"You already have a baby and you're just getting a wedding license today? Do you know that makes your little boy a technical bastard?"

Mo was icy. "So?" he countered. "That's what the man on the third floor said *you* are, and *you* seem to be doing all right!"

Two women met again after many years and began exchanging histories. "Whatever happened to your son?" asked one woman.

"Oh, what a tragedy!" moaned the other. "My son married a no-good who doesn't lift a finger around the house. She can't cook, she can't sew a button on a shirt, all she does is sleep. My poor boy brings her breakfast in bed, and all day long she stays there, loafing, reading, eating candy!"

"That's terrible," sympathized the first woman. "And what about your daughter?"

"Oh, she's got a good life. She married a man who's a living doll! He won't let her set foot in the kitchen. He gives her breakfast in bed, and makes her stay there all day, resting, reading, and eating chocolates."

A rabbi, a priest, and a minister were playing poker. Suddenly, the police burst into the room. "Sorry, gents, but gambling's illegal," said one of the officers, and he hustled the religious trio down to the court.

"I'm sorry about this," said the judge, "but now that you're here there's only one thing to do. Since you're all men of the cloth, I think I can trust your word. So I'll ask you if you were gambling, and whatever you answer, I'll believe you. We'll start with you, Father."

"Your Honor, surely it is important to be certain that we define what we mean by gambling. In a narrow, but entirely valid sense, what we describe as gambling is only truly so if there is a desire to win money, rather than merely to enjoy the suspense of the fall of cards. In addition, we might confine gambling to situations where the loss of money would be harmful, as—"

"Okay, Father," the judge interrupted. "I see that in the manner in which you define the word, you were not gambling. Now how about you, Reverend?"

The minister said, "I entirely agree with my learned colleague."

"Fine," said the judge. "And now you, rabbi. Were you gambling?"

The rabbi looked at his two friends, and then back at the judge, and asked, "With whom, Your Honor?"

A CRUISING SHIP was sailing near Iceland when the captain spied an iceberg right in his ship's path. He tried to steer around it, but found to his horror that something was wrong with the rudder. The ship wouldn't turn.

Maintaining his calm, the captain immediately wired for help, and ships and helicopters were dispatched. In the meantime, the captain tried to think of some way to keep the passengers from noticing the fearful peril ahead.

Then he remembered that there was a magician aboard. So he called the man in and explained the situation. "Please do a show for the passengers to keep them occupied," said the captain. "If it becomes unavoidable for us to hit the iceberg, I'll signal you. When you see me signal, just tell the audience that for your final act, you'll split the ship in two. By the time they realize you weren't fooling, help should arrive."

So the magician did as he was told, and put on a lively and entertaining show, pulling rabbits out of his hat and making things mysteriously disappear. Then he noticed the captain frantically signaling to him. Obediently, the magician announced: "Ladies and gentlemen, for my final illusion, I shall split this ship in two."

At that moment, the iceberg was reached. The ship rocked with the impact and listed dangerously to one side. The passengers fell into a state of panic. Half of them were thrown into the sea.

Amidst all the brouhaha Mr. Finkelstein, clinging to an upside-down railing, bumped into the magician. Shaking his head disapprovingly, Finkelstein snarled, "Wise guy!"

ABE SELTZER WAS PASSING a golf course when he was struck in the head by a golf ball.

Seething, Abe picked up the ball and gestured wildly at the player running anxiously toward him. "I'll sue you in court for five hundred dollars!" Abe shouted angrily.

The golfer tried to excuse himself. "I hollered 'Fore!'" he said.

"All right!" answered Abe, "I'll take it."

THE BLIND ABBOT

An old medieval tale tells of a blind abbot who had 20 prodigal monks under his care. He and his charges lived in the top story of a square tower which was arranged in nine cells. He himself occupied the center cell.

Each night it was his habit to patrol the abbey and to count his charges in order to make sure that the monks were all at home. His own peculiar method of tallying was to count nine heads for each wall. If he got a full count, he took it for granted that all were present.

Now a certain sly fellow arranged the beds so that two of the boys could leave of a night and make whoopee without the old codger suspecting any A.W.O.L.

On another night, this shrewd young fellow even contrived to bring in four comrades from a neighboring monastery for a party. He arranged the group so cleverly that when the abbot made his evening round, he still counted only nine heads along each wall.

A few months later, the boys decided to give a grand blow-out. They increased the attendance to 32, but still the abbot did not sense that anything was amiss.

And as a grand finale, they held one big gala super-affair, which 36 monks attended, but still the blind abbot counted but nine heads along each wall.

Now the problem is to discover how that wily brother arranged the monks in each cell so that 18, 20, 24, 32, and 36 friars were present, although the blind abbot in each case counted nine heads along each wall of the tower.

Solution on page 355

THE COUNTERFEIT COIN

A king of ancient days once wished to reward one of his wise men, so he had his servants lay before the sage nine coins and a balance scale.

Addressing the object of his largesse, the king said, "There are nine coins here. Eight of them are made of pure gold. One of them has been debased by a lesser metal, which of course, does not weigh as much as gold.

"Now," continued the king, "you will determine your own reward. If you weigh each coin separately, you will, of course, find out which coin weighs the least, and that one will obviously be the counterfeit coin. But if you proceed in that manner you will be obliged to use the balance scale nine times. You would then achieve the worst result, for every time you use the scale, you lose one coin. You can take 15 minutes to think over how to proceed. Since you are a very wise man, you will manage to use the balance scale the fewest possible number of times."

The sage retired for a few minutes, and then came back and addressed himself to the king. "Sire," he said, "I am now ready to pick the counterfeit coin." And he proceeded to do this, using the scale the least number of times necessary to determine which of the nine coins was the counterfeit.

HOW DID HE CONTRIVE TO FIND OUT?

HOW MANY TIMES DID HE USE THE SCALE?

Solution on page 356

THE LADY AND THE TIGER

In ancient days, a certain crafty king had a daughter as beautiful as he was vicious. Her charm and beauty attracted suitors from the four corners of the earth who came to sue for her hand.

But the king imposed harsh conditions. Each suitor was obliged to put up a fortune, if he even dared to try to win the maiden, a fortune which became forfeit to the crown if the suitor was unsuccessful. Then the candidate was given a number of difficult feats to perform. If he succeeded in overcoming these trials of strength and courage, he would then be led to a box which contained two slips of paper. On one there was written the name of the princess; on the other, the word *Tiger*. If he drew the slip with the word *Tiger* on it, he would be thrown into a cage, there to meet a cruel death.

Mathematically, his chances of winning the girl were even; but practically, his chances were nil because the unscrupulous monarch always put into the box two slips of paper on both of which was written the word *Tiger*.

After many suitors had met an untimely death in this manner, the princess had become aware of her father's deceit.

One day, a handsome young man came a-riding to the palace, and she immediately fell in love with him. Since she couldn't bear to see him be torn limb from limb by a vicious tiger, she told him of the king's stratagem and what lay in store for anyone who tried for her hand.

Undaunted, the young man announced that he was a suitor, and accomplished the feats of strength and other tasks set for him. Then he was led away to the box which held his fate.

But somehow he contrived to outwit the king.

HOW DID HE DO IT?

Solution on page 356

THE FIVE OFFICE BOYS

Five office boys were examined by their employer in reading, writing, arithmetic, geography, and history. The marking system was simple: 10 marks in all were awarded in each subject and divided among the boys.

When the examination was over, the results were announced in the following roundabout way:

The order of merit in the examination as a whole is: (1) Percy; (2) Walter; (3) Fred; (4) Cyril; (5) Foch. Each boy was tops in one subject. No two boys, in any one subject, were given the same mark.

Foch was tops in history; Walter in geography.

Fred was tops in reading. He received the same mark in writing as in arithmetic and the same mark in geography as in history.

Cyril was tops in writing and third in arithmetic.

In reading, Foch was second and Percy third.

Walter was not bottom in anything. In two subjects, Walter did better than Percy.

Foch gained as many marks in one subject as in the other four put together.

DRAW UP A TABLE SHOWING EACH BOY'S MARK
IN EACH SUBJECT.

Solution on page 356

THE SOCCER LEAGUE

Four teams—Arsenal, Hotspur, United, and Villa—take part in a soccer competition. Each team plays each of the others once. Two points are awarded for a win and one for a tie.

United scored five points; Hotspur, three points; Villa, one point. Thirteen goals were scored in all, seven of these by the Hotspur; the Arsenal scored no goals at all.

Hotspur beat Villa by four goals to one.

WHAT WAS THE SCORE IN THE GAME
BETWEEN VILLA AND UNITED?

Solution on page 356

✤

THE ADVENTUROUS SNAIL

Two philosophers were walking in a garden when one of them noticed a snail making the perilous ascent of a wall 20 feet high. Judging by the trail, the gentlemen calculated that the snail ascended three feet each day, sleeping and slipping back two feet each night.

"Pray tell me," said one philosopher to his companion, "how long will it take the snail to climb to the top of the wall and descend the other side. The top of the wall, as you know, has a sharp edge, so that when he gets there he will instantly begin to descend, putting precisely the same exertion into his daily climbing down as he did in his climbing up, and sleeping and slipping at night as before."

CAN YOU FIGURE OUT THE ANSWER?
(ASSUME THAT THE DAY IS EQUALLY DIVIDED
INTO 12 HOURS' DAYTIME AND 12 HOURS' NIGHT.)

Solution on page 356

MILITARY SECRETS

Four servicemen—Bob, Sam, Ken, and Tom—met at the USO. They were from different home states and belonged to four different branches of the Armed Services, and no two had the same hobby. Given the clues below, can you fill in the grid so that each soldier is matched with his state, service, and hobby?

PAR: 15 MINUTES

Solution on page 356

	Bob	Sam	Tom	Ken
State				
Hobby				
Service				

1. Ken is a Navy man.

2. The Army man likes to dance.

3. Tom likes to play baseball.

4. Sam is from Kansas.

5. The Army man is not from Kansas.

6. Someone collects stamps, but it's not the Marine.

7. Tom is not the Ohioan.

8. The Air Force man does not play cards, but one of the others does.

9. Bob is from Utah.

10. The Marine is from Maine.

THE BAFFLED BUTLER

Jacob Jones—the twice-married millionaire—was happy when the butler announced the arrival of Jones's three sons, his only remaining relatives, for his 70th birthday. As he ushered them into the parlor, the butler couldn't help but notice the strong family resemblance all three bore to old Jacob.

After the birthday visit was over and he was helping them on with their coats, the butler commented on this resemblance.

Joseph Jones, the first son to respond, said: "Actually, I'm not Jacob's natural son, I'm adopted. But my resemblance to him is not accidental. I wasn't born out of wedlock, and there haven't been any divorces in our family."

Robert Jones, the next son to speak, said: "I see Joseph's remarks have mystified you. This may help you, or it may further mystify you. He omitted mentioning that he's my half-brother, although he's only a step-brother to Edward here. On the other hand, he's also Edward's and my cousin."

Edward Jones, the last son to speak, said: "My brother Robert hasn't told you quite everything, either. He and I are the only two natural sons of Jacob, but we are also only half-brothers."

The butler was now totally confused. Only after he'd gotten pencil and paper, and drawn several trial diagrams, was he able to see that everything he'd been told could be true. Can you figure it all out?

PAR: 45 MINUTES

Solution on page 357

WHICH MAIL FOR WHICH MALE?

There are five mailboxes in the local post office in Pleasantville that belong to five male villagers. During months of sorting mail, the postal worker has gleaned certain facts about these five men. Using the 10 bits of information below as clues, you should be able to figure out which mailbox belongs to whom, and the occupation of each mailbox holder.

PAR: 4 MINUTES

Solution on page 357

	Box 1	Box 2	Box 3	Box 4	Box 5
Name					
Occupation					

1. Mike is a lawyer.

2. The owner of Box #3 is a grocer.

3. The plumber uses an end box.

4. Jim is a grocer.

5. Pat got Fred's mail in a mix-up.

6. Tom uses Box #2.

7. The lawyer is next to the doctor.

8. The farmer uses Box #2.

9. The lawyer uses Box #5.

10. Fred's mailbox is next to Tom's.

MATCH THEM UP

Six Senators and their wives are having a barbecue. The men are discussing the bills they wish to introduce before the Senate. You are eavesdropping and you pick up the information contained in the 14 clues below. Can you then figure out which bill each Senator is sponsoring? You should also be able to state with certainty the name of each Senator's wife, and their home states.

PAR: 10 MINUTES

Solution on page 357

Senator	Clawson	Jones	Henry	Johnson	Smith	Rooney
Bill						
State						
Wife						

1. Peggy married the Senator from Utah.

2. Senator Clawson is sponsoring a bill on military athletics.

3. Jane did not marry the Senator from Indiana.

4. The state of Ohio elected Jim Jones as a Senator.

5. The Senator from Maine is sponsoring a bill on the National Leaf.

6. Employment for the handicapped is being sponsored by Senator Henry.

7. Senator Johnson does not represent any state west of Ohio.

8. Senator and Mrs. Jill Clawson come from Sun City, Idaho.

9. Senator Henry is from Georgia.

10. The Indiana Senator wants to make St. Patrick's Day a national holiday.

VACATION VEXATION

Charlie Charleston, Dick Dixon, Edwin Edwards, and Nick Nichols all work for the National Fruitcake Company. Since they are senior executives, they are each allowed a whole month off, but no two can have the same month. Each has a favorite hobby and looks forward to his month off to enjoy it. Given the seven clues below, can you fill in the grid to indicate who goes on vacation when, and who does what on his vacation?

PAR: 5 MINUTES

Solution on page 357

	CC	DD	EE	NN
Hobby				
Month				

1. The camper takes his vacation in July.

2. Charlie hates fishing.

3. Nick loves to go sailing.

4. June is the month when the fisherman goes fishing.

5. Someone vacations in August, but it's not Charlie.

6. Dick vacations in December.

7. Someone skis, but it's not Ed.

TYPING TROUBLE

Steve has a very special typewriter. Each key has three things on it: a combination of two capital letters, a one- or two-digit number, and a symbol. Trouble is, Steve can't seem to memorize which figures go with which keys. Using the 11 clues given below, you should be able to figure out which letters, numbers and symbols are combined on each key and help Steve learn them. The sign = means "goes with " and the sign ≠ means "does not go with."

PAR: 30 MINUTES

Solution on page 357

1. **77 = BC**

2. **DF = @**

3. **5 ≠ %** or ***

4. **JK = &**

5. **94 ≠ GH**

6. **NP = 26**

7. **92 ≠ LM**

8. **36 = $**

9. **26 ≠ #**

10. **LM = ***

11. **& ≠ 92**

THE DORMITORY PUZZLE

The diagram below shows the floor plan of a girl's dormitory at Pruitt Prep School. Each room is occupied by a girl who comes from a different city. It is up to you to figure out, from the clues below, which girl occupies each room, and what city each one comes from.

PAR: 10 MINUTES

Solution on page 358

```
+----------------+----------------+
| 1              | 6              |
|                |                |
+----------------+----------------+
| 2              | 5              |
|                |                |
+----------------+----------------+
| 3              | 4              |
|                |                |
+----------------+----------------+
```

1. Kim is from New York.

2. The girl from Chicago occupies Room 4.

3. Lisa does not have a corner room.

4. A Kansas City girl lives between Kim and Tina.

5. The girl in Room 3 comes from Los Angeles.

6. A Cleveland girl is in the room between the girls from Chicago and Cincinatti.

7. Tina lives across the hall from Rita.

8. Ruth occupies Room 6.

9. Mona occupies Room 5.

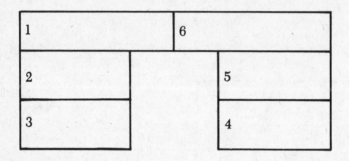

THE BOYS IN THE LOCKER ROOM

Five high school students are chatting in the locker room after a workout in gym. They have adjacent lockers, numbered 101-105. The boys are exchanging opinions about their favorite subjects and teachers.

Using the clues below, can you fill in the boxes to show who goes with each locker, and what subject and teacher each student prefers?

Seven minutes or under shows that your favorite subject is Logic.

Solution on page 358

	101	102	103	104	105
Student					
Subject					
Teacher					

CLUES:

1. Jerry's locker is next to Tom's.
2. Dave likes math the best.
3. Mr. Smith teaches German.
4. Bob likes shop class.
5. Mr. Bryon does not teach history.
6. Dave's favorite teacher is Mr. Green.
7. Mr. Brown teaches English.
8. Gene has locker 103.
9. Bob has locker 105.
10. Tom's locker is next to Gene's.
11. Jerry's best subject is history.
12. Mr. Brown does not teach Tom.
13. Mr. Jones does not teach Tom.

GRAB BAG

In this quiz, we have gathered together 24 questions pertaining to just about anything you can imagine. There was absolutely no method to our madness.

Check the answer you deem correct. Give yourself one point for each correct answer. A score of ten does credit to your capacity for retaining useless information; 15 is a track record to be proud of; and 20 earns you the triviata trophy of the year.

Answers on page 358

1. A cretin is:
   A person of low intelligence   A small wildflower
   An inhabitant of one of the Greek islands

2. The highest city in the world is:
   Lhasa, Tibet   Bogota, Columbia   Addis Ababa, Ethiopia

3. Who said, *"Hope springs eternal in the human breast?"*
   William Shakespeare   Alexander Pope   Arthur Godfrey

4. Venison is the meat of a:
   Buffalo   Yak   Deer

5. The country with the lowest life expectancy is:
   Guinea, Africa   Chad, Africa   Nigeria, Africa

6. A marimba is a:
   Cuban dance   Guatemalan stew
   Musical instrument which resembles a xylophone

7. The hottest city in the world is:
   Khartoum, Sudan   Timbuktu, Mali   Niamey, Nigeria

8. Atavism is:
   The study of birds   Very limited eyesight
   Reversion to characteristics in one's remote ancestors

9. "The Little Brown Wren" was the nickname of which Hollywood film star?
   Bette Davis   Olivia de Havilland   Natalie Wood

10. Someone referred to as Brobdingnagian is likely to be:
    Gigantic   A native of a town in Siberia   Puppet-like

11. A trapezoid is:
    A quadrilateral rectangle having only two sides parallel
    A snare used to catch especially wild animals
    An order of monks, which still flourishes in French-speaking
    Switzerland

12. *Song of Myself* is a long poem by:
    William Wordsworth   Walt Whitman
                    Henry Wadsworth Longfellow

13. The greatest harness-racing horse that ever lived was:
    Dancer's Image   Goldsmith Maid   My Friend, Flicka

14. Comestibles are:
    Things which catch fire easily   Eatables
                    Rubbers made of gutta percha and tin

15. The fastest hockey skater, Bobby Hull, has been timed at:
    19.7 mph   29.7 mph   49.7 mph

16. The Rosetta Stone is in:
    The British Museum   Luxor, Egypt   Tiffany's, New York

17. The opera *Il Trovatore* was written by:
    Arturo Toscanini   Gaetano Donizetti   Giuseppe Verdi

18. Mickey Wright is a great:
    Jockey   Golfer   Rock singer

19. New South Wales is located in:
    The British Isles   Australia   The Orkney Islands

20. The first person in history to swim the English Channel was:
    Matthew Webb   Allerondro Scalini   Johnny Weissmuller

21. Apiphobia is a fear of:
    Enclosed spaces   Cats   Bees

22. The Garden State is:
    California   Florida   New Jersey

23. The heaviest planet in the universe is:
    Venus   Jupiter   Earth

24. The Kentucky Derby is held at:
    Epsom Downs   Churchill Downs   Kentucky Downs

À LA MODE

Do you follow women's fashions? If so, this quiz is custom-made for you. Below are 27 questions. You have three choices. Check the answer you believe is correct.

A score of 12 says you are in vogue; 16 says you are a fashion plate; and a score of 21 means you're either a couturier or you know someone who is!

Answers on page 359

1. The mini-skirt was the rage in the:
   1900s   1930s   1960s

2. A designer noted for classic, conservatively-cut clothes is:
   Pierre Cardin   Pauline Trigere   Coco Chanel

3. A dress with the waistline just below the bust is said to be what style:
   Empire   Belle Epoque   Gibson Girl

4. The "flapper" look was the in-look of the:
   1890s   1920s   1950s

5. Crinoline is another name for:
   Bobby sox   A hoop skirt   Bloomers

6. The British "mod" look of the 1960s was introduced by designer:
   Bill Blass   Mary Quant   Yves St. Laurent

7. Before nylon was invented, stockings were generally made of:
   Rayon   Linen   Silk

8. Short pants disguised by a skirt front are known as:
   Hot pants   Pantaloons   Culottes

9. A burnoose is a type of:
   Hooded cloak   Mutton-sleeved blouse   Sunbonnet

10. A beret is a type of:
    Hat   Jacket   Petticoat

11. Bustles were worn in what century?
    Fifteenth   Nineteenth   Twentieth

12. A type of hooded robe with a mask worn at 17th-century costume balls was a:
    Doublet   Dirndl   Domino

13. A type of fur often used to trim royal robes is:
    Mink   Sable   Ermine

14. A skirt worn over a series of hoops extending horizontally from the waist, fashionable in the 16th and 17th centuries was:
    A farthingale   A patrouche   A simballet

15. A fichu is a type of:
    Shoelace   Boot   Shawl

16. Before the days of panty hose, women often wore:
    Chastity belts   Garter belts   Knee socks

17. A type of hat made popular by Jackie Kennedy was the:
    Pillbox   Pokebonnet   Tam O'Shanter

18. An Indian cotton fabric that "bleeds" when you wash it is:
    Mohair   Madras   Calico

19. The shirtwaist look was popularized by:
    Charles Dana Gibson   Amelia Bloomer   Emilio Pucci

20. Organdy is a fabric once considered particularly appropriate for:
    Widows in mourning   Maternity dresses
                    Young girls' pinafores

21. Peter Pan refers to a type of:
    Headgear   Collar   High-button boot

22. A ceremonial dress worn by Japanese women is the:
    Sari   Caftan   Kimono

23. A sweater that buttons up or down completely is a:
    Turtleneck   Cardigan   Pullover

24. A cummerbund is worn around the:
    Neck   Ankle   Waist

25. Unisex is a look of the:
    1870s   1930s   1970s

26. The fashion designer, Pauline Trigère, is:
    French   American   English.

27. Traditionally, the average family budget apportions what percentage for clothing?
    8%   15%   25%

HOOP-LA!

How much do you know about basketball? Below are 25 questions about America's biggest sport. See how many answers you know. You have three choices. Check the answer you believe is correct.

A score of 11 is good; 14 is superb; and 21 nets you a championship rating.

Answers on page 359

1. The longest collegiate basketball shot, estimated at 55 feet by Madison Square Garden officials, was made on March 14, 1946, by a 5'10" player named Ernie Calverley. He was playing for:
   Rhode Island State   Oklahoma Aggies   St. John

2. Who was the highest professional scorer in history?
   Larry Costello   Bob Petit   Wilt Chamberlain

3. The originator of modern basketball was:
   Abner Doubleday   Bill Tilden   James Naismith

4. Kareem Abdul-Jabbar was born with the name:
   Tom Chamberlain   Ferdinand Lewis Alcindor   Andy Wright

5. What team did Bill Russell play on?
   Los Angeles Lakers   Boston Celtics   New York Knickerbockers

6. A basketball attendance record was set in 1951, at Olympic Stadium in West Berlin, Germany. How many fans appeared to watch the Harlem Globetrotters' high jinks?
   50,000   75,000   100,000

7. The tallest basketball player in the history of the game was:
   Bob Lanier of Detroit   Mu Tieh-Chu
                    George Mikan of Minneapolis

8. The driving genius of the original Celtics was:
   Nat Holman   Dutch Leonard   James Naismith

9. Approximately how many high school basketball teams are there in America?
   10,000   20,000   50,000

10. The first country outside the United States to adopt basketball was:
    England   China   Canada

11. Worldwide, how does basketball rank among sports as a popular spectator sport:
    First   Third   Fifth

12. The only college team to win both the NCAA and the NIT championships in the same year was:
    New York City College   UCLA   New York University

13. Wilt Chamberlain's nickname is:
    Runty   The Stilt   Mr. Basketball

14. Women's basketball began in the:
    1840s   1890s   1920s

15. There are how many teams in the four divisions of the NBA?
    15   22   32

16. Who was the best professional foul shooter ever?
    Julius Erving   Oscar Robertson   Bill Sharman

17. Goaltending refers to:
    Interference with the ball on its final arch toward the basket
    Guarding the best forward on the opposite team
    Staying in your own court, so when a teammate gets the ball, he
    can throw it to you

18. The first intercollegiate basketball game, with seven men per team, was played in 1896. The teams were:
    Harvard and Princeton   Wesleyan and Yale
    University of Chicago and UCLA

19. Professional basketball games are played in four quarters. Each quarter lasts how many minutes?
    12   20   35

20. Basketball has been part of the Olympic Games since:
    1910   1936   1945

21. In basketball, it is illegal to:
    Dribble the ball   Roll the ball   Run holding the ball

22. What is the greatest number of points ever scored by a single player in one game:
    60   80   100

23. The time limit for an offensive team to make a shot is:
    15 seconds   24 seconds   38 seconds

24. The lowest free-throw percentage for the 1976-77 season was set by center Kim Hughes of the New Jersey Jets. His percentage was:
    .275   .325   .395

25. The men's basketball gold medal in the 1976 summer Olympics was won by what country?
    U.S.S.R.   Canada   U.S.

FOR BETTE DAVIS FANS

Heroines, harridans, harlots, and hags—Bette Davis played every kind of role, and so convincingly that many consider her America's best as well as most versatile film actress.

How much do you know about the woman who has been called America's "First Lady of the Screen?" Below are 23 questions. You have three choices. Check the answer you believe to be correct.

A score of 12 is fine; 15 is admirable; 18 is great; and 21 is Davis-tating.

Answers on page 359

1. Bette Davis's real name is:
   Bettina Dawes   Ruth Elizabeth Davis   Norma Jean Baker

2. Bette Davis was born in 1908 in:
   Lowell, Massachusetts   Savannah, Georgia
                   Hartford, Connecticut

3. Bette Davis studied dance with:
   Isadora Duncan   Martha Graham   Ruth St. Denis

4. Bette's famous line, "What a dump!" comes from what movie:
   Of Human Bondage   *Beyond the Forest*   *Jezebel*

5. Bette's first professional acting experience was with the stock company of a famous movie director. He was:
   Howard Hawks   John Huston   George Cukor

6. Bette Davis was not well known until she gave a brilliant performance as the sluttish Mildred Rogers in *Of Human Bondage*. The movie was based on a novel by:
   Theodore Dreiser   Leslie Howard   Somerset Maugham

7. Bette's co-star in *Mr. Skeffington* was:
   Leslie Howard   Claude Rains   Humphrey Bogart

8. *Jezebel*, one of Davis's best-loved movies, was made in:
   1930   1938   1948

9. Bette played a frumpy Bronx housewife in:
   The Little Foxes   *Juarez*   *The Catered Affair*

10. For 18 years, Bette Davis was under contract to what movie studio?
    United Artists   Paramount Pictures   Warner Brothers Studios

11. Davis made her movie debut in:
    1931   1933   1935

12. Bette played a character named Joyce Heath in:
    Dangerous   *Kid Galahad*   *A Marked Woman*

13. Which historical queen did Bette Davis play, in two different movies?
    Catherine the Great of Russia   Elizabeth I of England
    Queen Christine of Sweden

14. Bette's co-star in *Whatever Happened to Baby Jane?* was:
    Joan Fontaine   Joan Crawford   Olivia de Havilland

15. Bette's fourth husband was:
    Actor Gary Merrill   Recluse Howard Hughes
    Bandleader Harmon Nelson

16. "Fasten your seatbelts—it's going to be a bumpy night," is a line spoken by what Davis character?
    Charlotte Vale   Margot Channing   Joyce Heath

17. Bette Davis was the first woman elected president of the Academy of Motion Picture Arts and Sciences in:
    1938   1941   1961

18. Which of the following movies did Bette *not* star in?
    Watch on the Rhine   *The Old Maid*   *Sunset Boulevard*

19. Bette Davis has how many children?
    None   Three   Six

20. Davis played opposite George Arliss in what film?
    The Man Who Came to Dinner   *The Great Lie*
    The Man Who Played God

21. In *Bad Sister*, Davis's first movie, her male co-star was another tyro. His name was:
    Spencer Tracy   Humphrey Bogart   James Stewart

22. Bette Davis began her film career under contract to what studio:
    Warner Brothers   Universal   Columbia

23. Bette turned down the role of Scarlett O'Hara in *Gone With the Wind* because she thought her co-star was to be:
    Clark Gable   Errol Flynn   Humphrey Bogart

BITS AND PIECES

There is absolutely no system or common element to the 50 questions in this quiz, which makes it all the better for trivia buffs like you!

A score of 25 is good; 32 is excellent; 40 is nothing trivial.

Answers on page 359

1. A dog is generally considered to have aged as much in one year as a human ages in:
   Three years   Seven years   Eleven years

2. There is a statue in honor of sea gulls in:
   Los Angeles   Denver   Salt Lake City

3. The first Bible printed in the Eskimo language was made in:
   Alaska   France   Denmark

4. The first President to throw out the first ball of the baseball season was:
   Woodrow Wilson   Teddy Roosevelt   William Howard Taft

5. Typhoid Mary's real name was:
   Susan McNally   Mary McGraw   Mary Mallon

6. The first emperor of Rome was:
   Julius Caesar   Romulus   Augustus

7. America's first modern electric traffic light was on:
   Atlanta's Peachtree Street   New York's Fifth Avenue   Cleveland's Euclid Avenue

8. Great Britain's second largest metropolitan area is:
   Manchester   Birmingham   Leeds

9. The first flag of the state of Texas was made in:
   Texas   New York City   Georgia

10. The only one of his works that Michelangelo signed is:
    The *Last Supper* mural   The *Pieta*   The ceiling of the Sistine Chapel

11. The European nation that first used field artillery was:
    Holland   Prussia   France

12. The basic Guatemalan unit of currency is the :
    Sombrero   Quetzal   Peso

13. The Confederate constitution allowed a single presidential term of :
    Two years   Six years   Eight years

14. The original name for the hot dog was a :
    Coney Island   Steamer   Pig in a blanket

15. America's largest retail chain is :
    Sears   J.C. Penney   Woolworth's

16. The first Pulitzer Prize for poetry went to :
    Edward Arlington   Stephen Vincent   Robert Frost
    Robinson   Benet

17. The Florida State University football team is known as the :
    Sun Devils   Gators   Seminoles

18. The planet Earth is about :
    A billion years old   Four to five billion   Almost ten billion
                          years old   years old

19. The average area of a state in the U.S. is 72,302 square miles; the state that comes closest to this norm is :
    Wyoming   Pennsylvania   North Dakota

20. America's first left-handed President was :
    Thomas Jefferson   William Buchanan   James Garfield

21. The fastest bird in the world is :
    The roadrunner   The swift   The hummingbird

22. An inland European city that has more miles of canals than Venice is :
    Vienna, Austria   Hamburg,   Birmingham,
                       West Germany   United Kingdom

23. The modern nation you would visit to see the ruins of ancient Carthage is :
    Tunisia   Turkey   Algeria

24. Eric Blair wrote under the pen name of :
    H.G. Wells   Mark Twain   George Orwell

25. The most common surname in the United States is, of course, Smith; the name in second place is :

Johnson   Jones   Brown

26. The word "shampoo" was taken into English from :

Chinese   Cherokee   Hindi

27. Henry H. Blair has the distinction of being the first American to :

Have a flush toilet in   Buy a ticket for an   Die in a car accident
    his home   airplane ride

28. *Lineus longissimus* is Earth's largest species of worm; the longest specimen on record measured :

15 feet   40 feet   180 feet

29. A European nation with no official national anthem is :

Italy   Denmark   Switzerland

30. Alaska and Hawaii, of course, touch no other states; Maine touches only one other. Which two states touch eight others?

Missouri and   Texas and   Tennessee and
    Texas   Tennessee   Missouri

31. The world's largest freshwater fish is the :

Trout   Catfish   Sturgeon

32. Of the Seven Wonders of the Ancient World, how many were in what is now Egypt?

None   Two   Four

33. The atomic bomb dropped on Hiroshima, Japan, on August 6, 1945, had an explosive force equal to :

2,000 tons of TNT   20,000 tons of TNT   200,000 tons of TNT

34. The gestation period of an elephant is :

6 months   21 months   33 months

35. That St. Peter was the first pope is common knowledge. But who was the second pope?

Gregory   Pius   Linus

36. The heaviest organ in the human body is the :

Brain   Stomach   Liver

37. The United States' first golf course was in a suburb of :

Chicago   New York   Los Angeles

38. In what state besides Indiana is there an Indiana University?

    Michigan   Ohio   Pennsylvania

39. Rodrigo de Jerez is usually named as the first European to have :

    Set foot on the soil of   Called the New   Smoked tobacco
      the New World   World "America"

40. The Great Fire of London was in the year :

    1493   1666   1754

41. How many of the 50 states have completely man-made, arbitrary borders?

    None   Three   Seven

42. The world's oldest stock exchange is in :

    New York   Amsterdam   London

43. Harvey Kennedy became a multimillionaire because he invented the :

    Electric dishwasher   Shoelace   Windshield wiper

44. The 21st Amendment to the U.S. Constitution :

    Gave women   Introduced   Repealed
      the vote   prohibition   prohibition

45. The Kerensky Republic refers to a short-lived regime in :

    Poland   Hungary   Russia

46. America's first radio station with a regular broadcasting schedule was in :

    Boston   Pittsburgh   Baltimore

47. The first World Series was in 1903 and was won by :

    Boston   New York   Philadelphia

48. The world's largest rodents live in:

    North America   South America   Africa

49. The first President to wear a pair of men's long pants was :

    Thomas Jefferson   James Madison   Zachary Taylor

50. Every one of the 50 states has at least one official nickname except :

    Rhode Island   Iowa   Alaska

NATIVE HABITAT

Listed below are the names of 27 animals. Do you know where each animal commonly makes his home? You are given three possibilities.

Give yourself two points for each correct answer. If you score 20, that's good; 30 is excellent; 36 is outstanding; and 42 means you are an expert in this field. Congratulations.

Answers on page 360

1. The duckbilled platypus lives in:
   Africa   *Brazil*   *Australia*

2. The sloth lives in:
   Europe   *South America*   *South Africa*

3. The giraffe lives in:
   Burma   *Africa*   *Australia*

4. The gila monster lives in:
   United States   *French West Africa*   *Peru*

5. The reindeer lives in:
   Lapland   *Antarctic*   *Ecuador*

6. The lemur lives in:
   South America   *Australia*   *Madagascar*

7. The hippopotamus lives in:
   Iran   *Africa*   *Norway*

8. The rhinoceros lives in:
   India   *Argentina*   *New Zealand*

9. The giant armadillo lives in:
   United States   *South America*   *Italy*

10. The orangutan lives in:
    Indonesia   *Africa*   *Syria*

11. The koala lives in:
    Australia   *India*   *China*

12. The anteater lives in
    Egypt   *South America*   *Hawaii*

13. The elephant lives in:
    Africa   *Turkey*   *Chile*

14. The two-humped camel lives in:
    Arabia   *North Africa*   *Central Asia*

15. The musk ox lives in:
    Canada   *Russia*   *Chile*

16. The gorilla lives in:
    Burma   *African Congo*   *Spain*

17. The bison lives in:
    Argentina   *Alaska*   *United States*

18. The tiger lives in:
    Africa   *Europe*   *India*

19. The giant panda lives in:
    Samoa   *China*   *Venezuela*

20. The zebra lives in:
    Africa   *Madagascar*   *Borneo*

21. The aardvark lives in:
    Australia   *South America*   *Africa*

22. The ostrich lives in:
    South America   *Africa*   *Australia*

23. The kangaroo lives in:
    India   *Africa*   *Australia*

24. The leopard lives in:
    Africa   *Syria*   *Brazil*

25. The dingo lives in:
    Central America   *South America*   *Australia*

26. The okapi lives in:
    Australia   *South America*   *Africa*

27. The zebu lives in:
    Canada   *Norway*   *Tibet*

GAME FOR THE GOURMET

Are you a connoisseur of culinary specialties? The 26 questions below all concern the composition of gourmet dishes. There are three choices. Check the answer you believe to be correct.

A score of 12 is savory; 16 is delectable; and 21 is delicious!

Solution on page 360

1. Chicken Marengo is made with:
   White wine and tomatoes   Cognac and turnips   Saffron and beer

2. Eggs Benedict are poached eggs and ham served with:
   Hollandaise sauce   Sauce bearnaise   Brandied ketchup

3. Crêpes suzettes are:
   German apple pancakes   Brazilian potato dumplings
   French pancakes with a flaming orange sauce

4. A steak dish eaten virtually raw is:
   Steak Diane   Steak tartare   Salisbury steak

5. Chicken Tetrazzini is served on a bed of:
   Spinach   Brown rice   Spaghetti

6. Genoise is a:
   Cheese sauce   Cake   Pasta cooked in cream

7. Sukiyaki is a Japanese dish consisting primarily of:
   Beef and onions   Pork and cabbage   Veal and oyster sauce

8. Szechuan cooking is:
   Meatless   Spicy   Indigenous to Thailand

9. One of the ingredients of Sachertorte is:
   Gooseberry jam   Macadamia nuts   Apricot jam

10. Coquilles St. Jacques is made with:
    Shrimp   Filet of sole   Scallops

11. North African Couscous uses:
    Crushed grain   Potato flour   Steamed milk

12. Santa Lucia buns are made with:
    Allspice   Saffron   Chopped maraschino cherries

13. Croissants are:
    A Viennese dessert made with semi-sweet chocolate
    A Brazilian dish made with pork sausage
    A French roll made with lots of butter

14. An important seasoning in paella is:
    Oregano   Saffron   Cumin

15. Spaghetti al pesto is made with:
    A fresh basil sauce   An egg and cream sauce
                     A tomato and meat sauce

16. Southern-style spareribs are:
    Baked in orange juice and white wine
    Barbecued in a tomato and molasses sauce
    Parboiled and served plain

17. Zabaglione is an Italian dessert made with:
    Egg yolks, sugar, and wine   Ice cream   Cream and cheese

18. Chilis releños is a Mexican dish consisting of:
    Corn wafers stuffed with ground meat and drenched in
        tomato sauce
    Green peppers stuffed with meat or cheese
    Chicken with a spicy chocolate sauce

19. Lentils are a prime ingredient of:
    Soupe nicoise   Mulligatawny soup   French onion soup

20. A soupçon is:
    A heaping tablespoon   A dash   A cup-and-a-half

21. A Waldorf salad contains:
    Celery, apples, and walnuts   Tuna and anchovies
                     Croutons and bacon bits

22. Veal Parmigiana is made with:
    Mozzarella cheese and tomato sauce   Marsala and mushrooms
                     White wine, lemon juice, and herbs

23. Calzone are stuffed with:
    Ricotta cheese and sometimes ham   Shrimp and minced clams
                     Brazil nuts and sweet chocolate

24. Curry is composed of:
    Basil, thyme, and oregano   Cinnamon, cloves, and nutmeg
         Cumin, coriander, turmeric, and other pungent spices

25. Filet mignon is:
    A fish dish cooked in white wine and garnished with almonds
    A dessert made with bananas and ricotta cheese
    A choice steak dish, cooked in butter

26. If you ordered pommes soufflés, you would be eating:
    Apples   Cheese   Potatoes

IN YOUR CUPS

What do you know about booze? Below are 25 questions about alcoholic beverages. You have three choices. Check the answer you believe to be the right one.

A score of 16 is high; 18 is intoxicating; 21 is inebriating; and 23 certifies you as a bartender.

Answers on page 360

1. Vodka is distilled from:
     Blueberries   Potatoes   Juniper berries

2. Calvados is a French brandy made from:
     Oranges   Peaches   Apples

3. Dubonnet is generally served as:
     An after-dinner cordial   An apéritif   A chaser for whiskey

4. Aquavit is a Scandinavian liquor flavored with:
     Cloves   Chocolate liqueur   Caraway seed

5. Irish coffee is made with:
     Coffee and Kahlua   Coffee, whipped cream, and whiskey
          Coffee, vodka, and Cointreau

6. A Virgin Mary is:
     Vodka and tomato juice   Gin and tomato juice
          Plain tomato juice

7. A Grasshopper is made with:
     Crème de menthe, crème de cacao and cream
     Crème de menthe, kahlua, and vodka
     Sloe gin and mint leaves

8. The liqueur that tastes like licorice is:
     Crème de menthe   Kahlua   Anisette

9. Champagne *brut* is:
     Very dry   Very sweet   Very old

10. A Black Russian is made with:
     Kahlua and vodka   Kahlua and cream
          Crème de cacao and Jack Daniels

11. Bourbon is distilled from:
     Corn   Rice   Wheat

12. An Americano contains:

    Campari   Bourbon   Tequila

13. Rum is obtained from fermented:

    Potatoes   Sugar cane or molasses   Grain, such as rye or barley

14. Whiskey that is 86 proof contains what percent alcohol?

    43 percent   86 percent   100 percent

15. An Old Fashioned consists of:

    Whiskey, sugar, bitters, and club soda
    Bourbon, mint leaves, sugar, and water
    Gin, tonic, and a green olive

16. The initials *J* and *B* in J&B rare scotch stand for:

    James and Billy   Juice and Brew   Justerini and Brooks

17. A Margarita contains:

    Tequila, salt, lime juice, and Triple Sec
    Tequila, vodka, and kahlua
    Tequila, orange juice, sugar, and Cointreau

18. A Martini is made with:

    Gin, angostura bitters, and a maraschino cherry
    Gin, a dash of vermouth, and a green olive (or lemon twist)
    Gin, Campari, club soda, and a black olive

19. Tequila is distilled from:

    The mescal cactus   A special Mexican white grape
        The sap of the Mexican agave plant

20. Most wines contain what percent alcohol?

    2 to 4 percent   8 to 12 percent   15 to 20 percent

21. The favorite toast of the Italians is:

    Cin cin   Mama mia   Buon giorno

22. The portion of teetotalers in the United States is:

    ¼ of the population   ⅓ of the population   ½ of the population

23. A Side Car is made of:

    Cointreau, lemon juice, and brandy
    Vodka, white rum, and shaved ice
    Gin, white creme de menthe, and sugar

24. Porter is a:

    Vintage wine   Light beer similar to lager
        Dark beer made from malt

25. A one-ounce measure is a:

    Jigger   Pony   Shot

THIS AND THAT

Below are 24 questions on this, that, and the other thing. Check the correct answer.

A score of 12 makes you I don't know what; 18 makes you you know what; and 22 elects you as the Great Panjandrum.

Answers on page 360

1. New Orleans is the site of which football bowl?
   The Rose Bowl   The Sugar Bowl   The Orange Bowl

2. Verjuice is:
   A form of bog found in Wales   The juice of unripe grapes
   A form of rock and roll music played on woodwind instruments

3. An orthoepist is:
   An authority on correct pronunciation   A bone specialist
   A specialist in correcting faulty positions of the teeth

4. A sobriquet is:
   A nickname   A female vaudevillian   A redhead

5. Legally speaking, how many people must be involved, at the minimum, for an action to be called a riot?
   Two   Three   Five

6. If you are a gridiron fan, you are enthusiastic about:
   How waffles should be baked   Football
   Best methods of building an outdoor grill

7. Vermouth is made from:
   May wine flavored with juniper juice   Over-ripe grapes
   White wine flavored with aromatic herbs

8. Gin gets its special flavor from:
   Juniper berries   Thrice distilled Vermouth   Dutch bay leaves

9. A shofar is:
   A ram's horn used in Jewish ritual   A crook
   An obsolete spelling of chauffeur

10. What is the pronunciation of *leeward*, as used by nautical people?
    Loo-ward   Lurd   Lee-ward

11. The first woman who made a solo flight across the Atlantic was:
    Judy Splinters   Amelia Earhart   Amy Lovell

12. The Bertillon System identifies a:

    System of shorthand   Method of criminal identification
        Method of grading Civil Service employees

13. What famous orator, in the presence of Abraham Lincoln, delivered an address two hours long at the dedication of Gettysburg?

    Clarence Darrow   Edward Everett   Stephen Douglas

14. A theatrical performance in New York ran close to six hours. One hour was granted for intermission. The playwright was Eugene O'Neill. The play was:

    Ah, Wilderness!   *Strange Interlude*
        A Streetcar Named Desire

15. The first astronomer who used a telescope to observe the heavens was:

    Galileo   Copernicus   Maria Mitchell

16. Slalom Racing is one of the events of the Winter Olympics. Slalom Racing is:

    A race against time, skiing downhill   An uphill race
        A race skiing downhill, backwards

17. Whose portrait is on The United States ten dollar bill?

    Hamilton   Jackson   Washington

18. An alienist is:

    A specialist in diseases of the mind   A foreign spy
        A specialist in immigration problems

19. What state is divided not into counties but into parishes?

    Oklahoma   Massachusetts   Louisiana

20. The length of the Panama Canal is:

    22½ miles   32½ miles   50½ miles

21. The creator of Charlie McCarthy recently died. What was his name?

    Joseph McCarthy   Edgar Bergen   Mike Ronat

22. President Wilson went all out for the League of Nations. The President's first name was:

    Thomas   Woodrow   Roger

23. The symbol & is an abbreviation for the word *and*. The name for this symbol is:

    Anka   Ampersand   Amanda

24. Who was the inventor of the first zipper?

    Thomas Edison   Whitcomb Judson   George Talon

AN ANTHOLOGY OF OLOGIES

To label various special disciplines, English has borrowed roots from Greek and Latin. "The study of animals," for example, is called ZOOL-OGY. The word comes from the Greek ZOON, meaning "a living thing."

Below are definitions for 49 of these five-dollar words. Can you match up the words listed in the right-hand column with the definitions on the left? A score of 25 is good; 32 is excellent; 40 means your specialty is philology.

Answers on page 361

THE STUDY OF...

1. Evil spirits	_____	ECOLOGY
2. The heart	_____	GRAPHOLOGY
3. Aging	_____	PALEONTOLOGY
4. Insects	_____	ARCHAEOLOGY
5. Handwriting	_____	DEMONOLOGY
6. Weather and climate	_____	PENOLOGY
7. Word origins	_____	ONTOLOGY
8. Birds	_____	CETOLOGY
9. Dance	_____	CARDIOLOGY
10. The stars	_____	EPISTEMOLOGY
11. Existence, being	_____	CYTOLOGY
12. Whales	_____	OTOLOGY
13. Living tissue	_____	METEOROLOGY
14. Rocks	_____	LARYNGOLOGY
15. The sense of hearing	_____	OSTEOLOGY
16. The ear	_____	PAPYROLOGY
17. The skin	_____	ORNITHOLOGY
18. Wine	_____	ICHTHYOLOGY
19. Knowledge and thought	_____	PSYCHOLOGY
20. Poison	_____	EPIDEMIOLOGY
21. Water	_____	MYRMECOLOGY
22. China	_____	CHRONOLOGY

23.	Contagious diseases	_____	**ANTHROPOLOGY**
24.	Time sequence	_____	**TOXICOLOGY**
25.	Bones	_____	**GEOLOGY**
26.	Spiders	_____	**GENEALOGY**
27.	Women's diseases	_____	**ENTOMOLOGY**
28.	Ancient writing	_____	**OOLOGY**
29.	Fossils	_____	**ARANEOLOGY**
30.	Fish	_____	**AEROLOGY**
31.	The earth's crust	_____	**COPROLOGY**
32.	Ants	_____	**PETROLOGY**
33.	Drugs	_____	**HERPETOLOGY**
34.	Birds' eggs	_____	**CHOREOGRAPHY**
35.	Ancient papyri	_____	**TYPOLOGY**
36.	God	_____	**HYDROLOGY**
37.	Gems	_____	**GERONTOLOGY**
38.	One's ancestry	_____	**PALEOGRAPHY**
39.	Cells	_____	**ETYMOLOGY**
40.	The throat	_____	**THEOLOGY**
41.	Prisons and punishment	_____	**AUDIOLOGY**
42.	Human races and customs	_____	**GEMMOLOGY**
43.	Symbolic representations	_____	**OENOLOGY**
44.	Organisms in relation to their environment	_____	**ASTRONOMY**
45.	Reptiles (especially snakes)	_____	**PHARMACOLOGY**
46.	The mind, emotions and behavior	_____	**HISTOLOGY**
47.	Pornography in art and literature	_____	**GYNECOLOGY**
48.	The atmosphere in relation to flying	_____	**SINOLOGY**
49.	The past through its material remains	_____	**DERMATOLOGY**

WHO WAS THAT LADY?

Many great movies bear the heroine's name in the title. Do you remember what actresses played the memorable heroines in the 50 movies listed below?

You have three choices. Check the answer you think is correct.

A score of 35 shows female intuition; 40 is matriarchal; and 45 is worthy of a femme fatale.

Answers on page 361

Answers on page 361

1. *Stella Dallas*
   Joanne Woodward   Barbara Stanwyck   Marilyn Monroe

2. *Mildred Pierce*
   Joan Fontaine   Joan Crawford   Joan Blondell

3. *Alice Adams*
   Katharine Hepburn   Olivia de Havilland   Katharine Houghton

4. *Jezebel*
   Bette Davis   Vivien Leigh   Donna Reed

5. *Marjorie Morningstar*
   Elizabeth Taylor   Shelley Winters   Natalie Wood

6. *Anna Christie*
   Liv Ullman   Greta Garbo   Julie Christie

7. *Theodora Goes Wild*
   Shirley Temple   Sandra Dee   Irene Dunne

8. *Sadie Thompson*
   Gloria Swanson   Carole Lombard   Joan Crawford

9. *Ninotchka*
   Greta Garbo   Gloria de Haven   May Britt

10. *Madame X*
    Ruth Gordon   Ruth Chatterton   Claudette Colbert

11. *Julia*
    Karen Black   Lynn Redgrave   Vanessa Redgrave

12. *Camille*
    Janet Leigh   Greta Garbo   Jane Wyman

13. *Sarah and Son*
    Lucille Ball   Ruth Chatterton   Katharine Hepburn

14. *Marie Antoinette*

Norma Shearer   Celeste Holm   Judy Holliday

15. *Rebecca*

Merle Oberon   Joan Fontaine   Wendy Hiller

16. *Kitty Foyle*

Glenda Jackson   Ginger Rogers   Janet Suzman

17. *Annie Hall*

Diane Keaton   Jane Fonda   Lily Tomlin

18. *Madame Curie*

Irene Dunne   Greer Garson   Grace Kelly

19. *Gigi*

Jeanne Moreau   Jean Simmons   Leslie Caron

20. *Mrs. Miniver*

Bette Davis   Susan Hayward   Greer Garson

21. *Joan of Arc*

Marie Dressler   Ingrid Bergman   Joan Fontaine

22. *Sister Kenny*

Audrey Hepburn   Tuesday Weld   Rosalind Russell

23. *Violette*

Isabelle Huppert   Jeanne Moreau   Stephanie Audran

24. *All About Eve*

Joanne Woodward   Anne Baxter   Eva Marie Saint

25. *Irma La Douce*

Sophia Loren   Anna Magnani   Shirley MacLaine

26. *Juliet of the Spirits*

Giulietta Masina   Catherine Deneuve   Sophia Loren

27. *Mary Poppins*

Julie Andrews   Patricia Neal   Marsha Mason

28. *The Unsinkable Molly Brown*

Barbra Streisand   Barbara Stanwyck   Debbie Reynolds

29. *Georgy Girl*

Deborah Kerr   Lynn Redgrave   Sarah Miles

30. *Bonnie and Clyde*

Fay Wray   Faye Dunaway   Gena Rowlands

31. *Rachel, Rachel*

Raquel Welch   Mia Farrow   Joanne Woodward

32. *Isadora*
    Ann Bancroft   Vanessa Redgrave   Leslie Browne

33. *Anne of the Thousand Days*
    Genvieve Bujold   Simone Signoret   Luise Rainer

34. *The Prime of Miss Jean Brodie*
    Claudette Colbert   Janet Gaynor   Maggie Smith

35. *Alice Doesn't Live Here Anymore*
    Diane Keaton   Ellen Burstyn   Cybill Shepherd

36. *Myra Breckenridge*
    Ali McGraw   Candice Bergen   Raquel Welch

37. *Rosemary's Baby*
    Mia Farrow   Sissy Spacek   Maureen O'Hara

38. *The Americanization of Emily*
    Julie Christie   Julie Andrews   Judith Anderson

39. *Harold and Maude*
    Ruth Chatterton   Ruth Gordon   Bette Davis

40. *Hello, Dolly!*
    Barbra Streisand   Liza Minelli   Ruth Gordon

41. *Fanny*
    Simone Signoret   Jean Seburg   Leslie Caron

42. *Cleopatra*
    Elizabeth Taylor   Elizabeth Ashley   Mae West

43. *Daisy Miller*
    Mia Farrow   Cybill Shepherd   Tatum O'Neill

44. *The Perils of Pauline*
    Clara Bow   Lillian Gish   Pearl White

45. *McCabe and Mrs. Miller*
    Martha Scott   Julie Christie   Margaret Sullavan

46. *Carrie*
    Sissy Spacek   Tatum O'Neill   June Allyson

47. *Becky Sharp*
    Miriam Hopkins   Billie Burke   Loretta Young

48. *Auntie Mame*
    Rosalind Russell   Carol Channing   Maggie Smith

49. *Whatever Happened to Baby Jane?*
    Jill Clayburgh   Gloria Swanson   Bette Davis

50. *Lolita*
    Sue Lyon   Carol Baker   Tuesday Weld

WHERE, OH, WHERE?

You need not have seen all this world's sights to know where these land-mark monuments are located. In the blank spaces, write the name of the city in which (or near which) the monument is located.

Give yourself two points for every correct answer. Deduct one point for every incorrect answer. A score of 30 is worthy of Atlas; 36 is monumental; and 44 means you're a walking Michelin guide!

Answers on page 361

1. The Statue of Liberty is in _____.

2. The Wailing Wall stands in _____.

3. The Eiffel Tower is in _____.

4. The Great Pyramids stand near _____.

5. The Spanish Steps are in _____.

6. The Hermitage is in _____.

7. The Sphinx is near _____.

8. The Leaning Tower is in _____.

9. The Vatican is in _____.

10. The Empire State Building is in _____.

11. The Taj Mahal is in _____.

12. Saint Marks' Cathedral is in _____.

13. Big Ben is in _____.

14. The Blarney Stone is in _____.

15. The Kremlin is in _____.

16. La Scala Opera House is in _____.

17. The Alhambra is in _____.

18. The Golden Gate Bridge is in _____.

19. The Parthenon is in _____.

20. Westminster Abbey is in _____.

21. The Kaaba is in _____.

22. Notre Dame Cathedral stands in _____.

23. The Prado is in _____.

24. Faneuil Hall is in _____.

WHO SAID IT?

Below are listed 48 famous quotations, from the recent or distant past. Each phrase is associated with one particular person. You have the job of figuring out who made each of these famous statements. You have heard or read them all, at one time or another. Can you properly identify the sponsors?

Below each statement is a list of four names, one of which is the correct source for that phrase. Circle the letter in front of your choice.

A score of 26 is good; 33 is excellent; and 40 makes you a true historian.

Answers on page 361

1. *To thine own self be true.*
   a) Wordsworth
   b) Bible
   c) Shakespeare
   d) Plato

2. *Man proposes, but God disposes.*
   a) Daniel Webster
   b) Thoreau
   c) Thomas a Kempis
   d) John Wycliffe

3. *Love is blind.*
   a) Chaucer
   b) Shakespeare
   c) Keats
   d) Aristotle

4. *We will bury you.*
   a) Fidel Castro
   b) Idi Amin
   c) Adolf Hitler
   d) Nikita Krushchev

5. *A foolish consistency is the hobgoblin of little minds.*
   a) Thoreau
   b) Nathaniel Hawthorne
   c) Wordsworth
   d) Ralph Waldo Emerson

6. *Good-night, Mrs. Calabash, wherever you are.*
   a) Jimmy Durante
   b) Noel Coward
   c) Al Jolson
   d) Eddie Cantor

7. *We have nothing to fear but fear itself.*
   a) Winston Churchill
   b) Dwight Eisenhower
   c) Franklin Roosevelt
   d) Charles de Gaulle

8. *One small step for man; one giant leap for mankind.*
   a) John Glenn
   b) Neil Armstrong
   c) Virgil Grissom
   d) Frank Borman

9. *Look before you leap.*
   a) John Milton
   b) John Heywood
   c) Sir Thomas More
   d) Maimonides

10. *Honor thy father and thy mother.*
    a) Aeschylus
    b) Shakespeare
    c) Confucius
    d) Exodus, Old Testament

11. *The public be damned.*
    a) John D. Rockefeller
    b) Marie Antoinette
    c) William Vanderbilt
    d) Richard Nixon

12. *From each according to his ability, to each according to his needs.*
    a) Charles Darwin
    b) Karl Marx
    c) Leo Tolstoy
    d) Henry David Thoreau

13. *Am I my brother's keeper?*
    a) Isaac
    b) Jacob
    c) Cain
    d) Abel

14. *Something is rotten in the state of Denmark.*
    a) Hamlet
    b) Macbeth
    c) King Lear
    d) Othello

15. *To err is human.*
    a) Jesus Christ
    b) William Shakespeare
    c) Victor Hugo
    d) Jean Jacques Rousseau

16. *Don't count your chickens before they are hatched.*
    a) Sophocles
    b) Aesop
    c) Hans Christian Anderson
    d) The Brothers Grimm

17. *It is a riddle wrapped in a mystery inside an enigma.*
    a) Benjamin Disraeli
    b) Henry Fielding
    c) Jonathan Swift
    d) Winston Churchill

18. *How do I love thee? Let me count the ways.*
    a) John Keats
    b) Ralph Waldo Emerson
    c) Elizabeth Barrett Browning
    d) Robert Browning

19. *I am not a crook.*
    a) John Dillinger
    b) "Pretty Boy" Floyd
    c) Richard Nixon
    d) John Dean

20. *Rope a dope.*
    a) Joe Frazier
    b) Jonathan Swift
    c) Henny Youngman
    d) Mohammed Ali

21. *Religion is the opium of the people.*
    a) Karl Marx
    b) Charles Darwin
    c) Leon Trotsky
    d) Nikita Krushchev

22. *The buck stops here.*
    a) Theodore Roosevelt
    b) Harry Truman
    c) Lyndon Johnson
    d) John F. Kennedy

23. *Bah, humbug!*
    a) Charlie McCarthy   c) The Cowardly Lion
    b) Ebineezer Scrooge   d) Captain Hook

24. *It is a tale told by an idiot, full of sound and fury, signifying nothing.*
    a) William Faulkner   c) William Shakespeare
    b) Paul Simon   d) Aesop

25. *Damn the torpedoes! Go ahead!*
    a) Admiral Farragut   c) Douglas MacArhur
    b) Winston Churchill   d) Robert E. Lee

26. *I have been a stranger in a strange land.*
    a) Robert A. Heinlein   c) William Shakespeare
    b) Exodus, Old Testament d) Gospel of John, New Testament

27. *Frankly, my dear, I don't give a damn.*
    a) Rhett Butler   c) Charles Bovary
    b) Prof. Henry Higgins   d) Philip Marlowe

28. *The times they are a-changin'.*
    a) Pete Seeger   c) Arlo Guthrie
    b) Woody Guthrie   d) Bob Dylan

29. *A rose is a rose is a rose.*
    a) Dorothy Parker   c) Alice B. Toklas
    b) Gertrude Stein   d) Phyllis Diller

30. *Ask not what your country can do for you; ask what you can do for your country.*
    a) Franklin D. Roosevelt c) John F. Kennedy
    b) Robert F. Kennedy   d) Edward Kennedy

31. *Let them eat cake.*
    a) Mary, Queen of Scots c) Marie Antoinette
    b) Josephine   d) Alexandra, Empress of Russia

32. *Take my wife—please!*
    a) Jimmy Durante   c) Noel Coward
    b) Henny Youngman   d) David Steinberg

33. *We are not amused.*
    a) Marie Antoinette   c) Queen Victoria
    b) Queen Elizabeth I   d) Richard III

34. *I hear America singing.*
    a) Robert Frost   c) Lawrence Welk
    b) Allan Ginsburg   d) Walt Whitman

35. *Death, be not proud.*
    a) John Donne   c) William Shakespeare
    b) John Keats   d) William Wordsworth

36. *Carry on, and dread nought.*
    a) Admiral Farragut   c) Ralph Waldo Emerson
    b) Abraham Lincoln   d) Winston Churchill

37. *Give me liberty, or give me death!*
    a) Nathan Hale   c) George Washington
    b) Patrick Henry   d) Thomas Paine

38. *Out, out, damned spot!*
    a) Lady Macbeth   c) Desdemona
    b) Ophelia   d) Scarlett O'Hara

39. *I want to be alone.*
    a) Sarah Bernhardt   c) Ellen Terry
    b) Greta Garbo   d) Grace Kelly

40. *And she brings you tea and oranges that come all the way from China.*
    a) Paul Simon   c) Leonard Cohen
    b) Art Garfunkel   d) Bob Dylan

41. *Hope springs eternal in the human breast.*
    a) Alexander Pope   c) Ben Jonson
    b) John Dryden   d) Jonathan Swift

42. *Call me Ishmael.*
    a) Theodore Dreiser   c) Edgar Allan Poe
    b) William Faulkner   d) Herman Melville

43. *I never met a man I didn't like.*
    a) Roy Rogers   c) W.C. Fields
    b) Will Rogers   d) P.T. Barnum

44. *For dust thou art, and unto dust thou shalt return.*
    a) William Shakespeare   c) Genesis, Old Testament
    b) William Wordsworth   d) Matthew, New Testament

45. *May you live all the days of your life.*
    a) Jonathan Swift   c) Johnny Carson
    b) Dorothy Parker   d) Christopher Morley

46. *Remember the Alamo!*
    a) Daniel Boone   c) Daniel Webster
    b) Col. Sidney Sherman   d) Davy Crockett

47. *I had a dream.*
    a) Robert F. Kennedy   c) Franklin D. Roosevelt
    b) Winston Churchill   d) Martin Luther King

48. *This land is your land, this land is my land.*
    a) Joan Baez   c) Phil Ochs
    b) Woody Guthrie   d) Pete Seeger

SPORTS LEGENDS

You're not likely to find these outstanding athletes on the sports pages of today's newspapers, but you will certainly find them in the sports history books. Some go back only a few years; others go back half a century or so. Can you name the sport in which each of these champions excelled?

A score of 20 is good; 30 is excellent; 40 means you may be missing your calling if you're not already a sports reporter.

Answers on page 362

1. Ty Cobb _____
2. Bill Quakenbush _____
3. Ben Hogan _____
4. Cookie Gilchrist _____
5. H. Ellsworth Vines _____
6. Patty Berg _____
7. John Weissmuller _____
8. Jim Ryun _____
9. Jimmy Foxx _____
10. Jacques Plante _____
11. Babe Didrikson Zaharias _____
12. Bill Tilden _____
13. Benny Leonard _____
14. Dazzy Vance _____
15. Paavo Nurmi _____
16. Duke Kahanamoku _____
17. Jesse Owens _____
18. Goose Goslin _____
19. Walter Camp _____
20. Jack Johnson _____
21. Willie Shoemaker _____
22. Don Schollander _____
23. Jean-Claude Killy _____

24. Zack Wheat   _____

25. Francis Ouimet   _____

26. Pelé   _____

27. Roger Bresnahan   _____

28. Althea Gibson   _____

29. Rocky Graziano   _____

30. Mal Whitfield   _____

31. Jack Kramer   _____

32. Sid Luckman   _____

33. Ray Ewry   _____

34. Dixie Walker   _____

35. Johnny Revolta   _____

36. Red Grange   _____

37. Gertrude Ederle   _____

38. Archie Hahn   _____

39. Pancho Gonzales   _____

40. George Mikan   _____

41. Grover Cleveland Alexander   _____

42. Eddie Arcaro   _____

43. Sammy Baugh   _____

44. Alice Marble   _____

45. Henry Armstrong   _____

46. Doc Blanchard   _____

47. Wilma Rudolph Ward   _____

48. Don Budge   _____

49. Emil Zatopek   _____

50. Wally Moon   _____

HOW MUCH DO YOU KNOW ABOUT THE AMERICAN REVOLUTION?

Below, you will find 25 questions that will test your knowledge of events that occurred before, during, or immediately after the American Revolution. There are four choices given for each. Check the one you believe is correct.

A score of 16 is good; 19 is very good; and 22 marks you as a patriot and historian.

Answers on page 362

1. The king of England during the American Revolution was:
    George II   George III   George IV   George V

2. The first shots of the American Revolution were fired at:
    Lexington   Concord   Bunker Hill   Yorktown

3. In 1775, Ethan Allen and his Green Mountain Boys seized:
    Fort Tyler   Bennington   Fort Ticonderoga   Champlain

4. The influential pamphlet *Common Sense* was written by:
    Nathan Hale   Samuel Adams   Thomas Paine   Benjamin Franklin

5. The Declaration of Independence was signed in:
    New York   Boston   Philadelphia   Washington, D.C.

6. George Washington crossed the Delaware River to attack a British force stationed at:
    Chester   Phillipsburg   Trenton   Wilmington

7. The battle that is generally regarded as the most important of the American Revolution was:
    Saratoga   White Plains   Concord   Germantown

8. The last battle of the American Revolution was:
    Monmouth   Yorktown   Long Island   Saratoga

9. The American guerrilla leader known as the "Swamp Fox" was:
    John Barry   Horatio Gater
    Francis Marion   Thomas Sumter

10. John Paul Jones's ship was named the:
    Serapis   *Bon Homme Richard*   *Drake*   *Lexington*

11. The treaty that formally recognized the new nation of the United States was the Treaty of:
    Versailles   Paris   Quebec   Yorktown

12. The American Revolution began in 1775; it ended in:
    1776   1778   1779   1781

13. The British commander at the battle of Yorktown was:
    Howe   Cornwallis   Leger   Burgoyne

14. Of the following, the only state that was one of the original 13 states was:
    Vermont   Maine   South Carolina   West Virginia

15. The first person to sign the Declaration of Independence was:
    John Hancock   Benjamin Franklin
    Thomas Jefferson   Thomas Pinckney

16. The first capital of the United States was:
    Philadelphia   Boston   New York   Washington, D.C.

17. Betsy Ross's first flag contained this many stars:
    One   Six   Thirteen   Fifty

18. At the battles of Lexington and Concord, the total number of British casualties was closest to:
    20   200   2000   20,000

19. "Give me liberty or give me death." These words were spoken by:
    Patrick Henry   Nathan Hale
    Johnny Tremain   Benjamin Franklin

20. The battle of Bunker Hill was fought closest to the city of:
    Boston   Providence   Concord   Hartford

21. The first Vice-President of the United States was:
    John Quincy Adams   John Adams
    Samuel Adams   John Hancock

22. Valley Forge is located in the state of:
    New York   Pennsylvania   New Jersey   Virginia

23. The first Secretary of Treasury of the United States was:
    Thomas Jefferson   Alexander Hamilton
    Henry Knox   James Madison

24. The first state to ratify the Constitution was:
    Pennsylvania   Delaware   Rhode Island   Massachusetts

25. The chief authors of *The Federalist Papers* were James Madison, Alexander Hamilton, and:
    James Monroe   Thomas Pinckney
    John Jay   George Washington

TUBE TOPICS

In barely three decades, television has had a tremendous influence on everyone in America, notably on trivia buffs. As a relief from all manner of profound or platitudinous statements about television's place in society, try your hand at the 50 questions on TV history in this quiz.

A score of 20 is good; 30 is excellent; 40 means you've certainly been keeping your eyes and ears open.

Answers on page 362

1. The actress who played Miss Kitty on TV's *Gunsmoke* was

   _____

2. On the old *Dick Van Dyke Show*, the profession of next-door-neighbor Jerry was _____

3. Gene Barry played an independently wealthy Los Angeles police detective on a series entitled_____

4. Linda Lavin's series *Alice* is based on the film

   _____

5. *The Andy Griffith Show's* mythical setting, Mayberry, was in the state of _____

6. The train which played an important role in life at *Petticoat Junction* was named the _____

7. The actor who played Thurston Howell, the millionaire ship-wrecked on *Gilligan's Island*, was _____

8. A situation comedy set in a New York apartment house and starring Will Hutchins and Sandy Baron was entitled

   _____

9. What comedian used *The Smothers Brothers Comedy Hour* as a platform for his presidential campaign?_____

10. Robert Reed and Florence Henderson played the parents of a brood of six children in_____

11. The real name of the Beaver in *Leave It to Beaver* was

_____

12. Diahann Carroll played a nurse in one of the first series to feature a black in a starring role. The show was _____

13. In *The Beverly Hillbillies*, Buddy Ebsen put aside his dancing shoes to play a character named _____

14. Jack Lord portrays Steve McGarrett in _____

15. In *I Love Lucy*, the hometown of best friend Ethel Mertz is

_____

16. Jerry Van Dyke starred in *My Mother the Car*, in which an old jalopy is the reincarnation of his mother. The mother's voice coming out of the car is really actress _____

17. Peter Tork, Davy Jones, Micky Dolenz, and Mike Nesmith were the title characters in _____

18. Peter Duell and Judy Carne played newlyweds in a San Francisco sitcom, the name of which was _____

19. *Mr. Ed's* owner was played by_____

20. The OSI chief, played by Richard Anderson, who sends *The Six Million Dollar Man* on his missions is_____

21. The actor who played Adam Cartwright, the oldest son on *Bonanza*, was _____

22. Two performers, husband and wife, who have appeared on *Mission Impossible* and more recently on *Space: 1999* are

_____ and _____

23. The name of *Perry Mason's* outer-office secretary, who was almost never seen on camera, was _____

24. Julie Newmar played a beautiful lady robot in

_____

25. The actress who played the mother on *Father Knows Best* later
    played Mr. Spock's mother on *Star Trek*. She is the talented

    _____

26. An unsuccessful series based on the works of James Thurber starred
    William Windom as a Thurberesque cartoonist. The series was

    _____

27. Bill Cosby and Robert Culp played American secret agents
    masquerading as tennis bums in _____

28. *The Flying Nun* was set in _____

29. The father of *My Three Sons* was played by _____

30. The long-running game show *Jeopardy* was hosted by

    _____

31. Eddie Albert and Eva Gabor played cityslickers transplanted to a
    farm on the series titled_____

32. One of the most successful made-for-TV movies starred James Caan
    portraying a dying football player in _____

33. Both astronaut Tony Nelson (*I Dream of Jeannie*) and psychologist
    Dr. Robert Hartley (*The Bob Newhart Show*) had a scatter-
    brained best friend played by _____

34. The voices of Bugs Bunny and Daffy Duck, and also sound effects
    and comedic minor characters in *The Jack Benny Show* were
    provided by _____

35. Georgette, the wife of buffoonish newsman Ted Baxter on *The
    Mary Tyler Moore Show*, was played by actress

    _____

36. *The Man from U.N.C.L.E.* was sent on his perilous missions by Leo
    G. Carroll, who played the role of_____

37. Dick Benjamin and Paula Prentiss, real-life husband and wife,
    played a cartoonist and his wife in the sitcom _____

38. In an appearance on *The Tonight Show*, the actor who threw a tomahawk in one of television's most famous "bloopers" was

   _____

39. In *Family*, the sensitive and all too human mother is played by the very talented _____

40. Klem Kadiddlehopper and Freddie the Freeloader are characters created by_____

41. The leading role in *The Life of Riley* was played by Jackie Gleason and by the late _____

42. What military rank was held by Hogan in *Hogan's Heroes?*

   _____

43. In *Roots*, LeVar Burton and John Amos played different periods in the life of character _____

44. *Family Affair* starred Brian Keith as a "bachelor father." His "gentleman's gentleman" was played by _____

45. The network which scored a coup by being the first to show *Gone with the Wind* was_____

46. In *Lost in Space* Jonathan Harris played a despicable character named _____

47. Lt. Uhura, the communications officer aboard the *USS Enterprise* in *Star Trek*, was played by_____

48. George C. Scott played a New York social worker in

   _____

49. The Coneheads and "News Update" are among the most popular recurring features in NBC's _____

50. Coach Leroy Fedders drowned in a bowl of chicken soup prepared by the title character of the show _____

FAMOUS AMERICAN SLOGANS

It has been said that words can move mountains. Some words have certainly moved history.

Listed below are 20 phrases out of America's past. Each is associated with some particular man. Can you match the slogan with the man?

A score of 8 is good; 10 is excellent; and 15 puts you up with the experts.

Answers on page 363

1. "Give me liberty or give me death."
   Abraham Lincoln   *Patrick Henry*   *Thomas Jefferson*

2. "Remember the Alamo!"
   Admiral Dewey   *Sidney Sherman*   *Daniel Boone*

3. "We have nothing to fear but fear itself."
   Herbert Hoover   *Dwight Eisenhower*   *Franklin Roosevelt*

4. "I only regret that I have but one life to give for my country."
   Nathan Hale   *Paul Revere*   *Benedict Arnold*

5. "Don't fire until you see the whites of their eyes!"
   William Prescott   *General Israel Putnam*   *Daniel Webster*

6. "I have just begun to fight!"
   Admiral Farragut   *General Grant*   *John Paul Jones*

7. "We have met the enemy and they are ours."
   Robert E. Lee   *General Sherman*   *Commodore Perry*

8. "Go West, young man, and grow up with the country."
   Henry Raymond   *Horace Greeley*   *Brigham Young*

9. "Damn the torpedoes! Full speed ahead!"
   Stephen Decatur   *Admiral Farragut*   *Admiral King*

10. "Taxation without representation is tyranny."
    Thomas Jefferson   *Patrick Henry*   *James Otis*

11. "The world must be made safe for democracy."
    Herbert Hoover   *Warren Harding*   *Woodrow Wilson*

12. "We must all hang together, or assuredly we shall all hang separately."
    Benjamin Franklin   *Samuel Adams*   *John Hancock*

13. "Our country . . . may she always be in the right; but our country, right or wrong."
    James Madison   *John Adams*   *Stephen Decatur*

14. "Millions for defense, but not one cent for tribute."
    Charles Pinckney   *Thomas Paine*   *Alexander Hamilton*

15. "Sir, I would rather be right than President."
    Henry Clay   *Daniel Webster*   *Horace Greeley*

16. "You shall not crucify mankind upon a cross of gold."
    Grover Cleveland   *William J. Bryan*   *William Borah*

17. "These are the times that try men's souls."
    Thomas Paine   *George Washington*   *Franklin Roosevelt*

18. "I shall return!"
    Harry Truman   *Woodrow Wilson*   *Douglas MacArthur*

19. "Yesterday, December 7, 1941 — a date which will live in infamy —"
    Alfred E. Smith   *Franklin Roosevelt*   *Herbert Hoover*

20. "Fifty-four forty, or fight."
    Theodore Roosevelt   *William Allen*   *John Pershing*

THE LADY IN THE CASE

Each of the fifty virile words in this quiz has its feminine counterpart. It's a matter of "Cherchez la femme!"

You score 2 points for each correct answer. A score of 64 is good and 72 is very good. Scoring 80 or better indicates a very intelligent opinion on the female question.

Answers on page 363

1. Waiter _____

2. Master _____

3. Masseur _____

4. Tiger _____

5. Marquis _____

6. Rooster _____

7. King _____

8. Steward _____

9. Drake _____

10. Earl _____

11. Bullock _____

12. Couturier _____

13. Patriarch _____

14. Fox _____

15. Testator _____

16. Groom _____

17. Usher _____

18. Buck _____

19. Lord _____

20. Abbot _____

21. Dog _____

22. Bartender _____

23. Peacock _____

24. Monk _____

25. Monsieur _____

26. Aviator _____

27. Sire _____

28. Ram _____

29. Sultan _____

30. Duke _____

31. Colt _____

32. Maharaja _____

33. Blond _____

34. Boar _____

35. Lad _____

36. Kaiser _____

37. Stallion _____

38. Tsar _____

39. Fiancé _____

40. Best Man _____

41. Cob _____

42. Hero _____

43. Stag _____

44. Señor _____

45. Pierrot _____

46. Billy goat _____

47. Baronet _____

48. Gander _____

49. Sannup _____

50. Bull _____

IN THE BEGINNING

The opening lines of some of our great works of literature are quoted below. You have a choice of three sources. Can you identify which masterpiece each selection comes from?

A score of 12 is good; 16 is excellent; and 21 is masterful.

Answers on page 363

1. "When I was a small boy at the beginning of the century I remember an old man who wore knee-breeches and worsted stockings, and who used to hobble about the street of our village with the help of a stick."

    The Way of All Flesh, Samuel Butler
    Of Human Bondage, W. Somerset Maugham
    Nicholas Nickleby, Charles Dickens

2. "The studio was filled with the rich odour of roses, and when the light summer wind stirred amidst the trees of the garden there came through the open door the heavy scent of the lilac, or the more delicate perfume of the pink-flowering thorn."

    Portrait of the Artist as a Young Man, James Joyce
    The Picture of Dorian Gray, Oscar Wilde
    Camille, Alexander Dumas

3. "If music be the food of love, play on."

    The Magic Flute, libretto by Schikaneder, music by Mozart
    Twelfth Night, William Shakespeare
    The Art of Love, Ovid

4. "Late in the afternoon of a chilly day in February, two gentlemen were sitting alone over their wine, in a well-furnished dining-parlor, in the town of P_____, in Kentucky."

    The Devil and Daniel Webster, Stephen Vincent Benet
    Uncle Tom's Cabin, Harriet Beecher Stowe
    As I Lay Dying, William Faulkner

5. "On the first Monday of the month of April, 1625, the town of Meung, in which the author of the Romance of the Rose was born, appeared to be in as perfect a state of revolution as if the Hugenots had just made a second Rochelle of it."

    The Red and the Black, Stendhal
    Guy Mannering, Sir Walter Scott
    The Three Musketeers, Alexandre Dumas

6. "Where are Elmer, Herman, Tom and Charley,
   The weak of will, the strong of arm, the clown, the boozer, the
      fighter?
   All, all are sleeping on the hill."
   > *Annabel Lee*, Edgar Allan Poe
   > *The Concord Hymn*, Ralph Waldo Emerson
   > *Spoon River Anthology*, Edgar Lee Masters

7. "April is the cruelest month, breeding
   Lilacs out of the dead land..."
   > *The Waste Land*, T.S. Eliot
   > *Paradise Lost*, John Milton
   > *Romeo and Juliet*, William Shakespeare

8. "In my younger and more vulnerable years my father gave me some
   advice that I've been turning over in my mind ever since."
   > *Tom Sawyer*, Mark Twain
   > *The Great Gatsby*, F. Scott Fitzgerald
   > *The Sound and the Fury*, William Faulkner

9. "Call me Ishmael."
   > *The Book of Exodus*
   > *Pilgrim's Progress*, John Bunyan
   > *Moby Dick*, Herman Melville

10. "All happy families resemble one another; every unhappy family is
    unhappy in its own fashion."
    > *Anna Karenina*, Leo Tolstoy
    > *The Brothers Karamazov*, Fyodor Dostoievski
    > *Jane Eyre*, Charlotte Bronte

11. "A throng of bearded men, in sad-colored garments and gray,
    steeple-crowned hats, intermixed with women, some wearing hoods,
    and others bareheaded, was assembled in front of a wooden edifice,
    the door of which was heavily timbered with oak, and studded with
    iron spikes."
    > *The Scarlet Letter*, Nathaniel Hawthorne
    > *Silas Marner*, George Eliot
    > *The Inspector General*, Nikolai V. Gogol

12. "When in April the sweet showers fall and pierce the droughts of
    March to the root..."
    > *The Winter's Tale*, William Shakespeare
    > *The Canterbury Tales*, Geoffrey Chaucer
    > *Lines Written in Early Spring*, William Wordsworth

13. "The Jebel es Zubleh is a mountain fifty miles and more in length, and so narrow that its tracery gives it a likeness to a caterpillar crawling from the south to the north."

   The Snows of Kilimanjaro, Ernest Hemingway
   Ben-Hur, Lewis Wallace
   Robinson Crusoe, Daniel Defoe

14. "It is a truth universally acknowledged, that a single man in possession of a good fortune must be in want of a wife."

   Vanity Fair, William Thackeray
   Pride and Prejudice, Jane Austen
   Wuthering Heights, Emily Bronte

15. "It was the best of times; it was the worst of times."

   Common Sense, Thomas Paine
   The Decline and Fall of the Roman Empire, Sir Edward Gibbon
   A Tale of Two Cities, Charles Dickens

16. "In that pleasant district of merry England which is watered by the river Don, there extended in ancient times a large forest, covering the greater part of the beautiful hills and valleys which lie between Sheffield and the pleasant town of Doncaster."

   Tess of the D'Urbervilles, Thomas Hardy
   Roxana, Daniel Defoe
   Ivanhoe, Sir Walter Scott

17. "Now is the winter of our discontent
   Made glorious summer by this sun of York."

   Hamlet, William Shakespeare
   King Lear, William Shakespeare
   Richard III, William Shakespeare

18. "A spectre is haunting Europe—the spectre of communism."

   The Communist Manifesto, Karl Marx and Friedrich Engels
   Mein Kampf, Adolf Hitler
   The Second World War, Sir Winston Churchill

19. "It was love at first sight."

   Love Story, Eric Segal
   Daisly Miller, Henry James
   Catch-22, Joseph Heller

20. "Arms and the man I sing..."

   The Aeneid, Virgil
   The Iliad, Homer
   The Odyssey, Homer

21. "It was in the Gardens of Hamilcar at Megara, an outskirt of Carthage."

   King Solomon's Mines, H. Rider Haggard
   Salambo, Gustave Flaubert
   Andromache, Jean Baptiste Racine

22. "Scarlett O'Hara was not beautiful, but men seldom realized it when caught by her charm as the Tarleton twins were."

   Gone with the Wind, Margaret Mitchell
   Tender Is the Night, F. Scott Fitzgerald
   Little Women, Louisa May Alcott

23. "One thing was certain, that the *white* kitten had had nothing to do with it—it was the black kitten's fault entirely."

   Peter Pan, James Barrie
   Through the Looking Glass, Lewis Carroll
   Black Beauty, Anna Sewell

24. "'Well, Piotr, not in sight yet?' was the question asked on May the 20th, 1859, by a gentleman of a little over forty, in a dusty coat and checked trousers, who came out without his hat on to the low steps of the posting station at S_____."

   Madame Bovary, Gustave Faulbert
   The Inspector General, Nikolai V. Gogol
   Fathers and Sons, Ivan Turgenev

25. "Without, the night was cold and wet, but in the small parlor of Lakenam Villa the blinds were drawn and the fire burned brightly."

   The Monkey's Paw, W.W. Jacobs
   The Speckled Band, Sir Arthur Conan Doyle
   The Tell-Tale Heart, Edgar Allan Poe

POT-AU-FEU

We have here a stew of 28 unrelated bits and pieces of information. See how good a chef you are. Choose the answer you think is right.

Award yourself one point for each correct answer. A score of 13 makes the grade; 18 is commendable; and 23 earns you a cordon bleu.

Answers on page 363

Answers on page 363

1. Which country has the highest death rate?
   Panama   Angola   Bangladesh

2. A neophyte is a:
   New golf club   New type of carriage   Beginner

3. Katharine Hepburn's first movie was:
   Alice Adams   *A Bill of Divorcement*   *The Philadelphia Story*

4. The first Little League World Series took place in:
   1910   1947   1967

5. Which animal lives the longest?
   A camel   A tortoise   A parrot

6. Which of the following birds can *not* fly?
   The magpie   The bobwhite   The cormorant

7. A vendetta is a:
   Feud   Spanish marketplace   Large advertised sale

8. A backlist is:
   List of books published previously
   A published list of insurance prospects
   A list of retired military officers

9. The largest desert in the world is:
   The Great Gobi   The Sahara   Death Valley

10. Stephen Crane's novel *The Red Badge of Courage* was published in:
    1845   1895   1955

11. A troglodyte is:
    A cave-dweller   A large amphibian
    An attic window transparent to the sky

12. The largest bird in the world is the:
    Eagle   Ostrich   Emu

13. A famous battle of World War I was:
    The Battle of the Bulge   The Battle of the Marne
    The Battle of Waterloo

14. Kleig lights are:
    High powered laser beams   Bright lights used in the theatre
                Illegal illuminations used by smugglers

15. What President of the United States became Chief Justice of the Supreme Court after he left the Presidency?
    Taft   Polk   Buchanan

16. A pinafore is a:
    Type of musical instrument   Large safety pin   Children's apron

17. The last bare-knuckle fight was held in:
    1869   1889   1919

18. The most expensive food in the world, the white truffle of the Piedmont district of Italy, sells for about:
    $20 per pound $200 dollars per pound $2,000 per pound

19. The Thousand Islands are located:
    In the Southwest Pacific   In the Great Lakes   Off Alaska

20. A dromedary is a:
    Date   Camel   Mohammedan calendar

21. David slew Goliath with a:
    Slingshot   Trunk of a tree   Broadsword

22. The artist associated with the Sistine Chapel was:
    Leonardo da Vinci   Giotto   Michelangelo

23. A palimpsest is a:
    Grapefruit   Cordovan pocketbook
                Manuscript in which later writing
                is superimposed on earlier writing

24. What is meant by the phrase "killing the fatted calf?"
    Feasting and rejoicing   Wasting without limit
                Destroying one's source of sustenance

25. A knight errant was a:
    Knight who had fallen from grace   Wandering knight
            Knight in a chess game which has been turned into a king

26. The fur nutria comes from a large South American water rodent called a:
    Coypu   Weasel   Ferret

27. The capital of the State of Delaware is:
    Wilmington   Elsmere   Dover

28. The author of *Wuthering Heights* was:
    Charlotte Brontë   Emily Brontë   Jane Austen

PASSIONATE PAIRS

Below, you will find listed the names of 50 people, whose love affairs, in fiction, myth, and history, have become legendary.

Each name listed below is associated with one particular person, but that person's name has been left blank, Can you fill in the blanks and reunite the passionate pairs?

A score of 26 is fair; 34 is great; and 42 is top-notch.

Answers on page 364

1. Marc Antony and _____

2. Boaz and _____

3. Penelope and _____

4. Romeo and _____

5. William Randolph Hearst and _____

6. Tristram and _____

7. Rhett Butler and _____

8. Madame Pompadour and _____

9. Heloise and _____

10. Paris and _____

11. Lillian Hellman and _____

12. Robin Hood and _____

13. Dante and _____

14. Eurydice and _____

15. The Duke of Windsor and _____

16. Sir Lancelot and _____

17. Isis and _____

18. Simone de Beauvoir and _____

19. Pygmalion and _____

20. Robert Browning and _____

21. Ingrid Bergman and _____

22. Carole Lombard and _____

23. Napoleon and _____

24. Humphrey Bogart and _____

25. George Bernard Shaw and _____

26. Nell Gwynne and _____

27. Heathcliff *(Wuthering Heights)* and _____

28. John Alden and _____

29. Emma Hamilton and _____

30. Woodrow Wilson and _____

31. Katharine Hepburn and _____

32. F. Scott Fitzgerald and _____

33. Yoko Ono and _____

34. Prince Albert and _____

35. Pip *(Great Expectations)* and _____

36. Liv Ullmann and _____

37. Beatrice *(Much Ado About Nothing)* and _____

38. George Eliot and _____

39. Eugene Onegin and _____

40. L'il Abner and _____

41. Henry Miller and _____

42. Blanche DuBois *(A Streetcar Named Desire)* and _____

43. Carlo Ponti and _____

44. Popeye and _____

45. Mick Jagger and _____

46. Katherine *(The Taming of the Shrew)* and _____

47. Pyramus and _____

48. Jay Gatsby *(The Great Gatsby)* and _____

49. Justinian and _____

50. Jacob and _____

EMPORIA OF IMPORT

Do you like to shop? Do you know the names of the world's most famous stores, and can you name the cities in which they are located?

Below is a list of 25 outstanding emporia. Some of them have more than one branch, but in every case, the main branch is the one that is well-known. In the blank space, write the name of the city in which the main store is located.

A score of 11 is good; 14 is spiffy; and 19 indicates you've shopped around.

Answers on page 364

1. Neiman Marcus _____
2. Macy's _____
3. Selfridge's _____
4. G. Fox and Company _____
5. Filene's _____
6. G.U.M. _____
7. Galeries Lafayette _____
8. Den Permanente _____
9. Fauchon _____
10. Christiana Glasmagasin _____
11. Hammacher Schlemmer _____
12. Gimbel's _____
13. Jordan Marsh _____
14. Au Printemps _____
15. Harrod's _____
16. Marks and Spencer _____
17. Galerias Preciados _____
18. Saks Fifth Avenue _____
19. Fortnum and Mason _____
20. I. Magnin _____
21. Marshall Field _____
22. Sanborn's _____
23. F.A.O. Schwarz _____
24. Tiffany's _____
25. Gucci _____

WHO'S THE POET?

The following lines of poetry will probably sound very familiar, as they are often quoted. But do you know who penned them?

A score of 10 is good; 15 is excellent; 20 makes you a real literary maven!

Answers on page 364

1. *Drink to me only with thine eyes,*
   And I will pledge with mine.

   Matthew Arnold   Ben Jonson   Andrew Marvell

2. *I do not love thee, Doctor Fell,*
   The reason why I cannot tell;
   But this alone I know full well:
   I do not love thee, Doctor Fell.

   James Bowell   Thomas Brown   William Walsh

3. *She walks in beauty, like the night*
   Of cloudless climes and starry skies;

   Percy Bysshe Shelley   Lord Byron   Edwin Muir

4. *Quoth the raven, "Nevermore."*

   Alfred Lord Tennyson   Edgar Allan Poe   Dorothy Sayers

5. *Stone walls do not a prison make,*
   Nor iron bars a cage.

   Walt Whitman   Richard Lovelace   John Milton

6. *Parting is all we know of heaven*
   And all we need of hell.

   Archibald MacLeish   John Keats   Emily Dickinson

7. *True wit is nature to advantage dress'd*
   What oft was thought, but ne'er so well express'd.

   Alexander Pope   John Dryden   Jonathan Swift

8. *'Mid pleasures and palaces though we may roam,*
   Be it ever so humble, there's no place like home.

   Vachel Lindsay   John Howard Payne   Henry Wadsworth Longfellow

9. *Though I am old with wandering*
   Through hollow lands and hill lands,
   I will find out where she has gone,
   And kiss her lips and take her hands;
   And walk among long dapple grass,
   And pluck till time and times are done
   The silver apples of the moon,
   The golden apples of the sun.

   John Keats   William Butler Yeats   Carl Sandburg

10. *Shall I compare thee to a summer's day?*
    Thou art more lovely and more temperate.

    Edmund Spencer   Francis Bacon   William Shakespeare

11. *Miniver Cheevy, born too late,*
    Scratched his head and kept on thinking;
    Miniver coughed and called it fate,
    And kept on drinking.

    Robert Herrick   Edward Arlington Robinson   Edgar Lee Masters

12. *April is the cruelest month.*

    Geoffrey Chaucer   T.S. Eliot   Sylvia Plath

13. *How do I love thee? Let me count the ways.*
    I love thee to the depth and breadth and height
    My soul can reach, when feeling out of sight
    For the ends of Being and ideal Grace.

    Robert Browning   Elizabeth Barrett Browning   Sara Teasdale

14. *Tiger, tiger, burning bright*
    In the forests of the night,
    What immortal hand or eye
    Could frame thy fearful symmetry?

    Robert Graves   William Blake   William Carlos Williams

15. *As tho' to breathe were life.*

       Oscar Wilde   Alfred Lord Tennyson   Edgar Lee Masters

16. *The best laid schemes o' mice and men*
Gang aft a-gley.

       Thomas Moore   Robert Burns   William Butler Yeats

17. *When I was one-and-twenty*
    I heard a wise man say,
"Give crowns and pounds and guineas
    But not your heart away;
Give pearls away and rubies
    But keep your fancy free,"
But I was one-and-twenty,
    No use to talk to me.

       A.E. Housman   Conrad Aiken   Edna St. Vincent Millay

18. *Jenny kissed me when we met,*
Jumping from the chair she sat in;
Time you thief, who love to get
Sweets into your list, put that in!

Say I'm weary, say I'm sad,
Say that health and wealth have missed me:
Say I'm growing old, but add
Jenny kissed me.

       Robert Lowell   Walt Whitman   Leigh Hunt

19. *Give me your tired, your poor,*
Your huddled masses yearning to breathe free,
The wretched refuse of your teeming shore,
Send these, the homeless, tempest-tossed, to me:
I lift my lamp beside the golden door.

       Carl Sandburg   Emma Lazarus   Francis Scott Key

20. *Men seldom make passes*
    At girls who wear glasses.

       Dorothy Parker   Ogden Nash   Marianne Moore

FOR CHAPLIN FANS

Many film buffs consider Charlie Chaplin the greatest personage in motion-picture history. How much do you know about this beloved star and his movies?

Below are 25 questions. You have three choices. Check the answer you believe is correct.

A score of 14 is admirable; 21 means you're a movie aficionado; and 24 means you win the Chaplin Emmy.

Answers on page 364

1. A Charlie Chaplin sobriquet was:
   The Little Tramp   The Sheik   Pagliaccio

2. Charlie was born in:
   1859   1889   1905

3. How many times did Charlie marry?
   Two   Four   Six

4. Charlie Chaplin began his film career as an extra for which director?
   D.W. Griffith   Cecil Hepworth   Cecil De Mille

5. The leading lady who starred with Charlie in 35 films was:
   Marie Dressler   Lillian Gish   Edna Purviance

6. Which of these was the earliest Chaplin film?
   A Night Out   *City Lights*   *Monsieur Verdoux*

7. *The Great Dictator* is considered a satire on:
   Bismarck   Hitler   Nixon

8. Charlie Chaplin was born in what city?
   New York   London   Glasgow

9. In 1919, United Artists was formed by Chaplin, D.W. Griffith, Douglas Fairbanks, and:
   Mack Sennett   Mary Pickford   Spencer Chaplin

10. Charlie's last wife, Oona, was the daughter of:
    Samuel Beckett   Eugene O'Neill   William Gibson

11. Charlie's first feature length film (six reels) was:
    The Kid   *A Day's Pleasure*   *Modern Times*

12. In which Chaplin film is "the little fella" so starved that he cooks his shoelaces and eats them like spaghetti?
    City Lights   *The Kid*   *The Gold Rush*

13. Which character did Charlie play in *The Gold Rush?*
   Big Jim   The Lone Prospector   Black Larson

14. How long did it take to film *City Lights?*
   Six months   Two years   Four years

15. Which of these leading ladies was Chaplin's third wife?
   Claire Bloom   Marilyn Nash   Paulette Goddard

16. Charlie's last film, made in 1967, was:
   A Countess from Hong Kong   *The Great Dictator*
                  A King in New York

17. Charlie had how many children by his various wives?
   Two   Five   Eight

18. Charlie's leading lady in *Modern Times* was:
   Mary Pickford   Paulette Goddard   Pola Negri

19. After being attacked during the McCarthy Era as a "fellow trav-eler," Charlie Chaplin left the United States and settled in what country?
   Switzerland   England   U.S.S.R.

20. Chaplin did not return to the United States, following his exile, until what year?
   1965   1972   1977

21. Charlie was involved in a notorious paternity suit brought by starlet:
   Joan Barry   Lita Grey   Claire Windsor

22. What was the name of the dog befriended by Charlie in *A Dog's Life?*
   Fido   Scraps   Mergatroid

23. Which of Charlie's daughters has become a well-known actress in her own right?
   Josephine   Victoria   Geraldine

24. The idea for *Monsieur Verdoux*, which is based on the life of an infamous French murderer named Landru, was suggested to Charlie by:
   Alexander Korda   Orson Welles   Charles De Gaulle

25. Charlie Chaplin died in:
   1973   1977   1979

MOVIE MONIKERS

Each of the 40 names listed below is a character in a noteworthy film. Can you select the right film from the choices given? Then can you name the actor who played the role? Give yourself one point for each identification of the movie. Add two more points to your score if you named the right actor.

Scoring 80 points is good; 90 is excellent; 100 or more makes you a real cinéaste!

Answers on page 365

1. Luke Skywalker . . . . **PLAYED BY** _____
   Cool Hand Luke
   Star Wars
   A Fistful of Dollars

2. Pseudolus . . . . **PLAYED BY** _____
   Quo Vadis
   Ben-Hur
   A Funny Thing Happened on the Way to the Forum

3. Sam Spade . . . . **PLAYED BY** _____
   The Maltese Falcon
   Casablanca
   The African Queen

4. Sally Bowles . . . . **PLAYED BY** _____
   South Pacific
   My Sister Eileen
   Cabaret

5. Norman Bates. . . . . **PLAYED BY** _____
   The Exorcist
   Psycho
   Vertigo

6. Billy Hooker . . . . **PLAYED BY** _____
   Sweet Charity
   The Sting
   Butch Cassidy and the Sundance Kid

7. Martin Dysart. . . . . **PLAYED BY** _____
   Equus
   The Man Who Came to Dinner
   The Sun Also Rises

8. Melanie Wilkes. . . . . **PLAYED BY** _____
   Wuthering Heights
   Gone with the Wind
   Jezebel

9. Caligula . . . . **PLAYED BY** _____
   Quo Vadis
   The Robe
   Ben-Hur

10. Tom Joad . . . . **PLAYED BY** _____
   Tom Thumb
   The Grapes of Wrath
   Gentlemen's Agreement

11. Benjamin Braddock . . . . **PLAYED BY** _____
   All the President's Men
   The Graduate
   Great Expectations

12. Margo Channing . . . . **PLAYED BY** _____
   Gentlemen Prefer Blondes
   All About Eve
   Sunset Boulevard

13. Professor Marvel . . . . **PLAYED BY** _____
   The Wizard of Oz
   Around the World in Eighty Days
   Flash Gordon

14. Father Karras . . . . **PLAYED BY** _____
   Going My Way
   The Exorcist
   Heaven Can Wait

15. Larson E. Whipsnade. . . . . **PLAYED BY** _____
   The Bank Dick
   You Can't Cheat an Honest Man
   Never Give a Sucker an Even Break

16. Inspector Clouseau . . . . **PLAYED BY** _____
   Murder on the Orient Express
   Ten Little Indians
   The Pink Panther

17. Annie Sullivan . . . . **PLAYED BY** _____
   The Quiet Man
   Parnell
   The Miracle Worker

18. Jamie Tyrone . . . . **PLAYED BY** _____
   The Last Hurrah
   Long Day's Journey into Night
   On the Waterfront

19. Alvy Singer . . . . **PLAYED BY** _____
   The Pawnbroker
   The Front
   Annie Hall

20. Eliza Doolittle . . . . **PLAYED BY** _____
   Dr. Doolittle
   My Fair Lady
   A Star Is Born

21. Robert Stroud . . . . PLAYED BY _____
    Elmer Gantry
    The Bird Man of Alcatraz
    The Rainmaker

22. Dashiell Hammett . . . . PLAYED BY _____
    The Maltese Falcon
    The Last Goodbye
    Julia

23. Fletcher Christian . . . . PLAYED BY _____
    David Copperfield
    Hallelujah
    Mutiny on the Bounty

24. Hawkeye Pierce . . . . PLAYED BY _____
    M*A*S*H
    Catch-22
    The Lost Weekend

25. Norma Desmond . . . . PLAYED BY _____
    All About Eve
    Sunset Boulevard
    The Birth of a Nation

26. Elwood P. Dowd . . . . PLAYED BY _____
    Harvey
    Mr. Smith Goes to Washington
    The Philadelphia Story

27. Max Bialystock . . . . PLAYED BY _____
    The Producers
    The Great Ziegfeld
    Stage Door

28. Ensign Pulver . . . . PLAYED BY _____
    Operation Petticoat
    Anchors Aweigh
    Mister Roberts

29. Professor Harold Hill . . . . PLAYED BY _____
    The Music Man
    My Fair Lady
    The Paper Chase

30. Stanley Kowalski . . . . PLAYED BY _____
    On the Waterfront
    It Happened One Night
    A Streetcar Named Desire

31. Phileas Fogg . . . . PLAYED BY _____
    The Great Dictator
    Babes in Toyland
    Around the World in Eighty Days

32. Rufus T. Firefly . . . . PLAYED BY _____
    A Night at the Opera
    A Day at the Races
    Duck Soup

33. Captain Nemo . . . . **PLAYED BY** _____
       Journey to the Center of the Earth
       Captains Courageous
       Twenty Thousand Leagues Under the Sea

34. Hubbell Gardner . . . . **PLAYED BY** _____
       Bringing Up Baby
       High Society
       The Way We Were

35. Fielding Mellish . . . . **PLAYED BY** _____
       Sleeper
       Bananas
       Play It Again, Sam

36. Cuthbert J. Twillie . . . . **PLAYED BY** _____
       My Little Chickadee
       Million Dollar Legs
       The Old-Fashioned Way

37. Mortimer Brewster . . . . **PLAYED BY** _____
       Marty
       Some Like It Hot
       Arsenic and Old Lace

38. Fred C. Dobbs . . . . **PLAYED BY** _____
       The Treasure of the Sierra Madre
       The African Queen
       The Petrified Forest

39. Hedley Lamarr . . . . **PLAYED BY** _____
       The Producers
       Silent Movie
       Blazing Saddles

40. J. Pinkerton Snoopington . . . . . **PLAYED BY** _____
       If I Had a Million
       The Bank Dick
       Poppy

HOW TO SOLVE ALFABITS

The idea is to form as many words as you can out of the letters which compose the given title. The rules are quite simple:

1. Words must contain five letters or more. Letters may not be used more than once to form a word unless they appear more than once in the given word.

2. Adding an "s" to a four-letter word to form a five-letter word is not allowed. However, if "ies" or "es" is added, that is acceptable.

3. All forms of a given word may be used, provided the needed letters are contained in the given word. For example, both BEACH and BEACHES are acceptable; so are BABIES and BABIED; CLEAN, UNCLEAN, CLEANED, CLEANER, CLEANING are all acceptable, provided, of course, they can be formed from the letters in the given word.

4. Contractions, proper names and obsolete or archaic words are taboo. Reformed spellings (NITE for NIGHT, THRU for THROUGH) are excluded.

5. Foreign words which have been accepted into the English language are permitted, e.g. PIZZA, DEBACLE, MAVEN. But those that the dictionary indicates are still considered foreign are not acceptable, e.g. GESUNDHEIT, MUCHO, FEMME.

NOMENCLATURE

At least 140 words of five letters or more can be found in NOMENCLATURE. If you score 70 you're about average; 95 gives you a good name; and 120 indicates intellectual stature.

Answers on page 365

1. _____ 12. _____ 23. _____
2. _____ 13. _____ 24. _____
3. _____ 14. _____ 25. _____
4. _____ 15. _____ 26. _____
5. _____ 16. _____ 27. _____
6. _____ 17. _____ 28. _____
7. _____ 18. _____ 29. _____
8. _____ 19. _____ 30. _____
9. _____ 20. _____ 31. _____
10. _____ 21. _____ 32. _____
11. _____ 22. _____ 33. _____

34. _____

35. _____

36. _____

37. _____

38. _____

39. _____

40. _____

41. _____

42. _____

43. _____

44. _____

45. _____

46. _____

47. _____

48. _____

49. _____

50. _____

51. _____

52. _____

53. _____

54. _____

55. _____

56. _____

57. _____

58. _____

59. _____

60. _____

61. _____

62. _____

63. _____

64. _____

65. _____

66. _____

67. _____

68. _____

69. _____

70. _____

71. _____

72. _____

73. _____

74. _____

75. _____

76. _____

77. _____

78. _____

79. _____

80. _____

81. _____

82. _____

83. _____

84. _____

85. _____

86. _____

87. _____

88. _____

89. _____

90. _____

91. _____

92. _____

93. _____

94. _____

95. _____

96. _____

97. _____

98. _____

99. _____

100. _____

101. _____

102. _____

103. _____

104. _____

105. _____

106. _____

107. _____

108. _____

109. _____

110. _____

111. _____

112. _____

113. _____

114. _____

115. _____

116. _____

117. _____

118. _____

119. _____

120. _____

121. _____

122. _____

123. _____

124. _____

125. _____

126. _____

127. _____

128. _____

129. _____

130. _____

131. _____

132. _____

133. _____

134. _____

135. _____

136. _____

137. _____

138. _____

139. _____

140. _____

INSTITUTIONAL

There are at least 39 words of five or more letters that can be formed from INSTITUTIONAL.

A score of 19 is fair; 26 is impressive; 33 shows you went through an institution of higher learning.

Answers on page 366

1. _____	14. _____	27. _____
2. _____	15. _____	28. _____
3. _____	16. _____	29. _____
4. _____	17. _____	30. _____
5. _____	18. _____	31. _____
6. _____	19. _____	32. _____
7. _____	20. _____	33. _____
8. _____	21. _____	34. _____
9. _____	22. _____	35. _____
10. _____	23. _____	36. _____
11. _____	24. _____	37. _____
12. _____	25. _____	38. _____
13. _____	26. _____	39. _____

APHRODITE

There are at least 75 words of five or more letters that can be formed from the letters in APHRODITE. How many can you list?

A score of 40 is lovely; 50 is inspired; and 65 is absolutely God-like!

Answers on page 366

1. _____	26. _____	51. _____
2. _____	27. _____	52. _____
3. _____	28. _____	53. _____
4. _____	29. _____	54. _____
5. _____	30. _____	55. _____
6. _____	31. _____	56. _____
7. _____	32. _____	57. _____
8. _____	33. _____	58. _____
9. _____	34. _____	59. _____
10. _____	35. _____	60. _____
11. _____	36. _____	61. _____
12. _____	37. _____	62. _____
13. _____	38. _____	63. _____
14. _____	39. _____	64. _____
15. _____	40. _____	65. _____
16. _____	41. _____	66. _____
17. _____	42. _____	67. _____
18. _____	43. _____	68. _____
19. _____	44. _____	69. _____
20. _____	45. _____	70. _____
21. _____	46. _____	71. _____
22. _____	47. _____	72. _____
23. _____	48. _____	73. _____
24. _____	49. _____	74. _____
25. _____	50. _____	75. _____

DELIGHTFUL

There are at least 42 words of five or more letters that can be formed from the letters in DELIGHTFUL. How many can you list?

A score of 22 is lovely; 30 is delightful; and 38 is supreme joy.

Answers on page 366

1. _____	15. _____	29. _____
2. _____	16. _____	30. _____
3. _____	17. _____	31. _____
4. _____	18. _____	32. _____
5. _____	19. _____	33. _____
6. _____	20. _____	34. _____
7. _____	21. _____	35. _____
8. _____	22. _____	36. _____
9. _____	23. _____	37. _____
10. _____	24. _____	38. _____
11. _____	25. _____	39. _____
12. _____	26. _____	40. _____
13. _____	27. _____	41. _____
14. _____	28. _____	42. _____

TRIBULATION

At least 53 words of five letters or more can be formed from the letters in TRIBULATION. How many can you list?

A score of 27 shows you tried; 37 indicates no sweat; and 47 means it was a lark.

Answers on page 367

1. _____	7. _____	13. _____
2. _____	8. _____	14. _____
3. _____	9. _____	15. _____
4. _____	10. _____	16. _____
5. _____	11. _____	17. _____
6. _____	12. _____	18. _____

19. _____	31. _____	42. _____
20. _____	32. _____	43. _____
21. _____	33. _____	44. _____
22. _____	34. _____	45. _____
23. _____	35. _____	46. _____
24. _____	36. _____	47. _____
25. _____	37. _____	48. _____
26. _____	38. _____	49. _____
27. _____	39. _____	50. _____
28. _____	40. _____	51. _____
29. _____	41. _____	52. _____
30. _____		53. _____

WATCHMAKER

There are at least 44 words of five letters or more that can be formed from the letters in WATCHMAKER. How many can you list?

A score of 23 is timely; 30 shows all the wheels are turning; and 40 is a sign of precision.

Answers on page 367

1. _____	16. _____	30. _____
2. _____	17. _____	31. _____
3. _____	18. _____	32. _____
4. _____	19. _____	33. _____
5. _____	20. _____	34. _____
6. _____	21. _____	35. _____
7. _____	22. _____	36. _____
8. _____	23. _____	37. _____
9. _____	24. _____	38. _____
10. _____	25. _____	39. _____
11. _____	26. _____	40. _____
12. _____	27. _____	41. _____
13. _____	28. _____	42. _____
14. _____	29. _____	43. _____
15. _____		44. _____

ESCALATED

There are at least 33 words of five letters or more that can be formed from the letters in ESCALATED. How many can you list?

A score of 16 is on the level; 22 is uplifting; and 30 soars.

Answers on page 367

1. _____	12. _____	23. _____
2. _____	13. _____	24. _____
3. _____	14. _____	25. _____
4. _____	15. _____	26. _____
5. _____	16. _____	27. _____
6. _____	17. _____	28. _____
7. _____	18. _____	29. _____
8. _____	19. _____	30. _____
9. _____	20. _____	31. _____
10. _____	21. _____	32. _____
11. _____	22. _____	33. _____

CHAMPIONSHIP

We list 30 words of five or more letters that can be formed from the letters in CHAMPIONSHIP. How many can you find?

A score of 15 is in the running; 21 wins honors; and 27 takes first prize.

Answers on page 367

1. _____	11. _____	21. _____
2. _____	12. _____	22. _____
3. _____	13. _____	23. _____
4. _____	14. _____	24. _____
5. _____	15. _____	25. _____
6. _____	16. _____	26. _____
7. _____	17. _____	27. _____
8. _____	18. _____	28. _____
9. _____	19. _____	29. _____
10. _____	20. _____	30. _____

COMPOUNDED

There are at least 21 words of five or more letters to be formed from the letters in COMPOUNDED. How many can you find?

A score of 10 is average; 14 is interest-bearing; and 18 is an augmentation of mental riches.

Answers on page 367

1. _____	8. _____	15. _____
2. _____	9. _____	16. _____
3. _____	10. _____	17. _____
4. _____	11. _____	18. _____
5. _____	12. _____	19. _____
6. _____	13. _____	20. _____
7. _____	14. _____	21. _____

ANTICIPATION

At least 39 words of five or more letters can be formed from the letters in ANTICIPATION. How many can you find?

If you score 20, that's good; 26 shows you're an eager beaver; and with 34 you can expect honors.

Answers on page 368

1. _____	14. _____	27. _____
2. _____	15. _____	28. _____
3. _____	16. _____	29. _____
4. _____	17. _____	30. _____
5. _____	18. _____	31. _____
6. _____	19. _____	32. _____
7. _____	20. _____	33. _____
8. _____	21. _____	34. _____
9. _____	22. _____	35. _____
10. _____	23. _____	36. _____
11. _____	24. _____	37. _____
12. _____	25. _____	38. _____
13. _____	26. _____	39. _____

INTROVERT

We list 25 words of five or more letters that can be formed from the letters in INTROVERT. How many can you find?

A score of 12 is satisfactory; 16 is respectable; and 20 shows you're into words.

Answers on page 368

1. _____   9. _____   18. _____
2. _____   10. _____   19. _____
3. _____   11. _____   20. _____
4. _____   12. _____   21. _____
5. _____   13. _____   22. _____
6. _____   14. _____   23. _____
7. _____   15. _____   24. _____
8. _____   16. _____   25. _____
                     17. _____

DIMINUTIVE

There are at least 20 words of five or more letters to be formed from the letters in DIMINUTIVE.

A score of 10 is on the small side; 14 is sizeable; and 18 is huge.

Answers on page 368

1. _____   8. _____   14. _____
2. _____   9. _____   15. _____
3. _____   10. _____   16. _____
4. _____   11. _____   17. _____
5. _____   12. _____   18. _____
6. _____   13. _____   19. _____
7. _____   20. _____

GEOMETRY

We list just eight words of five or more letters that can be formed from the letters in GEOMETRY. Can you do better?

A score of 5 or more is solid.

Answers on page 368

1. _____   4. _____   6. _____

2. _____   5. _____   7. _____

3. _____   8. _____

LACHRYMOSE

We list 52 words of five or more letters that can be formed from the letters in LACHRYMOSE. How many can you find?

A score of 25 is nothing to cry about; 35 is worth a grin; and 45 earns a cheer.

Answers on page 368

1. _____   18. _____   36. _____

2. _____   19. _____   37. _____

3. _____   20. _____   38. _____

4. _____   21. _____   39. _____

5. _____   22. _____   40. _____

6. _____   23. _____   41. _____

7. _____   24. _____   42. _____

8. _____   25. _____   43. _____

9. _____   26. _____   44. _____

10. _____   27. _____   45. _____

11. _____   28. _____   46. _____

12. _____   29. _____   47. _____

13. _____   30. _____   48. _____

14. _____   31. _____   49. _____

15. _____   32. _____   50. _____

16. _____   33. _____   51. _____

17. _____   34. _____   52. _____

                      35 _____

PSYCHOLOGICAL

There are at least 45 words of five letters or more that can be formed from the letters in PSYCHOLOGICAL. How many can you list?

A score of 23 is normal; 30 is superior; and 40 is in the genius class!

Answers on page 368

1. _____	16. _____	31. _____
2. _____	17. _____	32. _____
3. _____	18. _____	33. _____
4. _____	19. _____	34. _____
5. _____	20. _____	35. _____
6. _____	21. _____	36. _____
7. _____	22. _____	37. _____
8. _____	23. _____	38. _____
9. _____	24. _____	39. _____
10. _____	25. _____	40. _____
11. _____	26. _____	41. _____
12. _____	27. _____	42. _____
13. _____	28. _____	43. _____
14. _____	29. _____	44. _____
15. _____	30. _____	45. _____

CONVENTIONAL

We have listed 80 words of five or more letters that can be formed from CONVENTIONAL. How many can you find?

A score of 40 is average; 55 is outstanding; and 70 is beyond the pale.

Answers on page 369

1. _____	28. _____	54. _____
2. _____	29. _____	55. _____
3. _____	30. _____	56. _____
4. _____	31. _____	57. _____
5. _____	32. _____	58. _____
6. _____	33. _____	59. _____
7. _____	34. _____	60. _____
8. _____	35. _____	61. _____
9. _____	36. _____	62. _____
10. _____	37. _____	63. _____
11. _____	38. _____	64. _____
12. _____	39. _____	65. _____
13. _____	40. _____	66. _____
14. _____	41. _____	67. _____
15. _____	42. _____	68. _____
16. _____	43. _____	69. _____
17. _____	44. _____	70. _____
18. _____	45. _____	71. _____
19. _____	46. _____	72. _____
20. _____	47. _____	73. _____
21. _____	48. _____	74. _____
22. _____	49. _____	75. _____
23. _____	50. _____	76. _____
24. _____	51. _____	77. _____
25. _____	52. _____	78. _____
26. _____	53. _____	79. _____
27. _____		80. _____

FRATERNITY

There are at least 52 words of five or more letters that can be formed from the letters in FRATERNITY. How many can you list?

A score of 25 gets you into the club; 35 puts you on the executive board; and 45 makes you the head.

Answers on page 369

1. _____   11. _____   21. _____
2. _____   12. _____   22. _____
3. _____   13. _____   23. _____
4. _____   14. _____   24. _____
5. _____   15. _____   25. _____
6. _____   16. _____   26. _____
7. _____   17. _____   27. _____
8. _____   18. _____   28. _____
9. _____   19. _____   29. _____
10. _____   20. _____   30. _____

31. _____	38. _____	46. _____
32. _____	39. _____	47. _____
33. _____	40. _____	48. _____
34. _____	41. _____	49. _____
35. _____	42. _____	50. _____
36. _____	43. _____	51. _____
37. _____	44. _____	52. _____
	45. _____	

EMBARRASS

We list 16 words of five letters that can be formed from the letters in EMBARRASS.

A score of 8 shouldn't embarrass you; 12 or more should make you downright proud.

Answers on page 369

1. _____	6. _____	12. _____
2. _____	7. _____	13. _____
3. _____	8. _____	14. _____
4. _____	9. _____	15. _____
5. _____	10. _____	16. _____
	11. _____	

MENDACIOUS

There are at least 70 words of five or more letters that can be found in MENDACIOUS. How many can you list?

A score of 35 shows honest effort; 48 is undeniably good; and 60 is truly magnificent.

Answers on page 369

Answers on page 369

1. _____
2. _____
3. _____
4. _____
5. _____
6. _____
7. _____
8. _____
9. _____
10. _____
11. _____
12. _____
13. _____
14. _____
15. _____
16. _____
17. _____
18. _____
19. _____
20. _____
21. _____
22. _____
23. _____

24. _____
25. _____
26. _____
27. _____
28. _____
29. _____
30. _____
31. _____
32. _____
33. _____
34. _____
35. _____
36. _____
37. _____
38. _____
39. _____
40. _____
41. _____
42. _____
43. _____
44. _____
45. _____
46. _____
47. _____

48. _____
49. _____
50. _____
51. _____
52. _____
53. _____
54. _____
55. _____
56. _____
57. _____
58. _____
59. _____
60. _____
61. _____
62. _____
63. _____
64. _____
65. _____
66. _____
67. _____
68. _____
69. _____
70. _____

FURNITURE

We list 20 words of five or more letters that can be found in FURNITURE. How many can you find?

A score of 10 is comfortable; 13 is handsome; and 17 is *dernier cri.*

Answers on page 370

1. _____   8. _____   14. _____
2. _____   9. _____   15. _____
3. _____   10. _____   16. _____
4. _____   11. _____   17. _____
5. _____   12. _____   18. _____
6. _____   13. _____   19. _____
7. _____   20. _____

MEDIOCRITY

There are at least 33 words of five letters or more that can be formed from the letters in MEDIOCRITY. How many can you find?

A score of 17 is run of the mill; 23 is above average; and 29 is a standout.

Answers on page 370

1. _____   12. _____   23. _____
2. _____   13. _____   24. _____
3. _____   14. _____   25. _____
4. _____   15. _____   26. _____
5. _____   16. _____   27. _____
6. _____   17. _____   28. _____
7. _____   18. _____   29. _____
8. _____   19. _____   30. _____
9. _____   20. _____   31. _____
10. _____   21. _____   32. _____
11. _____   22. _____   33. _____

HOW TO SOLVE CRYPTOGRAMS

A cryptogram is nothing more nor less than one of the milder forms of self-torture. You let someone twist words all out of shape for you, and you then take delight in wracking your brains over the mess to straighten out all the words again. A lot of people think crytograms are an awful lot of fun.

To tell you what a cryptogram is we'll tell you how to make one. Write down the alphabet, placing one letter on a line. Then write down opposite it a second alphabet, but mix up the letters so that no two letters on the same line are alike. Take care that you don't repeat any letter in your second alphabet. Then put equal signs in between letters which stand opposite each other. For example, you might decide to have A = D, B = X, C = Y, D = J, E = P, F = L, and so forth. So far, then, you have substituted a fictitious letter for each one of the real letters of the alphabet. Then take any sentence and substitute these fictitious letters for each one of the true letters which comprise each word of the sentence. You now have a cryptogram.

But given such a jargon, how does one go about unraveling it? Well, the prime principle of decoding a substitution cipher is to determine how frequently any letter occurs in the encoded sentence. This information generally provides a sound key to the solution.

Students of the English language have determined that the five vowels — A, E, I, O, U — comprise 40 percent of the letters in the words of the language; that the letters L, N, R, S and T, comprise 30 per cent of usage; and that the letters J, K, Q, X, and Z, all together, comprise but 2 per cent of usage. The remaining eleven letters are used to form 28 per cent of the words commonly employed in English.

The letter E appears most frequently. The word THE is the most common three-letter word. Thus, the first step to take is to count the number of times each letter appears in the cryptogram. If, for example, the letter Z appears 30 times in a cryptogram whereas no other letter appears more than 12 times, it is a pretty safe bet that the letter is either an E, T, A, or O, which happen to be the most common letters. If in the same crytogram the combination A B Z appears four or five times, it is a fairly safe bet that this combination represents the word THE. At this point, we know three letters, T, H, and E. By writing these letters, T, H, and E, in such corresponding spaces directly under the cryptogram where the letters A, B, and Z appear in the given text, we can begin to establish the form of at least some of the words. For example, in a two-letter word where the first letter is T, the second letter must be O, since there is no other common two-letter word which begins with T. In this way we gain the letter O. Now, we substitute for O, all along the line, and this process probably leads us to a determination of other letters.

If you are a novice in cryptography, your solution in *Par Time* is doing very well indeed. *Medal Scores* are included to give the tried crytographer something to shoot at.

PREVARICATION AS AN ART

PAR TIME: 28 minutes
MEDAL TIME: 19 minutes

Answer on page 370

GAB PLLI EGA SNII SQN
___ ____ ___ ____ ___

SVZSQ, FZS TS VNOZTVNR
_____ ___ __ _____

G DGA LP RLDN RNARN SL
_ ___ __ ____ _____ __

XALH QLH SL ITN HNII.
____ ___ __ ___ ____

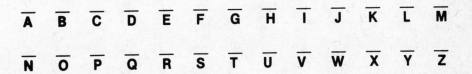

A B C D E F G H I J K L M
N O P Q R S T U V W X Y Z

BRAT AT A BALL

PAR TIME: 40 minutes
MEDAL TIME: 20 minutes

Answer on page 370

AGUFFQ AYRAUGUV AXTTQ
—————— ————————— —————

AUUOKNLTQ AXIFUV,
————————— ———————

AGKNNKTQ AIF XC LUG
————————— ——— —— ———

AIGATU AXR-AXR, YCV
—————— ———·——— ———

AUFFKNLTQ AUGYRWITYFUV
————————— —————————————

YF Y ATXVVKCM AYDU.
—— — ————————— —————

A̅ B̅ C̅ D̅ E̅ F̅ G̅ H̅ I̅ J̅ K̅ L̅ M̅

N̅ O̅ P̅ Q̅ R̅ S̅ T̅ U̅ V̅ W̅ X̅ Y̅ Z̅

ABSOLUTELY!

PAR TIME: 15 minutes
MEDAL TIME: 8 minutes

Answer on page 370

DRJ NMKW DRSMQ DRFD DRJ
___ ____ _____ ____ ___

FBDSCD HFMMND CJJ
_____ _____ ___

SC DRJ NGZSNEC
__ ___ _____

DRJ NMKW DRSMQ
___ ____ _____

DRFD DRJ OEGKSH HFM CJJ
____ ___ _____ ___ ___

SC DRJ NGZSNEC.
__ ___ _____

A̅ B̅ C̅ D̅ E̅ F̅ G̅ H̅ I̅ J̅ K̅ L̅ M̅

N̅ O̅ P̅ Q̅ R̅ S̅ T̅ U̅ V̅ W̅ X̅ Y̅ Z̅

THE POWER OF MUSIC

PAR TIME: 20 minutes
MEDAL TIME: 17 minutes

Answer on page 370

LRBU MR LRR NRBNDNH MR
____ __ ___ _____ __

LRRUINRB RER. NRREL
_____ ___ _____

LOOLRNRB, CZN LRBURNH
_____ ___ _____

MR MLD.
__ ___

A B C D E F G H I J K L M

N O P Q R S T U V W X Y Z

ERSE PHILOSOPHY

PAR TIME: 20 minutes
MEDAL TIME: 12 minutes

Answer on page 370

X HYT'R RVXTI RVOJO'M WTK
— — — — — — — — — — — — — — — — — — —

AYXTR XT ZOXTU XJXMV XP
— — — — — — — — — — — — — — — — — — —

KYS HYT'R ITYB RVWR RVO
— — — — — — — — — — — — — — — — — —

BYJNH XM UYXTU RY ZJOWI
— — — — — — — — — — — — — — — — — — —

KYSJ VOWJR OCOTRSWNNK.
— — — — — — — — — — — — — — — — — —

$\overline{A}$ $\overline{B}$ $\overline{C}$ $\overline{D}$ $\overline{E}$ $\overline{F}$ $\overline{G}$ $\overline{H}$ $\overline{I}$ $\overline{J}$ $\overline{K}$ $\overline{L}$ $\overline{M}$

$\overline{N}$ $\overline{O}$ $\overline{P}$ $\overline{Q}$ $\overline{R}$ $\overline{S}$ $\overline{T}$ $\overline{U}$ $\overline{V}$ $\overline{W}$ $\overline{X}$ $\overline{Y}$ $\overline{Z}$

THE CULT OF INCOHERENCE

PAR TIME: 20 minutes
MEDAL TIME: 15 minutes

Answer on page 370

UNMG N EIYBRI ARRUA BL

———— — —————— ————— ——

BZYMW ZR YA MLB KILSLCMQ

—————— —— —— ——— ————————

CMVRAA ZR ZYUARVS PNM'B

—————— —— ——————— ———— —

CMQRIABNMQ EZNB ZR ZNA

—————————— ————— —— ———

KCB QLEM LM KNKRI.

——— ———— —— —————

Ā B̄ C̄ D̄ Ē F̄ Ḡ H̄ Ī J̄ K̄ L̄ M̄

N̄ Ō P̄ Q̄ R̄ S̄ T̄ Ū V̄ W̄ X̄ Ȳ Z̄

TALISMAN

PAR TIME: 18 minutes
MEDAL TIME: 12 minutes

Answer on page 370

V OGGJ YRPWP BVZ VHQ RP

_ ____ _____ ___ ___ __

IVQP RSZ MWVEPW YG V

____ ___ _____ __ _

WVN VHQ V UGHP VHQ V

___ ___ _ ____ ___ _

RVHF GO RVSW.

____ __ ____

A̅ B̅ C̅ D̅ E̅ F̅ G̅ H̅ I̅ J̅ K̅ L̅ M̅

N̅ O̅ P̅ Q̅ R̅ S̅ T̅ U̅ V̅ W̅ X̅ Y̅ Z̅

RUBBING IT IN

PAR TIME: 50 minutes
MEDAL TIME: 30 minutes

Answer on page 370

MQ SBB XUG UMPPVF,
—— ——— ——— ———————

UVFGMWY ZMXGY MQ KMG,
——————— ————— —— ———

YSFFGP XUSZ MKB-YMZRY
—————— ———— ——— ———————

MP XUG AVFZVRUX TBSYX,
—— ——— ————————— —————

VY XUSX NMPXGZXMWY
—— ———— ———————————

NUPSYG "V XMBF IMW YM."
——————— — ———— ——— ——

$\overline{A}$ $\overline{B}$ $\overline{C}$ $\overline{D}$ $\overline{E}$ $\overline{F}$ $\overline{G}$ $\overline{H}$ $\overline{I}$ $\overline{J}$ $\overline{K}$ $\overline{L}$ $\overline{M}$

$\overline{N}$ $\overline{O}$ $\overline{P}$ $\overline{Q}$ $\overline{R}$ $\overline{S}$ $\overline{T}$ $\overline{U}$ $\overline{V}$ $\overline{W}$ $\overline{X}$ $\overline{Y}$ $\overline{Z}$

ONE-TRACK MIND

PAR TIME: 15 minutes
MEDAL TIME: 12 minutes

Answer on page 370

YRL IBXCI GHHA FOHAL
___ _____ ____ _____

YRL FEGA HM YRL
___ ____ __ ___

FHHAALLILO VRH
_____ ___

DLWLOYRLBLZZ ALIY
_____ ____

EZAQDN MHO GHMMLL.
_____ ___ _____

Ā B̄ C̄ D̄ Ē F̄ Ḡ H̄ Ī J̄ K̄ L̄ M̄

N̄ Ō P̄ Q̄ R̄ S̄ T̄ Ū V̄ W̄ X̄ Ȳ Z̄

SOUND PERCEPTION

PAR TIME: 24 minutes
MEDAL TIME: 18 minutes

Answer on page 370

PQG AMPB VQXPLV WP DWKS,
___ ____ _____ __ ____

MPL W WPODXLS MDD XFNMP
___ _ _____ ___ _____

MPL MDD FXFMD VQXPLV,
___ ___ _____ _____

SCOSSL WP WPGSFSVG M
_____ __ _____ _

IPQOI MG GJS LQQF.
_____ __ ___ ____

A̅ B̅ C̅ D̅ E̅ F̅ G̅ H̅ I̅ J̅ K̅ L̅ M̅

N̅ O̅ P̅ Q̅ R̅ S̅ T̅ U̅ V̅ W̅ X̅ Y̅ Z̅

FOLLY! FOLLY!

PAR TIME: 32 minutes
MEDAL TIME: 19 minutes

Answer on page 371

M EXT TDJ FMLV SDK JIV
_ ___ ___ ____ ___ ___

WDGQKYX WDG HKEEVHH,
_____ ___ _____,

UKJ M EXT FMLV SDK JIV
___ _ ___ ____ ___ ___

WDGQKYX WDG WXMYKGV—
_____ ___ _____—

ZIMEI MH "JGS JD
_____ __ ___ __

BYVXHV VLVGSUDAS."
_____ _____.

A B C D E F G H I J K L M

N O P Q R S T U V W X Y Z

ADVICE TO THE STRIFE-TORN

PAR TIME: 30 minutes
MEDAL TIME: 20 minutes

Answer on page 371

J F P C F X Q H Q W T P E I F
___ _____ ____

M Q K U, U N U W Q K Q J A E U H
____ ____ __ __ ____

K F Q T G J U W G U F X J K Q F H J
_____ ___ __ _____

A̅ B̅ C̅ D̅ E̅ F̅ G̅ H̅ I̅ J̅ K̅ L̅ M̅

N̅ O̅ P̅ Q̅ R̅ S̅ T̅ U̅ V̅ W̅ X̅ Y̅ Z̅

AH CHOO!

PAR TIME: 35 minutes
MEDAL TIME: 20 minutes

Answer on page 371

W   QELLOLU   H   QELLOL
_   _____   _   _____

WERT   RVL   HWP,
____   ___   ___

HEU   ET   TEL   XELA   KPTD
___   __   ___   ____   ____

AVLEIL   TP   AVLPL;
_____   __   _____

GYR   FTEJ   HEU   VHPU   ALPL
___   ____   ___   ____   ____

RVL   FTTXQ   TK   RVTQL,
___   _____   __   _____

WE   AVTQL   CWIWEWRS
__   _____   _____

W   QETOL!
_   _____

A̅   B̅   C̅   D̅   E̅   F̅   G̅   H̅   I̅   J̅   K̅   L̅   M̅

N̅   O̅   P̅   Q̅   R̅   S̅   T̅   U̅   V̅   W̅   X̅   Y̅   Z̅

YOUTH IS UNQUALIFIED

PAR TIME: 35 minutes
MEDAL TIME: 20 minutes

Answer on page 371

R V X   T B Y W X   Q V Z B A Y   E Z R   H X
___   _____   _____   ___   __

L Z B E W;   V X   Q V Z B A Y   V I C X
_____   __   _____   ____

A X I P E X Y   R Z   S E Z F   X C U A,
_____   __   ____   ____

E Z R   J P Z D   V U Q   Z F E   Q Z B A
___   ____   ___   ___   ____

H B R   J P Z D   A Z E W
___   ____   ____

Z H Q X P C I R U Z E.   S E Z F A X Y W X
_____   _____

Q V Z B A Y   H X   V U Q   W B U Y X,
_____   __   ___   _____

E Z R   K X P Q Z E I A   X M K X P U X E G X.
___   _____   _____

A   B   C   D   E   F   G   H   I   J   K   L   M

N   O   P   Q   R   S   T   U   V   W   X   Y   Z

252

THE SUPREME JUDGMENT

PAR TIME: 35 minutes
MEDAL TIME: 18 minutes

Answer on page 371

MAS OM SGI BKELAQ AD
___ __ ___ _____ __

SGI BQAVCIC RSQIIS,
___ _____ _____

MAS OM SGI RGAYSR EMC
___ __ ___ _____ ___

NKEYCOSR AD SGI SGQAMF,
_____ __ ___ _____

TYS OM AYQRIKZIR EQI
___ __ _____ ___

SQOYLNG EMC CIDIES.
_____ ___ _____

A B C D E F G H I J K L M

N O P Q R S T U V W X Y Z

253

ULTIMATE JUSTICE

PAR TIME: 35 minutes
MEDAL TIME: 25 minutes

Answer on page 371

U I U C C B U W R N Z Q B I E F P

__ _____ __ ____ ___

U N T F I B H F P M O O F N Q F Z

___ ___ _____ __ ____

R O N H F I O B X C O A F M

___ _____ ___

U I F O Q B M H F P M O.

_____ _____

A̅ B̅ C̅ D̅ E̅ F̅ G̅ H̅ I̅ J̅ K̅ L̅ M̅

N̅ O̅ P̅ Q̅ R̅ S̅ T̅ U̅ V̅ W̅ X̅ Y̅ Z̅

INESCAPABLE DEDUCTION

PAR TIME: 32 minutes
MEDAL TIME: 21 minutes

Answer on page 371

VIGX JHN VZ SIVA GKUTP
____ ___ __ ____ _____

HRQ SGHV YHUA QH YHUA;
___ ____ ____ __ ____

I QJHRPIUB DGKQKDP
_ _____ _____

PJHRQKUT: "JA'P RUXUHNU!"
_____ ___ _____

A B C D E F G H I J K L M
N O P Q R S T U V W X Y Z

LAMENT

PAR TIME: 20 minutes
MEDAL TIME: 10 minutes

Answer on page 371

JOWM XR WVK OW XVDIWLDY
_____ __ ___ __ _____

GOIMRJ, "O ZX EIVTR!
_____ _ __ _____

KVV XZWP JUYDIMRJ!"
___ ____ _____

A B C D E F G H I J K L M

N O P Q R S T U V W X Y Z

PLOY

PAR TIME: 35 minutes
MEDAL TIME: 29 minutes

Answer on page 371

IQKZ, JGDORZP AZ YT LRZK
____ _____ __ __ ____

FAYYDZJ AL XDZPMDPK,
_____ __ _____

R HDRJ ZAIQRZP.
_ ____ _____

A B C D E F G H I J K L M

N O P Q R S T U V W X Y Z

DISDAIN

PAR TIME: 30 minutes
MEDAL TIME: 20 minutes

Answer on page 371

LT WFFQTH VM AT VO KJ
—— —————— —— —— —— ——

K CVO V OKHT HKOL LT
— ——— — ———— ———— ——

LVHX'M FDHTDTH.
————— ———————

A̅ B̅ C̅ D̅ E̅ F̅ G̅ H̅ I̅ J̅ K̅ L̅ M̅

N̅ O̅ P̅ Q̅ R̅ S̅ T̅ U̅ V̅ W̅ X̅ Y̅ Z̅

PRAGMATISM

PAR TIME: 35 minutes
MEDAL TIME: 20 minutes

Answer on page 371

TN IHW GDFFHU GDUGS D
—— ——— —————— ————— —

ETPL HN KDPDLTRM,
———— —— —————————

EMUUMP UDXM D BMU SMF.
—————— ———— — ——— ———

A̅ B̅ C̅ D̅ E̅ F̅ G̅ H̅ I̅ J̅ K̅ L̅ M̅

N̅ O̅ P̅ Q̅ R̅ S̅ T̅ U̅ V̅ W̅ X̅ Y̅ Z̅

HOW TO SOLVE ACROSS-TICS

In the world of puzzle ratios, where the crossword puzzle would be held equivalent to a game of checkers, the ACROSS-TIC would be equivalent to a game of chess. It is the development *par excellence* of the word game.

If you've never done ACROSS-TICS before, a new glamorous world in puzzledom is now discovered for you.

The first thing to understand is that the diagram does not in any way resemble a crossword puzzle diagram. The words read only from left to right, and do not interlink.

The ACROSS-TIC contains a quotation from a book or a poem. The black squares in the diagram indicate the end of a word. If there's a white square at the end of the line and the next line following begins with a white square—then two possibilities exist. The white square at the end of the first line may actually be the end of a word, and the white square on the following line may represent the first letter of a new word. Or it may be that all the white squares, —those which end the first line and those which begin the following line—constitute a single word. This uncertainty constitutes one of the bafflements of the ACROSS-TIC puzzle.

With each ACROSS-TIC, you will find a list of definitions. The dashes alongside the definition indicate the number of letters in that particular word. The first thing you do is to read the definition and try to guess the word. It is a wise procedure to first run through all the definitions, in more or less rapid order, and then to write down those definitions which you are reasonably sure of.

Under each dash, you'll find a number. This number indicates a particular square in the diagram. You now fill in the letters of the words you have solved in the proper squares of the diagram. This will yield many hints towards a solution of other definitions. For example, if there's a three-letter word and you found that the first two letters are T H, the overwhelming likelihood is that the third box contains the letter E. Finding this E you now transcribe this particular letter by placing it on one of the dashes in the definition list. You do this by consulting the letter in the particular box in which you have written the E. If, for example, the box contains the keyed letter Q, you then know that the letter you wrote down is keyed to *Definition Q* and is to be placed in *Definition Q*.

By working this way, back and forth, you will be able to fill in letters from the diagram on the definition lines; and from the definition lines into the diagram. In other words, one solution helps the other.

Now and then, you will be forced to make a guess. Where, for example, in a five-letter word, the first two letters are G H, and the fourth one an S, it's a pretty safe bet that the word will be G H O S T. But where a four-letter word starts with the letters B A N, the fourth letter might be E, D, G, K or S; and you may be obliged to guess. This guessing is a temporary measure—a trial-and-error piece of business—which you employ until you find out for sure what the letter is. ACROSS-TIC puzzlers must be constantly armed with a nice, big eraser.

There's still another help you get in solving an ACROSS-TIC. The ACROSS-TIC gets its name and its particular flavor because of the fact that the initial letters of the given definitions, if read down, yield the name of the author of the quotation, followed by the name of the book or the name of the piece from which the quotation was taken. This may vary somewhat. The ACROSS-TIC may be the full name of the author, or just the last name of the author, or an initial or initials of the author followed by the last name. This may be followed by a designation of the kind of literary composition from which the quotation is taken, like *Shakespeare Play Macbeth,* or *Kilmer Poem Trees.* Where the author is anonymous, the name of the author would, of course, be omitted. What must be kept in mind is that the ACROSS-TIC device is used in a free manner, and there is no hard and fast rule which will indicate what the initial letters are going to spell out. However, you can be assured that the source of the quotation will always appear in the ACROSS-TIC.

Although some of the definitions will at first sight appear impossible of solution and beyond your ken of knowledge, you will find that merely makes the puzzle intriguing. A good ACROSS-TIC solver never employs encyclopedias or other reference books. It's considered cricket to check your definition in a dictionary for the purpose of authenticating your solution at any point in the game. But the ACROSS-TIC is not an exercise in research—it's rather a game, a pleasant pastime with a great amount of challenge. You will find that, although you may be obliged at the start to resort to reference helps, the real fun comes when you can dope out the solution of an "impossible definition" through conjecture and by force of your fuller experience in dealing with word structure.

Definitions are based on those found in *Webster's International Dictionary, Second Edition.* Where the word *compound* appears after a definition, it indicates that the word is hyphenated. Where a bracket contains a phrase like *four words,* it means that the definition consists of four words, like the expression *Out of this world.* No obsolete or archaic words or spellings are used at any time in the ACROSS-TIC puzzle.

Pleasant sailing!

ACROSS-TIC NO. 1

DEFINITIONS   WORDS

A   Early form of Sanskrit

__ __ __ __ __
102 64 42 26 169

B   Site of crucial battle (333 B. C.) won by Alexander the Great

__ __ __ __ __
97 192 66 146 53

C   Only actress to win two "Best Supporting" Oscars (2 wds.)

__ __ __ __ __ __ __ __ __ __ __ __ __ __
147 190 125 54 177 4 32 75 108 44 152 184 90 18

D   U. S. national monument in New Mexico (2 wds.)

__ __ __ __ __ __ __ __ __ __ __
120 160 76 126 10 145 165 109 178 40 24

E   Serpent

__ __ __ __ __ __ __ __
103 16 187 52 132 28 195 122

F   1953 Fred Astaire movie (2 wds.)

__ __ __ __ __ __ __ __ __ __ __ __
36 153 106 133 1 113 69 186 58 193 23 85

G   U. S. national forest in Idaho & Wyoming

__ __ __ __ __ __ __
116 198 156 130 51 5 83

H   Low-grade iron ore

__ __ __ __ __ __ __ __
74 188 13 144 98 30 123 61

I   Weary, drawn, and tired in appearance; author of *She* and *King Solomon's Mines*

__ __ __ __ __ __ __
171 163 99 114 158 35 142

J   Collections of property; large landholdings

__ __ __ __ __ __ __
180 9 170 121 139 94 77

K   River embankment

__ __ __ __ __
29 140 105 62 89

L   Suited to a purpose

__ __ __ __ __ __ __ __
155 22 6 67 115 100 80 200

M   Female silent movie star Mabel . . .

__ __ __ __ __ __ __
183 34 65 175 128 101 86

N   Famous conservationist; twice governor of Pa. (2 wds.)

__ __ __ __ __ __ __ __ __ __ __ __ __ __
39 182 143 59 194 3 48 176 136 151 162 111 70 96

O   Released; detached

__ __ __ __ __ __ __ __ __
134 164 37 174 189 14 117 161 179

P   Circumference

__ __ __ __ __
12 82 46 112 95

Q   Petty swindler; con man (colloq.)

__ __ __ __ __ __ __
91 8 55 181 135 38 199

R   Mythological poetry of Scandinavia

__ __ __ __
20 107 45 84

S   Large diving bird of the hawk family

__ __ __ __ __ __
150 138 63 19 79 92

T   Famous fat, jolly Shakespearean character

__ __ __ __ __ __ __ __
167 43 196 149 119 141 2 56

U   Metallic musical instrument, often used with drums

__ __ __ __
33 49 166 131

V   Gaseous hydrocarbons

__ __ __ __ __ __ __
57 31 127 118 137 7 197

W   Gaelic

__ __ __ __
154 60 25 148

X   Active volcano in California

__ __ __ __ __ __
104 47 185 159 71 11

Answers on page 371

				1 F			2 T	3 N	4 C	5 G								
6 L	7 V	8 Q	9 J	10 D	11 X		12 P	13 H	14 O	15 Z²	16 E	17 Y	18 C					
	19 S	20 R	21 Z	22 L	23 F	24 D	25 W	26 A	27 Z¹	28 E	29 K	30 H	31 V					
32 C		33 U	34 M	35 I		36 F	37 O	38 Q			39 N	40 D						
41 Z	42 A		43 T	44 C	45 R		46 P	47 X	48 N			49 U						
50 Y		51 G	52 E	53 B		54 C	55 Q	56 T	57 V			58 F						
	59 N	60 W	61 H	62 K		63 S	64 A	65 M	66 B	67 L	68 Z							
69 F	70 N	71 X	72 Z²	73 Y	74 H		75 C	76 D	77 J	78 Z¹	79 S							
80 L	81 Y	82 P	83 G		84 R	85 F	86 M		87 Z²	88 Z	89 K							
90 C	91 Q	92 S		93 Z¹	94 J	95 P	96 N	97 B	98 H	99 I		100 L						
101 M	102 A	103 E	104 X	105 K	106 F	107 R		108 C	109 D		110 Y	111 N						
112 P	113 F	114 I	115 L		116 G	117 O	118 V	119 J		120 D	121 J	122 E						
123 H		124 Z²	125 C		126 D	127 V	128 M	129 Z²	130 G	131 U	132 E							
	133 F	134 O	135 Q		136 N	137 V	138 S	139 J	140 K	141 T	142 I							
143 N	144 H	145 D	146 B	147 C	148 W	149 T		150 S	151 M		152 C	153 F						
154 W		155 L	156 G	157 Z	158 I	159 X		160 D	161 O		162 N							
163 I	164 O		165 D	166 U	167 T	168 Z¹	169 A	170 J		171 I	172 Y							
	173 Z²	174 O	175 M	176 N	177 C	178 D		179 O	180 J	181 Q	182 N	183 M	184 C					
185 X		186 F	187 E	188 H	189 O		190 C	191 Z¹	192 B		193 F							
194 N	195 E	196 T	197 V		198 G	199 Q	200 L											

DEFINITIONS · WORDS

A 1935 Katherine Hepburn movie (2 wds.)
86 30 124 148 118 98 7 183 74 60

B Disreputable; vulgar
160 201 51 67 174 22 95

C Stiff fabric of silk, nylon, etc.
94 165 52 66 193 134 206

D Having a horny covering on the feet
115 73 12 199 39 152

E Major Pacific fleet anchorage, W W II
13 196 78 110 143 32

F Oared
137 48 16 111 87

G Official misconduct or neglect
182 29 72 187 204 53 166 130 89 10

H Unyielding; rock-hard
59 178 68 157 140 19 101

I Bantered; needled; having bands
26 100 194 153 55 162

J Heavy gaseous element
49 185 125 20 34

K 17th century French dance
80 17 40 104 147 120 71

L Witchcraft; talisman; black magic
105 69 177 159 15

M Dictionary
6 127 186 205 14 175 79

N Wagner opera (2 wds.)
90 171 119 180 82 3 168 64 131 45 31 114

O Felon
58 173 93 81 207 149 135

P Leading contemporary (1933 -) Soviet poet
9 154 192 88 97 109 77 203 133 138 37

Q Gained; caught in a seine
113 161 11 76 188 106

R Placing stress upon
83 35 155 24 141 169 191 42 103

S Examination by touch
27 108 151 128 50 1 84 65 139 25 189 57

T Coroner's investigation
56 176 96 150 36 190 126

U By-product
91 179 170 18 85 44 116 197

V U. S. inventor (1818-1903) of machine gun
43 33 163 129 144 117 4

W Large wine bottle
38 132 23 136 47 181 112 200

X Bring into harmony
61 107 21 167 184 75

Y Type of temporary bridge built on cylinders
145 5 122 202 164 198 62

Z ". . . did from their color fly," *Julius Caesar* (3 wds.)
2 63 142 54 195 92 121 28 46 99 146 158 172

Z¹ Uttered mournful, long cries

$\overline{102}\ \overline{156}\ \overline{8}\ \overline{70}\ \overline{41}\ \overline{123}$

Answers on page 372

				1 S	2 Z	3 N		4 V	5 Y	6 M	7 A
8 Z¹	9 P	10 G		11 Q	12 D	13 E	14 M	15 L		16 F	17 K	18 U
	19 H	20 J	21 X		22 B	23 W	24 R	25 S	26 I		27 S	28 Z
29 G	30 A	31 N	32 E	33 V	34 J	35 R	36 T		37 P	38 W		39 D
40 K	41 Z¹	42 R		43 V	44 U	45 N	46 Z		47 W	48 F	49 J	
50 S	51 B	52 C	53 G	54 Z	55 I		56 T	57 S		58 O	59 H	60 A
	61 X	62 Y		63 Z	64 N	65 S	66 C	67 B	68 H	69 L	70 Z¹	71 K
	72 G	73 D	74 A	75 X	76 Q	77 P	78 E	79 M	80 K		81 O	82 N
83 R	84 S		85 U	86 A	87 F		88 P	89 G		90 N	91 U	
92 Z	93 O	94 C	95 B		96 T	97 P	98 A	99 Z	100 I	101 H	102 Z¹	
103 R	104 K	105 L	106 Q		107 X	108 S	109 P	110 E	111 F		112 W	113 Q
114 N		115 D	116 U	117 V	118 A	119 N	120 K		121 Z	122 Y	123 Z¹	
124 A	125 J	126 T	127 M	128 S	129 V	130 G	131 N	132 W	133 P	134 C		135 O
136 W	137 F	138 P	139 S	140 H	141 R	142 Z	143 E	144 V	145 Y		146 Z	147 K
	148 A	149 O	150 T	151 S	152 D		153 I	154 P		155 R	156 Z¹	157 H
158 Z	159 L	160 B	161 Q	162 I		163 V	164 Y		165 C		166 G	167 X
168 N	169 R		170 U	171 N	172 Z	173 O	174 B	175 M	176 T	177 L	178 H	
179 U	180 N	181 W	182 G		183 A	184 X		185 J	186 M	187 G	188 Q	189 S
190 T	191 R	192 P	193 C		194 I	195 Z	196 E	197 U		198 Y	199 D	
200 W	201 B	202 Y	203 P	204 G	205 M	206 C	207 O					

ACROSS-TIC NO. 3

264

	DEFINITIONS	WORDS

A Show business superstar, made broadway debut in *Word I* (full name, 2 wds.)
187 27 64 219 178 10 93 171 205 214

B Cutting into; sharp, penetrating
53 189 67 1 158 31 141 118

C Having a ribbed surface
32 213 131 57 201 112

D 1932 Marx Brothers movie (2 wds.)
137 84 154 99 26 167 8 38 203 211 157 119 59

E Command; urgent, necessary, compelling
58 179 159 80 176 33 125 5 200 140

F "The fairest meadow . . .," Oliver Wendell Holmes, *Chanson* (3 wds.)
150 60 107 73 3 217 132 82 48 25 161 191 139

G Anesthetic
111 18 126 76 183

H Bulging; protuberant (said of the moon)
120 177 101 164 63 98 17

I 1938 Broadway musical hit by Cole Porter (4 wds.)
81 151 22 117 66 170 36 110 138 97 6

J Former official native name for Tokyo
186 116 202 45

K Slipknot loop used by hangman
54 174 68 11 102

L Jewish university located in New York City
190 122 162 37 13 75 92

M Temple on the Acropolis
136 121 29 108 44 210 91 149 193 15

N Distribute; assign
105 69 144 41 130 218 185 24

O Based on hearsay
96 175 42 168 30 103 14

P Plant of the milkweed family
194 207 52 77 148 61 46 115 95 156 181

Q Protested; demurred; spoke against
160 195 19 87 135 47 127 9

R Political party of Hamilton and Adams (1789-1816)
83 71 12 212 89 109 197 163 206 147

S Pervade; pass through; enter stealthily
74 23 133 172 215 51 104 88 146 199

T Aircraft engine housing
34 208 72 166 90 4 155

U " . . . hard lodging and thin weeds," *Love's Labour's Lost* (3 wds.)
79 143 16 50 124 35 188 173 106 56 180 128 100 40

V Uneasy; fearful; worried
129 86 21 169 43 204 196 62 209 184 7 153

W Scene of major Civil War battle, 1864 (2 wds.)
28 114 2 198 70 142 94 123 216

X "This diamond he greets . . .," *Macbeth,* (3 wds.)
78 55 182 85 65 145 192 49 152 134 39 113 20 165

				1 B		2 W	3 F	4 T	5 E	6 I	7 V
8 D	9 Q		10 A	11 K		12 R	13 L	14 O		15 M	16 U	17 H
18 G		19 Q	20 X	21 V	22 I	23 S	24 N	25 F	26 D		27 A	28 W
29 M	30 O	31 B	32 C	33 E	34 T	35 U		36 I	37 L	38 D	39 X
40 U	41 N	42 O	43 V	44 M	45 J	46 P		47 Q	48 F	49 X		50 U
51 S	52 P	53 B	54 K		55 X	56 U		57 C	58 E	59 D	60 F	61 P
62 V	63 H	64 A		65 X	66 I		67 B	68 K	69 N	70 W	71 R	72 T
73 F	74 S	75 L	76 G	77 P	78 X		79 U	80 E	81 I	82 F		83 R
84 D	85 X		86 V	87 Q	88 S	89 R	90 T		91 M	92 L	93 A	94 W
95 P	96 O		97 I	98 H	99 D	100 U		101 H	102 K		103 O	104 S
105 N	106 U	107 F	108 M	109 R	110 I	111 L	112 C		113 X	114 W	115 P	116 J
117 I	118 B	119 D		120 H	121 M	122 L	123 W	124 U		125 E	126 G	127 Q
	128 U	129 V	130 N	131 C	132 F	133 S	134 X	135 Q	136 M		137 D	138 I
139 F	140 E	141 B	142 W	143 U		144 N	145 X	146 S	147 R	148 P	149 M
150 F	151 I		152 X	153 V	154 D	155 T		156 P	157 D	158 B	159 E	160 Q
161 F	162 L	163 R	164 H	165 X	166 T		167 D	168 O	169 V		170 I	171 A
	172 S	173 U		174 K	175 O	176 E		177 H	178 A	179 E	180 U	181 P
182 X	183 G	184 V	185 N	186 J		187 A	188 U	189 B	190 L		191 F	192 X
	193 M	194 P		195 Q	196 V	197 R	198 W	199 S	200 E	201 C	202 J
203 D	204 V	205 A	206 R		207 P	208 T	209 V		210 M	211 D	212 R
213 C	214 A	215 S	216 W		217 F	218 N	219 A

DEFINITIONS	WORDS

A   Tie down, as over a ship's hatch

<u>62</u> <u>83</u> <u>193</u> <u>107</u> <u>11</u> <u>39</u>

B   Playful webfooted, furry mammal related to the mink and weasel

<u>141</u> <u>189</u> <u>44</u> <u>115</u> <u>12</u>

C   1941 Barbara Stanwyck-Gary Cooper movie (3 wds)

<u>20</u> <u>9</u> <u>176</u> <u>143</u> <u>89</u> <u>102</u> <u>182</u> <u>98</u> <u>35</u> <u>70</u>

D   Evil spirit

<u>82</u> <u>36</u> <u>14</u> <u>170</u> <u>71</u> <u>153</u> <u>114</u> <u>208</u> <u>138</u>

E   "Best men are moulded . . .," *Measure for Measure* (3 wds.)

<u>45</u> <u>63</u> <u>207</u> <u>129</u> <u>73</u> <u>93</u> <u>5</u> <u>186</u> <u>27</u> <u>111</u> <u>197</u>

F   Brood or nest of pheasants

<u>130</u> <u>38</u> <u>152</u> <u>164</u>

G   Baseball or football arenas

<u>150</u> <u>171</u> <u>106</u> <u>124</u> <u>26</u> <u>49</u>

H   "Their images I loved . . .," Shakespeare, *Sonnets* (4 wds.)

<u>85</u> <u>60</u> <u>205</u> <u>34</u> <u>140</u> <u>103</u> <u>4</u> <u>50</u> <u>25</u> <u>196</u> <u>123</u>

I   Not concentrated; spread out; scattered

<u>132</u> <u>13</u> <u>177</u> <u>101</u> <u>68</u> <u>58</u> <u>185</u>

J   Reveal; make known

<u>81</u> <u>10</u> <u>33</u> <u>133</u> <u>154</u> <u>108</u>

K   Pitcher who hurled four no-hit games (2 wds.)

<u>149</u> <u>19</u> <u>46</u> <u>178</u> <u>86</u> <u>69</u> <u>134</u> <u>157</u> <u>165</u>

L   Designating the sweat glands

<u>175</u> <u>24</u> <u>1</u> <u>88</u> <u>59</u> <u>187</u> <u>120</u>

M   Obstructed; delayed; blocked

<u>151</u> <u>23</u> <u>119</u> <u>53</u> <u>203</u> <u>173</u> <u>28</u>

N   1949 Broadway musical (3 wds.)

<u>125</u> <u>184</u> <u>29</u> <u>109</u> <u>139</u> <u>55</u> <u>94</u> <u>76</u> <u>169</u> <u>3</u> <u>163</u> <u>79</u>

O   Famous singing group in the opera *Lucia*

<u>8</u> <u>190</u> <u>54</u> <u>195</u> <u>180</u> <u>128</u>

P   Subordinate associate; helper

<u>74</u> <u>144</u> <u>160</u> <u>211</u> <u>84</u> <u>147</u> <u>91</u>

Q   Outstanding U. S. female tennis star (1923 -) (2 wds.)

<u>21</u> <u>87</u> <u>142</u> <u>113</u> <u>118</u> <u>212</u> <u>145</u> <u>179</u> <u>181</u> <u>95</u> <u>40</u> <u>2</u>

R   Famous U. S. aircraft carrier sunk in W W II; a New York main thoroughfare

<u>97</u> <u>201</u> <u>30</u> <u>188</u> <u>57</u> <u>210</u> <u>112</u> <u>161</u> <u>75</u>

S   Fitted one within another

<u>209</u> <u>105</u> <u>16</u> <u>183</u> <u>199</u> <u>67</u>

T   Capital of ancient Media

<u>155</u> <u>135</u> <u>96</u> <u>7</u> <u>43</u> <u>110</u> <u>66</u> <u>77</u>

U   Place from which a pilot or captain conns a ship

<u>174</u> <u>136</u> <u>65</u> <u>47</u> <u>202</u> <u>172</u> <u>92</u> <u>117</u> <u>192</u> <u>56</u>

V   Sugar compound

<u>206</u> <u>159</u> <u>121</u> <u>99</u> <u>200</u> <u>166</u> <u>18</u> <u>137</u> <u>156</u> <u>51</u>

W   Wobble; sway; waver

<u>122</u> <u>61</u> <u>131</u> <u>37</u> <u>168</u> <u>48</u>

X Large constellation south of Hercules

148	17	198	72	42	167	204	90	32

Y Grim; ghastly; horrible

78	127	104	15	41	162	146

Z British poet (1878-1917): "Adlestrop," "The Owl," "Lights Out" (2 wds.)

22	191	6	31	80	52	64	126	100	158	194	116

Answers on page 372

		1 L	2 Q	3 N	4 H	5 E			6	2 7 T	8 O		9 C
10 J	11 A	12 B	13 I	14 D	15 Y	16 S			17 X	18 V	19 K	20 C	21 Q
22 Z	23 M		24 L	25 H	26 G	27 E	28 M			29 N	30 R	31 Z	32 X
33 J	34 H	35 C	36 D	37 W	38 F	39 A	40 Q		41 Y	42 X	43 T		
44 B	45 E	46 K	47 U	48 W	49 G	50 H	51 V	52 Z		53 M	54 O	55 N	
56 U	57 R	58 I	59 L	60 H	61 W			62 A	63 E	64 Z		65 U	66 T
67 S	68 I	69 K	70 C	71 D		72 X	73 E		74 P	75 R	76 N		
77 T	78 Y	79 N	80 Z	81 J	82 D	83 A	84 P		85 H	86 K		87 Q	
88 L		89 C	90 X	91 P		92 U	93 E		94 N	95 Q	96 T	97 R	
98 C	99 V		100 Z	101 I	102 C	103 H	104 Y	105 S		106 G	107 A		
108 J	109 N	110 T	111 E		112 R	113 Q	114 D	115 B		116 Z	117 U	118 Q	
119 M	120 L	121 V	122 W	123 H	124 G		125 N	126 Z	127 Y	128 O		129 E	
130 F	131 W		132 I	133 J	134 K		135 T	136 U	137 V	138 D	139 N		
140 H	141 B	142 Q	143 C	144 P		145 Q	146 Y		147 P	148 X	149 K	150 G	
151 M	152 F	153 D	154 J	155 T	156 V		157 K		158 Z	159 V	160 P	161 R	
162 Y		163 N	164 F	165 K	166 V	167 X	168 W		169 N	170 D		171 G	
172 U	173 M		174 U	175 L	176 C	177 I	178 K	179 Q	180 O		181 Q	182 C	
	183 S	184 N	185 I		186 E	187 L	188 R	189 B	190 O	191 Z		192 U	
193 A	194 Z	195 O	196 H	197 E		198 X	199 S		200 V	201 R	202 U	203 M	
	204 X	205 H	206 V		207 E	208 D	209 S	210 R	211 P	212 Q			

DEFINITIONS   WORDS

A Medicinal
— — — — — —
96 192 109 49 5 170

B Wandering; homeless
— — — — — — —
31 100 176 140 62 73 124

C 1934 Broadway musical hit by Cole Porter (2 wds.)
— — — — — — — — — — — —
30 148 59 38 61 119 179 40 9 88 198 166

D Legendary drug which brings forgetfulness
— — — — — — — —
76 32 139 173 6 105 110 58

E Common prefix meaning prelude or within
— — — — —
164 136 14 183 120

F Group of Norwegian islands
— — — — — — — —
116 147 89 28 135 52 101 162

G Sentinel
— — — — — — —
69 163 34 155 84 115 50

H Legal order which prevents or restrains
— — — — — — — — — —
67 122 3 152 57 95 181 189 39 63

I Harmonious; in agreement with
— — — — — — — — —
71 184 82 26 125 121 149 94 42

J Mythical monster with features of an eagle, horse and lion
— — — — — — — — — —
15 81 112 102 123 64 45 132 47 185

K Family of Jewish patriots, who revolted in 175 B. C.
— — — — — — — — —
168 93 154 99 177 157 16 86 144

L Anxious; impatient; showing keen desire
— — — — —
106 194 77 143 17

M Outstanding male red-headed U. S. pre-W W II tennis player (2 wds.)
— — — — — — — —
27 141 68 195 158 85 130 169

N Congenital scaly skin disease
— — — — — — — — — —
70 107 51 159 29 2 190 197 91 134

O Large U. S. national forest in Arizona
— — — — — — — —
60 113 18 4 97 146 126 48

P "The world . . . to make thee rich," *Romeo and Juliet* (3 wds.)
— — — — — — — — — — — —
117 90 142 44 25 80 87 8 104 193 171 35

Q Popular type of pasta
— — — — — — — —
127 53 138 98 22 75 191 13

R "They kept the . . . of their way," Gray, *Elegy* (2 wds.)
— — — — — — — — — — — — — —
79 137 7 21 186 161 36 156 74 118 41 133 167 103

S Ornamental stand or compartmented dish
— — — — — — —
24 114 46 37 12 165 72

T Light, sweet white Italian wine
— — — — — — —
43 129 54 172 153 150 78

U Ambassador's residence; person or group sent on an official mission
— — — — — — —
111 55 1 160 66 188 128

V Covered with scales
— — — — — — — —
174 151 196 131 23 175 10 65

W Duty; tax
— — — — — —
178 83 33 19 187 108

X Projecting platform for a ship's gun
— — — — — — —
145 182 56 20 180 11 92

		1 U	2 N		3 H	4 O	5 A	6 D	7 R	8 P
9 C		10 V	11 X	12 S	13 Q	14 E	15 J	16 K	17 L		18 O
19 W	20 X	21 R	22 Q	23 V	24 S	25 P	26 I		27 M	28 F	
29 N	30 C	31 B	32 D		33 W	34 G	35 P	36 R	37 S		38 C
39 H		40 C	41 R	42 I		43 T	44 P	45 J	46 S		47 J
48 O	49 A		50 G	51 N	52 F	53 Q	54 T		55 U	56 X	57 H
58 D	59 C		60 O	61 C	62 B	63 H	64 J	65 V	66 U		67 H
68 M		69 G	70 N	71 I	72 S	73 B	74 R	75 Q	76 D	77 L	
78 T	79 R	80 P		81 J	82 I	83 W	84 G	85 M	86 K	87 P	
88 C	89 F		90 P	91 N	92 X	93 K	94 I	95 H	96 A	97 O	98 Q
	99 K	100 B	101 F		102 J	103 R	104 P	105 D	106 L	107 N	108 W
	109 A	110 D	111 U		112 J	113 O	114 S	115 G	116 F	117 P	118 R
119 C	120 E	121 I		122 H	123 J	124 B		125 I	126 O	127 Q	128 U
	129 T	130 M	131 V	132 J	133 R	134 N	135 F		136 E	137 R	138 Q
139 D	140 B	141 M	142 P	143 L	144 K	145 X	146 O	147 F	148 C	149 I	150 T
	151 V	152 H	153 T	154 K	155 G	156 R		157 K	158 M	159 N	
160 U	161 R	162 F	163 G		164 E	165 S		166 C	167 R	168 K	169 M
	170 A	171 P	172 T	173 D	174 V		175 V	176 B	177 K	178 W	179 G
180 X	181 H		182 X	183 E	184 I	185 J	186 R	187 W	188 U	189 H	190 N
191 Q	192 A	193 P		194 L	195 M	196 V	197 N	198 C			

ACROSS-TIC NO. 6

DEFINITIONS   WORDS

A) Clever or humorous
    remark
    $\overline{49}$ $\overline{173}$ $\overline{104}$ $\overline{4}$ $\overline{64}$ $\overline{33}$ $\overline{142}$ $\overline{161}$ $\overline{152}$

B) In a lazy, indifferent
    way
    $\overline{182}$ $\overline{63}$ $\overline{17}$ $\overline{155}$

C) Buddhist holy city; Far
    Eastern capital
    $\overline{197}$ $\overline{112}$ $\overline{15}$ $\overline{53}$ $\overline{136}$

D) Type of printing
    $\overline{27}$ $\overline{180}$ $\overline{71}$ $\overline{208}$ $\overline{108}$ $\overline{75}$ $\overline{95}$ $\overline{42}$ $\overline{187}$ $\overline{10}$ $\overline{153}$

E) Demand; require
    $\overline{54}$ $\overline{181}$ $\overline{43}$ $\overline{81}$ $\overline{123}$ $\overline{22}$

F) Draw out; cause to be
    revealed
    $\overline{79}$ $\overline{193}$ $\overline{48}$ $\overline{127}$ $\overline{97}$ $\overline{12}$

G) Compassion; sorrow
    $\overline{137}$ $\overline{18}$ $\overline{148}$ $\overline{199}$ $\overline{113}$ $\overline{196}$ $\overline{128}$ $\overline{91}$

H) "Once more ___, dear
    friends, once more,"
    Henry V, (3 words)
    $\overline{52}$ $\overline{103}$ $\overline{201}$ $\overline{140}$ $\overline{195}$ $\overline{2}$ $\overline{69}$ $\overline{171}$ $\overline{164}$ $\overline{24}$ $\overline{188}$
    $\overline{130}$ $\overline{45}$

I) Souvenir of Atlantic
    City
    $\overline{44}$ $\overline{149}$ $\overline{99}$ $\overline{66}$ $\overline{165}$

J) Having a marked,
    special, appealing
    flavor
    $\overline{47}$ $\overline{93}$ $\overline{122}$ $\overline{8}$ $\overline{172}$

K) Tyrannical; hard to
    put up with
    $\overline{144}$ $\overline{135}$ $\overline{25}$ $\overline{109}$ $\overline{176}$ $\overline{57}$ $\overline{38}$ $\overline{210}$ $\overline{162}$ $\overline{89}$

L) Low point
    $\overline{61}$ $\overline{168}$ $\overline{86}$ $\overline{28}$ $\overline{177}$

M) Famous American
    "Hoosier" poet,
    1807-1892 (last name)
    $\overline{179}$ $\overline{92}$ $\overline{194}$ $\overline{9}$ $\overline{138}$ $\overline{116}$ $\overline{30}$ $\overline{189}$

N) In 1944, GIs fought
    among these French
    countryside features
    $\overline{19}$ $\overline{192}$ $\overline{134}$ $\overline{184}$ $\overline{167}$ $\overline{211}$ $\overline{34}$ $\overline{160}$ $\overline{74}$

O) University town in
    Pennsylvania
    $\overline{102}$ $\overline{11}$ $\overline{205}$ $\overline{175}$ $\overline{131}$ $\overline{55}$

P) Shot full of holes; ques-
    tioned
    $\overline{13}$ $\overline{126}$ $\overline{96}$ $\overline{114}$ $\overline{85}$ $\overline{39}$ $\overline{147}$

Q) Wife of Orpheus
    $\overline{198}$ $\overline{76}$ $\overline{101}$ $\overline{6}$ $\overline{117}$ $\overline{94}$ $\overline{29}$ $\overline{156}$

R) Herman Wouk's prize-
    winning book, play,
    and movie (3 words)
    $\overline{191}$ $\overline{23}$ $\overline{100}$ $\overline{202}$ $\overline{46}$ $\overline{73}$ $\overline{141}$ $\overline{151}$ $\overline{59}$ $\overline{132}$ $\overline{1}$
    $\overline{111}$ $\overline{174}$ $\overline{88}$

S) Chicago settlement,
    founded in 1889 by
    Jane Addams (2 words)
    $\overline{166}$ $\overline{37}$ $\overline{146}$ $\overline{133}$ $\overline{5}$ $\overline{58}$ $\overline{120}$ $\overline{78}$ $\overline{186}$

T) Spanish river
    $\overline{204}$ $\overline{157}$ $\overline{68}$ $\overline{32}$

U) Pretend (2 words)
    $\overline{90}$ $\overline{50}$ $\overline{150}$ $\overline{67}$ $\overline{119}$ $\overline{3}$ $\overline{107}$ $\overline{77}$ $\overline{163}$ $\overline{169}$ $\overline{139}$

V) Casual; unrehearsed

159	36	65	125	20	183	87

W) Plain objects on human faces

70	206	110	154	31

X) Ancient collection of Norse poetry; Icelandic epic

118	72	21	200

Y) Major industrial city in Ohio

170	83	145	7	56	80	178	106	124	35

Z) 1941 Triple Crown winner

41	203	129	121	16	209	82	190	62

Z¹) Fit into a budget; bear the cost of; supply

60	207	98	26	158	40

Z²) Victory; favorable result

115	84	143	105	14	185	51

Answers on page 373

1 R	2 H	3 U		4 A	5 S	6 Q	7 Y	8 J		9 M	10 D	11 O	12 F
13 P	14 Z²	15 C	16 Z	17 B	18 G		19 N	20 V	21 X		22 E	23 R	24 H	
25 K	26 Z¹	27 D	28 L	29 Q	30 M		31 W	32 T		33 A	34 N	35 Y	36 V	37 S
38 K	39 P	40 Z¹		41 Z	42 D	43 E		44 I	45 H	46 R	47 J		48 F	
49 A	50 U	51 Z²		52 H	53 C	54 E	55 O	56 Y		57 K	58 S		59 R	60 Z¹
61 L	62 Z		63 B	64 A	65 V	66 I	67 U	68 T	69 H	70 W	71 D		72 X	73 R
74 N	75 D	76 Q	77 U	78 S	79 F	80 Y		81 E		82 Z	83 Y	84 Z²	85 P	86 L
	87 V	88 R	89 K		90 U	91 G		92 M	93 J	94 Q	95 D		96 P	97 F
98 Z¹	99 I	100 R	101 Q	102 O	103 H	104 A		105 Z²	106 Y	107 U	108 D	109 K	110 W	
111 R		112 C	113 G	114 P		115 Z²	116 M	117 Q	118 X	119 U	120 S	121 Z	122 J	123 E
	124 Y	125 V	126 P	127 F	128 G		129 Z		130 H	131 O	132 R	133 S	134 N
135 K	136 C	137 G	138 M	139 U		140 H	141 R		142 A		143 Z²	144 K	145 Y	146 S
147 P		148 G	149 I	150 U	151 R		152 A	153 D		154 W	155 B	156 Q	157 T	158 Z¹
159 V	160 N	161 A		162 K	163 U	164 H	165 I		166 S	167 N	168 L	169 U	170 Y
171 H	172 J		173 A	174 R	175 O	176 K	177 L	178 Y	179 M	180 D	181 E	182 B	183 V	184 N
	185 Z²	186 S	187 D	188 H	189 M	190 Z	191 R	192 N		193 F	194 M	195 H	196 G	197 C
198 Q		199 G	200 X	201 H	202 R	203 Z	204 T	205 O		206 W	207 Z¹		208 D	209 Z
210 K	211 N												

HOW SELF-ASSERTIVE ARE YOU?

Are you an introvert, extrovert, or ambivert? The introvert is concerned with inner emotions, reflection, and subjective thinking. The introvert tends to shy away from people and find self-assertion uncomfortable. The extrovert is a doer, interested in action, other people, the outside world. The extrovert tends to have a clear idea of goals and enjoys manipulating people and events to achieve goals. The ambivert shares about equally the traits of the other two. All of us possess both introvert and extrovert qualities, but most of us lean a bit more in one direction than the other.

To find out where you fall, choose the one of the three solutions given for each question or situation which comes nearest to the way you believe you would react.

Answers on page 373

1. A traffic cop stops you and says, "This is the main street of Moose-town, not a race track." He starts writing you a ticket. Would you:
   a. Swallow hard and keep still.
   b. Say you were only going thirty.
   c. Smile and say, "Now, Buddy, let's talk this over."

2. If you were asked to give a talk at a meeting, would you:
   a. Feign illness and not go.
   b. Prepare a speech, but read it.
   c. Be glad for the chance to say what you think.

3. A friend invites you to a picnic, saying she will meet you there and introduce you to the gang. Upon arriving, you find that she has not yet shown up. Would you:
   a. Stand apart from the group waiting until she arrives.
   b. Introduce yourself to the group and tell them you are waiting for your friend.
   c. Join the group in what they are doing and then lead them in a game you enjoy.

4. You are walking down a street in which a truck loaded with barbed wire is parked. You see a woman dash across the street, catching her skirt on trailing strands of wire, which tear away a large strip of material. Would you:
   a. Blush and walk by pretending not to have noticed.
   b. Yell at the truck driver.
   c. Go to the woman and offer to help her.

5. You are planning a new venture, but have not yet completed the arrangements. A good friend asks you what is new. Would you:
   a. Say nothing and keep your plans to yourself.
   b. Tell him you are contemplating a change, but have not completed your plans.
   c. Tell him you're glad he asked and tell him the whole story.

6. Your boss has just given you an order which you happen to know will be disadvantageous to him. Would you:
   a. Take the order obediently and say nothing.
   b. Acknowledge his authority, but tell him if you follow this order, it will have bad results.
   c. Explain to him in detail why it is not a good thing to do.

7. Someone else has just been given the promotion you had hoped would fall to you. Would you:
   a. Feel personally slighted, and wonder what they don't like about you.
   b. Admit you're disappointed, and analyze why the other person deserved it more than you did.
   c. Have a talk with the boss about it.

8. You are entertaining a visitor who tends to monopolize the conversation. Would you:
   a. Let him talk on and enjoy himself.
   b. Try to draw others into the conversation.
   c. Interrupt him and direct the conversation yourself.

WOULD YOU MAKE A GOOD COUNTER-SPY?

Every boy and girl has sent a secret message at some time or other. Some amateur cryptographers have grown up to become important members of their country's secret service. It takes a special kind of skill to figure out secret codes. You have to be able to see relationships and manipulate abstract symbols.

This quiz will tell you whether you should apply for a job with the CIA.

Answers on page 374

1. Can you decipher this famous statement made by Benjamin Franklin?

   ETSAWSEKAMETSAH

2. Decode this quotation from the Book of Jeremiah (I:19.)
   GSVB HSZOO MLG KIVEZRO ZTZRMHG GSVV

3. Decode this simple numerical cipher and you will have a well-known American slogan.
   9-14 7-15-4 23-5 20-18-21-19-20

4. The following pattern is a variation of a coding system developed by the ancient Greeks.

	1	2	3	4	5
1	A	F	L	Q	V
2	B	G	M	R	W
3	C	H	N	S	X
4	D	IJ	O	T	Y
5	E	K	P	U	Z

   Use the above code to decipher this famous quotation attributed to General Patton.
   53-54-44 43-33-13-45 11-23-51-24-42-31-11-33-34 43-33
   22-54-11-24-41 44-43-33-42-22-32-44

5. If the hymn *ROCK OF AGES* is written:

   TQEM QH CIGU

   What is the title of this famous song?

   COGTKEC VJG DGCWVKHWN

6. This code and its variations has been called by different names, such as the pigpen cipher because of its shape, or the Rosicrucian or Masonic cipher because of its use by those organizations. It also played a role in the Civil War.

A	D	G
B ·	E ·	H ·
C ··	F ··	I ··
J	M	P
K ·	N ·	Q ·
L ··	O ··	R ··
S	V	Y
T ·	W ·	Z ·
U ··	X ··	

Using the above code, decipher this statement:

OBSERVATION TEST

There may not be anything wrong with your vision, but how observant are you? Here are 15 questions to test how carefully and accurately you perceive things. Write your answers in the blanks or circle the correct answer. Allow yourself 10 minutes to complete the test.

Give yourself 10 points for each correct answer. A score of 70 is passing fair; 100 shows you have a keen eye; and 120 or better makes you a veritable Sherlock Holmes.

Answers on page 374

1. How many surfaces does this

   object have? _____

2. Which two figures are identical?

   (a)   (b)   (c)   (d)   (e)   (f)

3. Which two figures are identical?

   (a)   (b)   (c)   (d)   (e)   (f)

4. Which two figures are identical?

   (a)   (b)   (c)   (d)   (e)   (f)

5. Which two figures are identical?

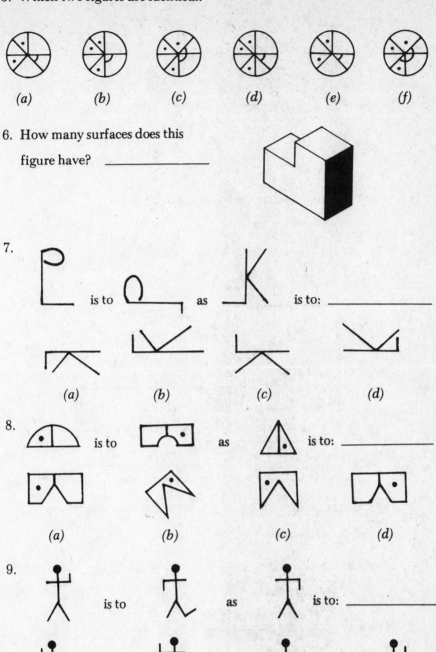

(a)   (b)   (c)   (d)   (e)   (f)

6. How many surfaces does this figure have? _____

7. [figure] is to [figure] as [figure] is to: _____

    (a)   (b)   (c)   (d)

8. [figure] is to [figure] as [figure] is to: _____

    (a)   (b)   (c)   (d)

9. [figure] is to [figure] as [figure] is to: _____

    (a)   (b)   (c)   (d)

10.

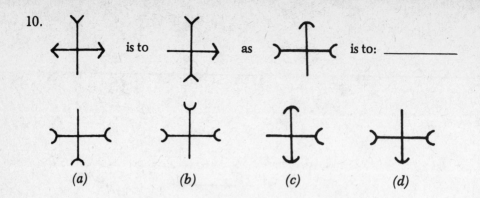

Questions 11-15 are based on the following figures:

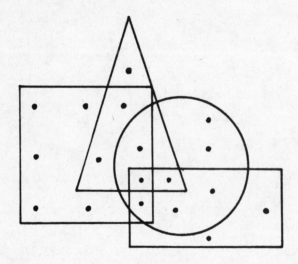

11. How many dots are in the triangle, but not in the circle?

   _____

12. How many dots are common to the rectangle, triangle, and circle?

   _____

13. How many dots are common to the circle, square, and triangle?

   _____

14. How many dots are common to the rectangle and square?

   _____

15. How many dots are common to all four figures: the square, the rectangle, the circle, and the triangle? _____

ARE YOU VAIN?

There is a considerable difference between having self-confidence or self-respect and being conceited or boastful. Actually, the person who knows his own abilities and is proud of his accomplishments finds it unnecessary to brag. It is the person who is unsure of himself who finds it necessary to make himself feel better by boasting. "To be a man's own fool is bad enough, but the vain man is everybody's." (William Penn).

This test will help you assess whether you truly value yourself, or hide your uncertainty behind your vanity.

Answers on page 374

1. What is your reaction to the picture at right?
    a. It is a symbol of vanity.
    b. It depicts friendship.
    c. It has no special meaning to me.

	YES	NO
2. Do you spend more money on your clothing and your appearance in general than you can afford?	___	___
3. When eating out with friends, do you tend to overtip the waiter?	___	___
4. Do you often surreptitiously try to glance at yourself in mirrors and at your reflection in the store windows you pass?	___	___
5. Do you dress appropriately for your age?	___	___
6. Are you personally hurt when someone criticizes your work?	___	___
7. Are you willing to admit when you are wrong?	___	___
8. Do you go out of your way to mention important people you know? Are you a name-dropper?	___	___
9. Do you feel that if you want anything done right you have to do it yourself?	___	___
10. Do you sometimes exaggerate or tell "little white lies" in order to impress others?	___	___

HOW SOCIABLE ARE YOU?

When they are in a social group, some people chatter on and on like an endless tape recording. They seem to feel free to sermonize or interrupt. Relating to others involves listening as much as talking. According to research studies, and contrary to popular belief, women do not talk more than men. It is a matter of personal makeup, not a sex characteristic.

This test will help you determine how popular with, or sensitive to, others you are.

Answers on page 374

1. Write your initials on one of the blocks in this diagram.

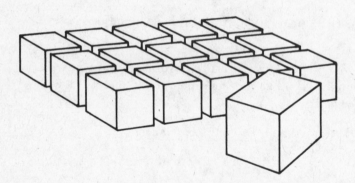

2. Which of these punctuation marks do you find most pleasing: A, B, C, or D?

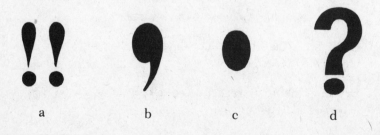

    a   b   c   d

3. If you were to select a painting for your living room, which would you prefer?
   a. A Parisian café scene.
   b. A seascape.

4. How would you prefer to spend an evening?
   a. Reading a book.
   b. At a party.
   c. At the theater or a movie.

	YES	NO
5. Do you spend much time thinking about your possessions?	___	___
6. Are your memories more concerned with happy moments than with unpleasantness?	___	___
7. Do you find looking at the sea, desert, mountains, and fields soothing?	___	___
8. Are you economically comfortable with no money worries for the future?	___	___
9. Do you wish you had more relatives and more opportunity to visit with them?	___	___
10. Would you like to attend more parties?	___	___
11. Do you have a secret goal you are working to achieve?	___	___
12. Do you watch your health carefully?	___	___
13. Do you know something about the care of a garden or potted plants?	___	___
14. Do you have good aim (shooting, bowling, hammering, etc.)?	___	___

HOW DETERMINED ARE YOU?

There is an old, old saying, "Where there's a will, there's a way." Educators, psychologists, and employers often note that those who fail are not necessarily less intelligent or less gifted than those who succeed, but are easily discouraged, possess little perseverance, and tend to view life with the anticipation of failure rather than success. This test evaluates your own attitudes.

Answers on page 375

1. You are planning to wallpaper your den. Which of the patterns shown below would you most likely select?

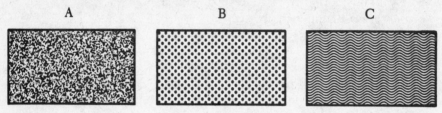

A   B   C

Put yourself in the following situations and check the reaction nearest your own.

2. You have an important appointment. Your car has a flat a mile from the place of the meeting. You would:
   a. Wait for help.
   b. Walk to the meeting.
   c. Change the tire.

3. You will be starting a new job shortly. You would:
   a. Take courses and/or read materials which may help you.
   b. Try to learn on the job.
   c. Keep your eyes and ears open for another position in case your new one doesn't work out.

4. Your romance is on the rocks. You would:
   a. Look for someone else who appreciates you.
   b. Hope that time will heal the wound.
   c. Seek help from a counselor, psychologist, or psychiatrist.

5. Do you every say or think, "I'm going to get that done if it kills me?"
   a. Never.
   b. Occasionally.
   c. Quite often.

6. You have just started a new hobby, such as learning to play golf, make ceramics, build a boat, or hook a rug. You are moving slowly in this endeavor and encountering many problems. You would:
   a. Abandon the whole idea.
   b. Finish off what you started any old way.
   c. Try to learn from your errors and improve your skill.

7. When you are trying to solve a problem, does the solution come to you in your sleep?
   a. Occasionally.
   b. Never.
   c. Quite often.

8. When you undertake something, either on the job or as a hobby, do you have a distinct reason for what you are doing?
   a. Never.
   b. Sometimes.
   c. Almost always.

9. You have a heavy cold. You would:
   a. Continue with your normal activity, doing the best you can.
   b. Go home to get a rest.
   c. Follow your doctor's orders to the letter.

10. You want something that costs a considerable amount of money, such as a trip to Europe, new furniture, or a car. You would:
    a. Put the desire out of your mind as an impossible dream.
    b. Figure out a budget and save consistently for your objective.
    c. Pray for an unexpected windfall.

HOW WELL-LIKED ARE YOU?

With a very few neurotic exceptions, everyone wants to be accepted and liked. Indeed, some pay a high price to appear popular—from trying to buy friendships with money to the misuse of sex to gain attention. The real test of how well-liked you are is the everyday behavior of those around you, and whether you have friends you can depend on during an emergency.

The following test will help you assess whether or not people really like you.

Answers on page 375

1. Which of the three drawings marked A, B, & C comes closest to describing how you feel with people around?

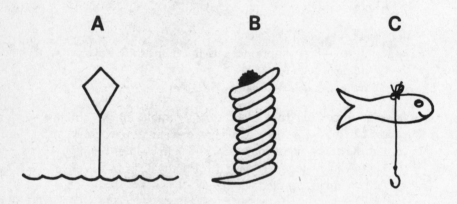

2. When you are confined to your home or the hospital because of illness:
   a. Many people call or send cards.
   b. You sit it out pretty much alone.
   c. Several of your best friends check in.

3. When you run into a group of friends:
   a. All of them say hello.
   b. Most keep on with their conversations.
   c. Some greet you more enthusiastically than others.

4. People you know:
   a. Seem to go out of their way to be nice to you.
   b. Are preoccupied with their own lives.
   c. See you when it is convenient.

5. If you are short of money:
    a. Many people are there to help you.
    b. Everyone else is broke, too.
    c. There is always someone you can depend on.

6. When you have a birthday:
    a. Many people remember the date.
    b. You have to hint for cards and presents.
    c. Some old standbys never forget.

7. People come to you for advice or help:
    a. Often.
    b. Seldom or never.
    c. On certain kinds of problems.

8. Which statement best describes your feelings?
    a. I like most people.
    b. I feel estranged from many people.
    c. I am highly selective in choosing my friends.

9. If you were asked to help in a community drive, you would:
    a. Make the time to participate actively.
    b. Beg off for some reason.
    c. Work a little to show your support.

10. When you return from a vacation:
    a. People call and come to welcome you home.
    b. No one seems to notice that you were away.
    c. You call friends to tell them you are back.

11. You are chosen to be the leader or decision maker:
    a. Many times.
    b. Never.
    c. Sometimes.

12. You are:
    a. Occasionally the brunt of a joke.
    b. Often teased.
    c. A self-effacing humorist.

13. When with people much older or younger than you, you:
    a. Find their conversation genuinely interesting.
    b. Are bored.
    c. Try to look interested even if you are not.

14. Generally speaking you:
    a. Confide in those close to you.
    b. Go to many people with your tales of woe.
    c. Try to solve your own problems.

CAN YOU KEEP A SECRET?

The ability to keep a secret requires self-control which is an important feature in the mature personality. The blabbermouth is disliked socially, and is a hazard in business. At the international level, the security of nations sometimes depends on silence. Walter Winchell, the noted columnist, said, "I usually get my stuff from people who promised somebody else that they would keep a secret." This test will tell how well you rate as a "secret risk."

Answers on page 376

1. Don't think! In the drawing room below there are two loose blocks. There are also three empty spaces in the mass of blocks. Draw lines from block A and block B to the hole or holes of your choice.

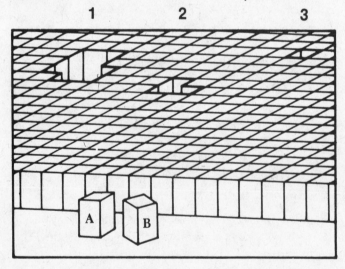

2. Think! In the situations given below, check the answer that best describes what you would do:

    A. A friend who is going to be given a surprise party in an hour comes to your house in dirty clothes covered with paint. You would:

a. Alert him about the party so he can change.
b. Say nothing.
c. Hint about his clothing.

B. A child tells you what Santa Claus is bringing him. You would:
   a. Alert his parents to what he wants.
   b. Listen with pleasure.
   c. Respond with what Santa is bringing to you.

C. You can select only one magazine. Your choice would be a:
   a. News or family publication.
   b. Confession or gossip magazine.
   c. Hobby, sports, or trade periodical.

D. A friend tells you of a secret romance. You would:
   a. Bind your other friends to secrecy and tell them the news.
   b. Record the news in your diary.
   c. Say nothing.

E. An employer confides that he is going to fire a staff member. You would:
   a. Warn the employee to look for a new job.
   b. Let information come through channels.
   c. Confidentally tell others on the staff.

F. When people confide secrets to you, you:
   a. Feel flattered and enjoy it.
   b. Wish people would not involve you.
   c. Enjoy passing the secret along.

3. Don't think! Put your initials on one of the two boxes below.

A   **B**

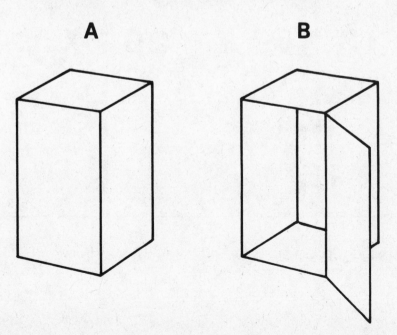

HOW WELL DO YOU CONCENTRATE?

In our world of noise and constant interruptions and demands, it is easy to become so distracted that you can't concentrate on the task at hand. The art of working under pressure is one which can be developed. Use this test as a starting point to evaluate how well you are able to concentrate. There is no time limit. Work at your normal speed.

Answers on page 376

1. Study the group of numbers on the left to find the relationship that will tell you what number is represented by X in the other group on the right.

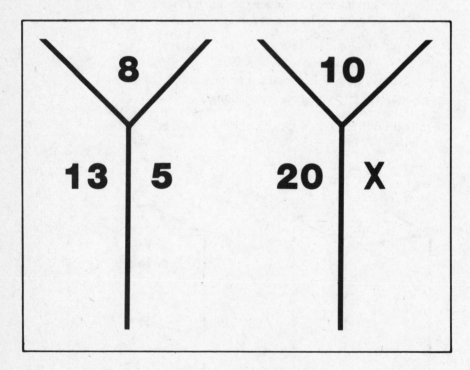

2. If FRANCE is spelled numerically as 61811435, what countries do these two groups of numbers spell?
   a. 19161914 _____   b. 92011225 _____

3. What is the second vowel in the name of the month that follows October? _____

4. What is the second letter in the name of the day which is the day that comes after the day after Friday? _____

5. Which letter in the word DEMAND is nearest the end of the alphabet? _____

6. Study the following pairs of words. One pair does not follow the pattern of the others. Which one do you think it is?

   goat:tug   boat:tab   sad:does   blind:did   dug:good

7. Follow the instructions given below, step by step to fill in the missing letters.

   _ _ S _ _ _ U _ Z _ _ _ _

   S is between N and W. Z comes between X and K. T should be placed before U. R comes after W. A comes before N. M comes after X. F should be placed to the right of M. L is the next to the last letter as you read to the right.

8. In the diagram below, the 12 blocks form a square with 4 blocks on each side. Can you rearrange the 12 blocks so there will be 5 blocks on each side of the block pattern?

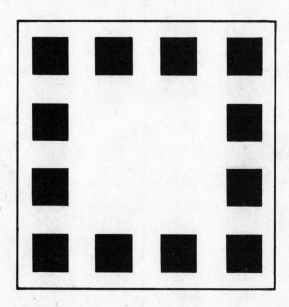

DO YOU FEEL INFERIOR?

Many of us harbor feelings of inadequacy. Some seek attention and sympathy by explaining in detail what sorry messes they are. Psychiatrists say that often the blustery and boastful person is, in reality, trying to hide feelings of inferiority; and the quiet little guy or gal may be warm and snug with inner security.

Answer the questions below to help determine whether or not you nurture a sense of inferiority.

Answers on page 376

1. Which illustration in the drawing below would best describe your usual mood when you awake to face a new day?

2. When you are asked to do an important job you didn't expect, how do you react? Check the drawing which best describes your immediate reaction.

3. You are trying to solve a problem when someone comes and silently looks over your shoulder. You would:
   a. Feel jittery.
   b. Be flattered.
   c. Put his presence in the back of your mind.

4. When an acquaintance fails on a project, you often:
   a. Are secretly pleased.
   b. Try to fill the breach.
   c. Worry almost as much as if it were your own error.

5. If someone makes you the brunt of a joke, you:
   a. Wait for the moment when you can tell an embarrassing story about him.
   b. Add to the story and make it more ludicrous.
   c. Explain the serious side of the situation.

6. With an unlimited amount of money, you would:
   a. Buy the luxuries you most want.
   b. Go all out with new possessions.
   c. Save it.

7. If you were invited to meet an important celebrity, you would:
   a. Be pleased to have the opportunity.
   b. Find an excuse for not going.
   c. Buy new clothing and nervously plan your behavior.

8. You think that:
   a. Most people are better than you.
   b. Everyone has strengths and weaknesses.
   c. Few have your assets and abilities.

9. If you won a trophy, you would:
   a. Place it in a conspicuous spot in your home.
   b. Let your family or friends suggest where you should put it.
   c. Tuck it away.

10. You sincerely believe:
    a. There is nothing you do really well.
    b. You do many things fairly well.
    c. You excel in one or two worthwhile skills.

ARE YOU A PLEASURE TO BE WITH?

At one time or another, each of us has said about some person, "I like him, but he annoys me." Then there are those who give a soothing quality to life.

Most of us are not aware of some of our social habits and behave automatically and unconsciously. Before criticizing others, it is wise to study yourself to find out if you have any characteristics which, according to psychological studies, are bothersome to others.

In order to try to see yourself as others see you, be as honest as you can in answering these questions.

Answers on page 377

Answers on page 377

	YES	NO
1. Do you have several stock phrases you use constantly?	___	___
2. Are you careless about your table manners and/or smoking habits?	___	___
3. Do you tend to keep touching the person with whom you are carrying on a conversation?	___	___
4. Do you try to shock or entertain people by telling off-color stories?	___	___
5. Does time mean so little to you that you are often late or wear out your welcome by staying too long?	___	___

6. Do you rattle coins in your pocket or play with car keys? ___ ___

7. When sitting or standing, is it difficult for you to keep your feet still? ___ ___

8. Do you find it hard to know what to do with your hands? Are you constantly moving them—twiddling your thumbs, touching your hair, etc.? ___ ___

9. When attending a group event (movie, lecture, church, etc.) are you prone to whisper to your neighbor? ___ ___

10. Do you squirm in your clothing constantly adjusting your belt, fingering your tie, straightening your skirt, stockings, or trousers? ___ ___

11. Do you bite your fingernails? ___ ___

12. Do you leave your clothing and personal property strewn about your home or office? ___ ___

13. Do you enjoy arguing or contradicting others? ___ ___

14. Is your voice much louder (or much softer) than the average person's? ___ ___

15. Are your feelings easily hurt? ___ ___

16. Is your conversation centered around yourself and your activities? ___ ___

17. Are you a "conversation hog," monopolizing the talk for prolonged periods of time? ___ ___

18. Do you avoid looking into the eyes of the person you are having a conversation with? ___ ___

CROSSWORD PUZZLE NO. 1

Solution on page 377

ACROSS

1. Smarted
6. Bulk
10. Bridge
14. Pith helmet
15. Encourage
16. Story
17. Major wire service (abbr.)
18. Cereals
20. Gained
22. China, e.g.
23. Came upon
25. Fixed routine
27. Vex
29. Support
31. Be inclined
33. Foot part
34. Dog type
36. "Money is the ____ of all evil"
38. Witch's concoction
41. Minister
44. Shortly
46. No in Dundee
47. Article
48. Close eyes (falconry)
50. Disorder
52. Yes in Yucatan
53. Eye infection
55. Notices
57. Linger
59. Rip
61. Light source
63. Society column word
64. Deteriorate
66. Anger
68. Balance
71. Contemporary
74. Turns to the right
76. Extinct bird
77. ____ snail's pace (2 words)
78. Cry of pain
80. Genuine
82. Two (prefix)
83. Streetwear for Caesar
85. Raise
87. Ideal
89. Opposite of 33 across
90. Allot
91. Serves at a tea

DOWN

1. Post office purchase
2. Imbiber
3. Northern Michigan (abbr.)
4. Recent (prefix)
5. Mechanism
6. Overcome
7. College degree
8. Stitch
9. Cease
10. Thoroughfare (abbr.)
11. Part of a horse's leg
12. Toward shelter
13. Approach
19. Nipper
21. Mesh
24. Outdoes
26. Long-lived Biblical character
28. Weep
30. Sets
32. Entrance
35. Leaves
37. Labor
39. Comfort
40. Fence in water
41. "What is ____ is prologue"
42. Prefix for bellum or diluvian
43. Angler's implement
45. *High* ____ (1952 Gary Cooper film)
49. Tragic king
51. Layer
54. Ground gained in football
56. Pollution
58. Abound
60. Poor man's caviar
62. Capital of South Dakota
65. Endeavor
67. Confederate hero
69. Solemn
70. Animal appendages
71. Arithmetic (colloquial)
72. Indian tribe
73. Average
75. Coarse hominy
79. Tiny
81. John (British slang)
84. Gangster Capone
86. Toward
88. German pronoun

CROSSWORD PUZZLE NO. 2

Solution on page 377

ACROSS

1. Light beams
5. I hear (Latin)
10. In favor of
13. Bicycle part
14. High-stakes car race (2 words)
16. Andean mammal
17. Some
18. Chosen few
19. Paddle
20. Many (slang)
22. Orant's "over and out"
23. Baseball great Cobb, the "Georgia Peach"
24. Finished
25. Community
28. "There is Nothing Like a ____" (*South Pacific*)
29. Ancient Greek battleground; long footrace
33. Centuries-old board game
35. Douglas and Nichols
36. Alter ____
37. Curse
38. Cavities
39. Underdone
40. Suffix meaning "full of"
41. Doorways
42. Tortoises' nemeses

43. Type of athlete
45. Gland
46. Powder
47. Take on
48. Monogram of famous rabbit
50. Volcano product
53. Body of water
54. Hawaiian food staple
55. Greeting to eaters of 54 across
57. Cigarette by-product
58. River in British Columbia
60. Cycle race
62. Master of ceremonies
63. Busy insect
64. Uptight
65. Raced

DOWN

1. Pass on
2. Jewish month
3. Sweet potato
4. Single skis
5. Term in printing or marbles
6. Vessels
7. 24-hour period
8. With it
9. Poem
10. Proper
11. Sacrament

12. Beasts of burden
13. Scheme
15. Factory
21. "____ if by land..."
24. Hyphen
25. Appropriates
26. Metalliferous rocks
27. Used to be
28. Inhibit
29. Distance runner
30. Valentine symbol
31. Monster
32. Negative responses
33. Sounds like a dove
34. Lock part
35. Musical work
38. "____ off"
39. Ethnic group
41. Risible antelope
42. Barriers
44. Western state
45. Clamor
47. Steed
48. Afflicted by ennui
49. Wait
50. Greek meat staple
51. Lily plant
52. Cast a ballot
53. Go by
54. College in NYC
56. Play part
57. Weight
59. Mischievous child
61. Prefix: again

CROSSWORD PUZZLE NO. 3

Solution on page 378

ACROSS

1. Shape at an angle
6. Effervescent drink
10. October birthstone
14. Breathing
15. Neat
16. Chemical weapon
17. Old Scratch
18. Shakespearean villain
19. Ireland
20. Greek letter
21. Slight depression
23. Hair curler
25. Peddle
27. American Indian
28. Be in debt
29. Paddle
31. Buzzard
35. Ride a bike
38. Mineral springs
40. Mythical land
41. Dodge
42. Owns
43. Cow's stomach
45. Tennis term
46. Darling
47. About 70% of you
48. Perfidy
51. Obtained
52. Total
53. Doctors' org.

55. I used to be (Latin)
59. Symbol
62. Move fast
64. Inventor Whitney
65. Strong wind
66. British school
68. Mete
70. Adhesive
71. Persecutor of Christians
72. Paris's river
73. Level
74. Forest animal
75. Gait-setting horse

DOWN

1. Foundations
2. Fill with joy
3. Essential
4. Woman's name
5. Give temporarily
6. Backbone
7. Make a speech
8. Archaeological site
9. Romantic
10. Fluffy breakfast fare
11. Bucket
12. Land measure
13. Lupine look
22. Slip
24. Nocturnal bird

26. Burden
30. British beverage favorite
31. Flower container
32. Single
33. Cord
34. German river
35. Hide
36. At any time
37. Appointment
38. Repel
39. Butter serving
43. ". . . ____ if by sea"
44. Appraise
46. Laud
49. Dormant
50. "A Boy Named ____" (song by Johnny Cash)
51. Fuel
53. Idolize
54. Estate house
56. Souvenir
57. By oneself
58. Bishop's hat
59. Ingredients in 10 down
60. Grain for brewing
61. Color of melancholy
63. Fastener
67. Golfer's pedestal
69. Grassland

CROSSWORD PUZZLE NO. 4

Solution on page 378

ACROSS

1. Walk
5. In between
9. Athena's birds
13. Absent
14. Ice cream receptacle
15. Trick or ____
16. Back of the neck
17. Joining of two streams
19. Be mistaken
20. Distress signal
21. Catch some rays
22. Morning moisture
23. Ease
25. Taste
27. Small lake
28. Repeals
33. Part of a platform
35. Recede
36. Bull (Spanish)
37. Charged particle
38. Ladder parts
39. Stain
40. Walkway
42. Press
43. Rise in ground
45. Together (French)
47. Indefinite word
48. *Charlotte's* ____
49. Cork
52. Novel by H. Rider Haggard
55. British beverage
57. Dine
58. Permissive
59. Popular candy
62. Television (slang)
63. Regions
64. Gaelic
65. Cupid
66. Requirement
67. Envisions
68. Cute

DOWN

1. Wooden plank
2. Sentient
3. Ladies' trouser style (2 words)
4. Face part
5. Harmony
6. Bullwinkle, e.g.
7. Tavern
8. Handy
9. Mineral source
10. Travel
11. Irish product
12. Goulash
15. Garment
18. Gaelic girls
20. Done for
24. "...His only begotton ____"
26. Word from a Poe title
28. "Home on the ____"
29. Border
30. Pseudonym (French, 3 words)
31. Word with race or strip
32. Angered
33. Conduit
34. Roman ears, to Marc Antony
35. Roll up
38. Bridge term
41. Chop
43. Source
44. Prankster
46. Allots
47. Part of the good ol' U.S. of A.
49. One of five
50. Prelude to parturition
51. Put forth
52. Bridge
53. "____ lies..."
54. Fencer's instrument
56. Surname of actors Leon and Ed
60. Former slang word for home
61. Wrath
62. Word used with 43 down

297

CROSSWORD PUZZLE NO. 5

Solution on page 378

ACROSS

1. Set of tools
4. Parrot
9. Rascal
14. Mountain in Sicily
15. "Joyful, Joyful, We ____ Thee" (hymn)
16. Work
17. Inferred
19. At a distance
21. Italian pronoun
22. Coop
23. Seafaring group
24. Varnish ingredient
25. River in Texas
28. Crate
29. Price of transportation
30. Comedian King
31. Ship's record
32. Streetcar
34. Tease
35. Navy women
37. Compile
40. "____ Ain't Necessarily So" (*Porgy and Bess*)
41. Sleeveless cloak
42. Scruff
44. Singular of 21 across
45. Drainage ditch
47. Rare
49. Wrong
50. Brainstorm
52. Rear, to members of 23 across
53. Singer Perry ____
54. Wan

56. South American nation
58. Abyss
59. Playwright Burrows
60. Camp unit
61. Old card game
62. Soldier
63. Verdi opera
64. Jet routes
68. Proverb
70. Nervous
72. Estuary (Spanish)
73. More recent
74. Egresses
75. Likely

DOWN

1. Child
2. Chemical suffix
3. Small portion
4. Medieval weapons
5. Arabian seaport
6. Food fish
7. Southern state (abbr.)
8. Rubs against
9. Cabbage salad
10. Train part
11. From (Latin)
12. Tooth
13. Surname of actor Vincent
18. "Once ____ a time"
20. Measurements of length

23. Canary's home
24. Tibetan monk
25. The City of Light
26. Chosen few
27. Mr. Calloway
28. Small harbors
29. Renown
31. "____ of luxury"
33. Absorbed
35. Suffix for silver or hard
36. Army acronym now in general use
38. Bangs
39. Biblical city of sin
41. Give over
43. Social insect
46. Trick
48. Supermarket aid
49. Large snake
51. Copied
53. Dog breed
54. Heathen
55. Tolerate
57. Growing out of
58. Hearts
60. Level
61. Enumerate
63. ____ of reason
64. Black cuckoo
65. Coach Parseghian
66. Lyricist Harburg
67. Stayed put
69. ____, shucks!
71. Prefix meaning former

CROSSWORD PUZZLE NO. 6

Solution on page 378

ACROSS

1. Guard
5. Smooth
9. Lion's trademark
13. Broadway hit of the late 60s
14. Layer
15. Young eel
17. Key
18. Direction indicator
20. Computer food
21. Reliable
23. Mr. Sharif or General Bradley
25. Ablaze
26. Señorita
28. Hole in a needle
29. Swedish coin
30. Gulf
33. Swindled
35. Las Vegas hotel
37. ____ *Town*
38. Is broadcast
41. Fido and Tabby
43. Venerate
44. Heroic poem
48. Satires
51. Mouths (Latin)
52. Be buoyant
55. Tiny
56. Playful aquatic mammal
58. Cut off
59. Partner of royal scepter
61. Farm sight
63. Diamonds (slang)
64. Subjunctive or conditional
66. Boon
70. Vat
72. Banish
74. Director Kazan
75. Brew tea
77. Tied
78. Hotel commodity
79. Novelist Ferber
80. Wise
81. Tennis terms

DOWN

1. "____ is my Son, in whom..."
2. ____ *of Eden*
3. Moses' river
4. Fantasizes
5. Corsets
6. Ventilation
7. Famous fiddler
8. One-humped camels
9. Musical note
10. Stale
11. Arthurian utopia
12. Withdraw
16. Prices
19. Appian ____
22. Coin to stop on
24. Advice (archaic)
27. Fights an imaginary opponent (compound)
30. Krupke or Muldoon
31. Tint
32. Game-show host Fleming
34. Battery terminal
36. Manipulate
39. Discolor
40. Golfer's tool
42. Health resort
45. Marijuana (slang)
46. Anger
47. *My Mother the* ____
49. Comic-book hero
50. Food fish
52. Flutters
53. Find
54. Revealed
57. "...the topless ____ of Ilium"
60. Fish product
62. Miss Dunne
65. Prima donna
67. Lily plant
68. Disturbance
69. Hoover and Aswan
71. Barbie's boyfriend
73. Support
76. Mr. Kettle

CROSSWORD PUZZLE NO. 7

Solution on page 378

ACROSS

1. Small wheeled vehicle
5. Coffee cup
8. Stage
12. Proportion
13. Bull (Spanish)
14. Center
15. Tiny quantity
16. Van Cliburn's instrument
17. Gain
18. Japanese Buddhism
19. Advise
20. Lairs
22. Recluse
24. Speaker part
27. Tree
28. Matches
29. Behold
30. "Too many cooks spoil the ___"
33. Count
34. Launching platform
35. Mature
36. Kind of nut
37. Deceased
38. Insect
39. Jutlanders
40. Small bird
41. "Parting ___ such sweet sorrow"
42. Cuts into cubes
43. "Ich ___ ein Berliner" (John F. Kennedy)

44. Take away
46. Big cat
50. Hawaiian dance
51. Irritate
52. Bustle
53. Parched
55. Itinerary
57. Decorate
58. Piece of jewelry
59. Singer Williams
60. Minos' island
61. Dessert item
62. Letter
63. Intentions

DOWN

1. Provide food
2. Do penance
3. Border
4. *A Farewell ___ Arms* (Hemingway)
5. Whimper
6. Vase
7. Benevolence
8. Play parts
9. Breakfast fare
10. Slip up
11. Quill

12. Demolish
13. Car part
16. Walkway
19. Want
21. Mysterious (variant)
23. Ship's officer
24. ___ of Hoffman
25. Gladden
26. Western show
28. Scalps
30. Hair feature
31. Wash
32. Choose
33. Doctrine
34. Golfer's term
36. Card game
37. Tiny bits of cloth
39. Use a telephone
40. Grape, e.g.
42. Tedious routine
43. Bundle
45. Concentrate
46. Sympathy
47. Sultan's playground
48. Prepares for publication
49. Caesar's city
51. Discourteous
53. Circle part
54. Estuary
56. Indefinite pronoun
57. Three (prefix)
60. The Golden State (abbr.)

CROSSWORD PUZZLE NO. 8

Solution on page 378

ACROSS

1. Stuff
5. Cry of grief
9. Ancient Greek community
14. Self (prefix)
15. African nation
16. Escape
17. Skier's milieu
19. Pale
20. Bravery
21. Place of worship
23. Black in Bologna
25. Work unit
26. Nervous
28. Presence of mind
30. French pronoun
31. Ambled
35. Acquires
37. Malt beverage
38. Brings up
40. Lucifer
43. Thing
45. Student's study aids (slang)
47. Tedious person
48. Long-running morning news program
50. Reaches across
52. Fresh
53. Hastened
55. Most silent
57. The Keystone State (abbr.)
59. Speaks
61. Fencer's weapon
62. Wave (Spanish)
64. Peruse
66. Cuts
70. Stylish shop
72. Small fruit
74. Danger
75. Novelist Zola
76. "Be it ____ so humble…"
78. Miss Moreno
79. Adored
80. "____ to you!"
81. Appear

DOWN

1. Throw
2. Pass judgment
3. Particle
4. Swabbed
5. Morning
6. Statute
7. Astronaut Shepherd
8. Muscle
9. Dedicates
10. Actress Le Gallienne
11. Masculine
12. Aromas
13. Twilled fabric
18. Senior
22. Wading bird
24. Falsify
27. Periods of time
29. Knife
31. Attend
32. Singing voice
33. Requirements
34. Falls
36. Blarney, e.g.
39. Declare
41. Greek war god
42. Salamander
44. Atlas contents
46. Small pieces
49. Longed for
51. Nap
54. Color
56. Simple tools
57. Impersonated
58. Texas tourist attraction
60. Vaults
63. Came to earth
65. Prima donna
67. Pennsylvania city
68. Ceremony
69. Close noisily
71. Arena cheer
73. Prized possession
77. Again (prefix)

CROSSWORD PUZZLE NO. 9

Solution on page 379

ACROSS

1. Reverberate
5. Arrangement
10. Flagellate
14. Regretted
15. Homily
16. Was borne
17. Signal for motion (2 words)
19. Man or Wight
20. Aged
21. Baseball terms
22. Part of Ireland
24. Paroxysms
25. Small insect
26. "When in the ____ . . ."
29. Obverse (slang, 2 words)
33. Be in harmony
34. Urgent request
35. King (Latin)
36. Taunt, reproach
37. Blessings
38. Actress Storm
39. One of the Gabors
40. Aaron and family
41. Provide food
42. Miss (Sp.)
44. Most docile
45. Buddies
46. College in New York City
47. Rise
50. Players
51. Make lace
54. At what time?
55. Flexibility
58. Ore deposit
59. Wash
60. Cupid
61. Beginning
62. Amphetamines (slang)
63. Note

DOWN

1. Therefore
2. Ringlet
3. Obey
4. Lyric poem
5. Pay homage
6. Corrects
7. Labels
8. Expression of distaste
9. Certain flowers
10. Arm parts
11. Welcomer
12. Inactive
13. British lord
18. Din
23. Circuits
24. Gratis
25. Valleys
26. Cells
27. Pointed arch
28. Name of eight popes
29. ____ the Red Menace
30. Angry
31. Removes (editor's term)
32. Put forth
34. Harbors
37. Makers
38. Contest
40. Cereal ingredient
41. Desert plants
43. Began
44. Savored
46. Behind the times
47. Cobbler's tools
48. Footwear
49. Yield
50. Sugar source
51. Hour
52. Fissionable particle
53. Novice
56. Sass
57. Rotary part

CROSSWORD PUZZLE NO. 10

Solution on page 379

ACROSS

1. Courage
6. Hair
10. Display
14. Tolerate
15. "...what ____ lurks in the..."
16. Hatteras, e.g.
17. Snooze
18. *Quid pro quo* (3 words)
20. Half a score
21. Element #82, symbol Pb
23. Touches
24. Satiety
25. Secure
27. Beset
30. Kind of song
34. Play
35. Audacious one
36. Pale
37. Model
38. Certain jails
39. Poverty
40. Diamonds (slang)
41. Sole
42. Feydeau play
43. Slum building
45. Vocation
46. Apply oil (slang)
47. Hourglass filler
48. Reference book
51. Power
52. Mr. Reiner
55. Feature of some airplanes
58. Breathing
60. Gentlemen
61. Connecticut college
62. Kind of car
63. Fencer's instrument
64. Well-known garden
65. Produce

DOWN

1. Huge
2. Competent
3. Legal claim on property
4. Poem
5. Image
6. Tin, e.g.
7. Eager
8. Insect egg
9. Gnome
10. Conceal
11. Loathing
12. Iridescent stone
13. Dampens
19. Proposal
22. Antlered animal
24. Celebrity
25. Fabric
26. Metric units
27. Confess
28. Vestige
29. Swindled
30. Peter or Paul
31. Conscious
32. Terpsichore's art
33. Join
35. Robot airplane
38. Small blister
39. Protectorate
41. Divert
42. Dream
44. Pass
45. Container
47. Tocsin
48. Church part
49. Fall
50. Folk tales
51. Remove (printing)
52. Go by car
53. Washington office
54. Curb
56. Soap ingredient
57. Young man
59. Hawaiian necklace

CROSSWORD PUZZLE NO. 11

Solution on page 379

ACROSS

1. Weapon's handle
5. Grind
9. Fat
14. Culture medium
15. Object of admiration
16. Hindu queen
17. Talk wildly
18. Star stage
19. Tidiness
20. Said
22. Flightless bird
24. Actor Randall
25. Pronoun
26. Tyke
28. Poker stake
30. Electricity
32. Kind of window
36. Extraterrestrial
39. Report
41. Anger
42. Golf stroke
43. Cut
44. Leave out
45. Summer in St. Moritz
46. Piece of 39 across
47. Lock
48. Mexican shawl
50. Prominent person
52. Bath powder
54. Constellation
55. Compass point

58. Shoo!
61. Spanish article
63. Commotion
65. Alarm
67. Skater's milieu
69. Wait
70. Socrates' forum
71. Margarine
72. Verve
73. Article of faith
74. Noted satellite
75. Minus

DOWN

1. Spartan
2. Christian love
3. Be partial
4. Star ____
5. Small fish
6. Altar promise (2 words)
7. Part of promise of 6 down
8. South American mammal
9. Gold (Italian)
10. Haggle
11. Within (prefix)
12. Witnessed
13. Strange (variant)
21. Short jacket

23. Beneath
27. Tent
29. Craggy hill
30. Caress
31. Bird
33. Speechless action
34. Greek goddess of discord
35. Soaks flax
36. King Kong and kin
37. Stringed instrument
38. Journey to Juvenal
40. Flower part
43. Facade
44. Globe
46. Mineral spring
47. Implement
49. Garb
51. Call over
53. Billiards shot
55. Expression of enjoyment
56. Ice-cream concoctions
57. Small birds
58. Expectorated
59. Prison
60. Soon (archaic)
62. Farm building
64. Son of Adam
66. Feline
68. New (comb. form)

CROSSWORD PUZZLE NO. 12

Solution on page 379

ACROSS

1. Sapphire, e.g.
4. Paper case
9. Seizes
14. Reverence
15. Surprise
16. Livy's language
17. Dominate
19. It is (16 across)
20. Straw
21. Thus
22. Skin ailment
24. Deity
25. *It Had to Be* ___
26. 1978 musical film starring John Travolta
29. Statute
30. Dispatched
31. Gambles
32. State
33. Nothing
34. Curved molding
35. Embrace
36. Common metal
39. Italy's largest river
40. Goal
41. Nut
42. Midwestern state (abbr.)
43. Mission
46. As of now
47. Lamented
49. Strange
50. Small quantity
51. Dull finish
52. Aria
54. Limb

55. Puts off
56. "___ for one..."
57. Greek letter
58. Allot
59. Cicero's six
60. Penguin's relative
61. Goal (French)
62. Spice
66. Manifest
68. Mitigated
70. Steal from
71. Musical notations
72. Word of comfort
73. Cockpit

DOWN

1. A gift
2. Female sheep
3. Checkers
4. Scale note
5. Overweight
6. Whip
7. 19 across in German
8. All-purpose interjection
9. Happy
10. Actor Walston
11. Directional preposition
12. Native American mammal
13. Nose
18. Elizabethan-age explorer
20. Geronimo's greeting
23. Lummox

24. Giddy
25. Bark
26. Feel blindly
27. Demanding nature
28. Adjectival suffix
29. Dawdle
30. Slight taste
32. I am (16 across)
33. Egg drink
35. Secreted
36. Chopped
37. Devoid
38. ___ *of Spring*
40. Plus
41. Conducted
44. Pastry
45. Confusion
46. Starchy vegetable
47. Home of Richard Burton
48. Schedule abbreviation
50. Three (prefix)
51. NY museum
52. Enjoy
53. Martini adjunct
54. Inquire
55. Hinder
57. Sets
58. Calliope, e.g.
60. Mr. Carney
61. Nonsense!
63. Bow
64. Indian region
65. Diminish
67. Spanish for 19 across
68. And (16 across)
69. Concerning (16 across)

CROSSWORD PUZZLE NO. 13

Solution on page 379

ACROSS

1. Jason's ship
5. Wild hog
9. Apiece
13. Farm structure
14. Plead
15. Missile
17. Over
18. Swamp grass
19. Condition
20. Corrects
22. Unproductive
24. Letter
25. Dine
26. Mediterranean, e.g.
27. Contained
28. Verbose
31. Unwed
33. Conceit
34. Auto
35. European capital
39. Historical period
40. Spigot
41. Tattle
42. *All about* ____ (1950 film)
43. Human
45. Pastry
46. Mr. Majors
47. Accord
49. Mix
51. Kodak product
54. Innovative
55. As well
56. Tennis term
57. Vegetable
58. Precipitated
62. Coronet
64. Price
67. Current
68. Legate
69. Scorch
70. Level
71. Obtains
72. Tortoise's rival
73. Torn

DOWN

1. Top
2. Chamber
3. Blood
4. Laid bare
5. Explode
6. Metalliferous rock
7. Epoch
8. Blush
9. Simple
10. Skill
11. Desire
12. *Grand* ____ (1932 film classic)
16. Marijuana (slang)
21. 24 hours
23. Loose overcoat
26. Knight's title
27. Solicitous person
28. Cry
29. Monster
30. Bellow
31. Patsy
32. Biblical character
34. Dog
36. Remove from type
37. Kiln
38. Lack
40. 2,000 pounds
41. Operate
44. Amount
45. Receive applause
48. Look for
49. Large snake
50. Loaf
51. Clotho, e.g.
52. Cake cover
53. Permission
55. That place
57. Country (French)
59. Abide
60. Sir Anthony ____
61. Depression
63. Decay
65. Word of discovery
66. Sailor (slang)

CROSSWORD PUZZLE NO. 14

Solution on page 379

ACROSS

1. Smooth
5. Monsters
10. Dice
14. Without (Latin)
15. Lean
16. Hanged patriot
17. Nose around
19. Gaelic
20. Toward shelter
21. Elongated fish
22. Winglike structures
24. Minister
26. Make a web
27. Eye infections
28. Hurry
31. Western heelwear
32. Pharmacist's abbreviation
34. Fall flower
35. Celestial bodies
36. *Mal de* ___
37. Spit out
38. Discoloration
39. Red or white
40. Get-up-and-go
41. Severe
42. Networks (anat.)
43. Tin (chem. symbol)
44. Indian woman's garment (var.)
45. Lost weight

46. Cut off
47. Wraith
48. Football team
50. Great ___
51. Lawyers' organization
54. Carry on
55. Tasty
57. Composer of *Bolero*
59. State with certainty
60. Suit fabric
62. Woman's name
63. Mentally healthy
64. German author
65. Actress Barbara ___

DOWN

1. To be (Latin)
2. Climbing plant
3. Organic compound
4. New (comb. form)
5. Bone (Latin)
6. Gather piece by piece
7. Infrequent
8. Naval rank (abbr.)
9. Skier's maneuver
10. Pursues
11. Stops
12. Margarine
13. Equal
18. Treatise

23. Type of equation (abbr.)
25. Makes public
26. Mulligatawny, e.g.
27. Iberian nation
28. Door fasteners
29. Colorado resort
30. Pace
31. Gaze intently
32. Lamp resident
33. Footstep
35. Pilot
36. Catcher's glove
38. Power
39. Cry
41. Rescue
42. Stairway part
44. Harsh
45. Hubbub
46. Gables or hills
47. Walks in water
48. Historical periods
49. Volcanic flow
50. Bucks' mates
51. Eager
52. Venerable English historian
53. Astronaut Sheperd or actor Hale
56. Be obliged to
58. Malt beverage
61. Of (Sp.)

FUNNY ADS

From an Indianapolis paper:
Now you can buy six different products to protect your car from your Mobil dealer.

✤

From a Long Island paper:
For Sale—Large crystal vase by lady slightly cracked.

✤

Personal in the La Marque, Texas Times:
Unemployed diamonds for sale at big discount. New four-diamond wedding ring. Slightly used seven-diamond engagement ring. Bought in burst of enthusiasm for $550, sentimental value gone, will sacrifice for $250.

✤

From the Help Wanted column in a Baltimore paper:
Would you lie to sell real estate? If so, call for an appointment to see us today. We will train.

✤

From the Long Beach, Cal. Tri-Shopper:
Jointer-Plane—used once to cut off thumb. Will sell cheap.

✤

From the Clifton Forge, Va. Daily Review:
Save regularly in our bank. You'll never reget it.

✤

In the merchandise columns of the Philadelphia Inquirer:
Tombstone slightly used. Sell cheap. Weil's Curiosity Shop.

✤

From a Dayton paper:
Now on the market—a Norelco shaver for women with three heads.

✤

From the Bargain Hunter:
Before you put your baby on the floor, clean it with a Power carpet sweeper.

✤

From the Sumner, Ia. Gazette:
For Sale: 1974 Chevy Nova in first clash condition.

From the Abilene Gazette:
For Rent or Sale: Six room house in shady neighborhood.

♔

From the Abilene, Tex. Reporter-News:
$10 reward for south side apartment. Large enough to keep young wife from going home to mother. Small enough to keep mother from coming here.

♔

Personal in a New York paper:
Young man who gets paid on Monday and is broke by Wednesday would like to exchange small loans with a young man who gets paid on Wednesday and is broke by Monday.

♔

From an advertising circular for a sporting goods store:
Special on golf clubs for good players with movable heads.

In the personal columns of a rural weekly:
Anyone found near my chicken house at night will be found there next morning.

♔

In Shears, the journal of the box-making industry:
Situation Wanted—by young woman 21 years of age. Unusual experience includes three years Necking and Stripping. Address Dept. 0-2, Shears.

♔

From a Missouri paper:
Wanted—Men, women and children to sit in slightly used pews on Sunday morning.

From the Grand Rapids Press:

Gelding—spirited but gentle. Ideal for teen-ager. For sale by parents whose daughter has discovered boys are more interesting than horses.

Classified ad in the New York Herald Tribune:

Man wanted to work in dynamite factory; must be willing to travel.

From the Atlanta Journal:

Wanted—A mahogany living room table, by a lady with Heppelwhite legs.

From the Charleston Chronicle:

Help Wanted, part-time. Smart young man to help butcher. Must be able to cut, wrap, and serve customers.

From a Parsons, Pa. paper:

Easter Matinee—Saturday Morning 10:30 a.m. Every child laying an egg in the door man's hand will be admitted free.

From the Hartford Times:

Front room, suitable for two ladies, use of kitchen or two gentlemen.

From the Birmingham Age-Herald:

Wanted—Farm mule. Must be reasonable.

From a Burns, Oregon paper:

Why go elsewhere to be cheated when you can come here?

From the Washington Post:
Sale: Oak dining room tables, seating 14 people with round legs, and 12 people with square legs.

♔

From the Help Wanted column of the Long Island Press:
Housekeeper, sleep in, must be fond of cooking children and housecleaning.

♔

From a Jamesville, Iowa paper:
Get rid of aunts. T—does the job in 24 hours. 25¢ per bottle.

♔

From a Chatham, Ontario paper:
Special foul dinner, 45¢.

♔

From an El Paso paper:
Widows made to order. Send us your specifications.

♔

From a New York paper:
Sheer stockings—Designed for dressy wear, but so serviceable that lots of women wear nothing else.

♔

From a Montesan, Wash. paper:
For sale—A full blooded cow, giving three gallons milk, two tons of hay, a lot of chickens and a cookstove.

♔

From a Willimantic, Conn. paper:
Wanted—A strong horse to do the work of a country minister.

♔

From The New York Times:
Situation wanted—Houseworker, plain crook, reliable.

♔

From a Jacksonville paper:
Man, honest, will take anything.

HOW TO SOLVE DIAMONDS

The idea is to form as many words as you can using combinations of some or all of the nine letters in the diamond. But there are certain restrictions to be observed:

1. The words must be of four letters or more.

2. Each word must contain the large letter that is in the center of the diamond.

3. Each letter in the diamond may be used only once.

4. Find one word which uses all nine letters.

5. All forms of a word are allowed, provided the letters are available. Thus, plurals, past tense, and comparative forms are all allowed.

6. Proper nouns, contractions, hyphenated, and obsolete forms are not allowed. Only one spelling of a word is acceptable; for example, *theater* or *theatre* may be used, but not both.

7. Give yourself one point for each word you list, and an additional 5 points if you get the nine-letter word.

THIS HAS PULL

At least 43 words of four letters or more (each including A) can be formed from the letters in this diamond. How many can you list?

Take five additional points if you get the nine letter word. A score of
25 is lightweight; 32 is a heavy score; and 40 is worthy of a champ.

Answers on page 380

1. _____	15. _____	30. _____
2. _____	16. _____	31. _____
3. _____	17. _____	32. _____
4. _____	18. _____	33. _____
5. _____	19. _____	34. _____
6. _____	20. _____	35. _____
7. _____	21. _____	36. _____
8. _____	22. _____	37. _____
9. _____	23. _____	38. _____
10. _____	24. _____	39. _____
11. _____	25. _____	40. _____
12. _____	26. _____	41. _____
13. _____	27. _____	42. _____
14. _____	28. _____	43. _____
	29. _____	

WAY-OUT

We found 48 words of four or more letters (including M) in this diamond. How many can you list?

A score of 25 is neat; 35 or more is sparkling.

Answers on page 380

1. _____   17. _____   33. _____

2. _____   18. _____   34. _____

3. _____   19. _____   35. _____

4. _____   20. _____   36. _____

5. _____   21. _____   37. _____

6. _____   22. _____   38. _____

7. _____   23. _____   39. _____

8. _____   24. _____   40. _____

9. _____   25. _____   41. _____

10. _____   26. _____   42. _____

11. _____   27. _____   43. _____

12. _____   28. _____   44. _____

13. _____   29. _____   45. _____

14. _____   30. _____   46. _____

15. _____   31. _____   47. _____

16. _____   32. _____   48. _____

ENCHANTÉ

There are at least 46 words of four letters or more that can be formed from the letters in this diamond, each containing the letter G. How many can you list?

Don't forget to take five points if you get the nine-letter word. A score of 25 is charming; 32 is enchanting; and 40 is devastating.

Answers on page 380

1. _____	16. _____	32. _____
2. _____	17. _____	33. _____
3. _____	18. _____	34. _____
4. _____	19. _____	35. _____
5. _____	20. _____	36. _____
6. _____	21. _____	37. _____
7. _____	22. _____	38. _____
8. _____	23. _____	39. _____
9. _____	24. _____	40. _____
10. _____	25. _____	41. _____
11. _____	26. _____	42. _____
12. _____	27. _____	43. _____
13. _____	28. _____	44. _____
14. _____	29. _____	45. _____
15. _____	30. _____	46. _____
	31. _____	

MORAL UPLIFT

We found 88 word of four letters or more (each containing T) in the letters of this diamond. How many can you list? Take five points for getting the nine-letter word.

A score of 50 is passing fair; 60 shows conviction; and 75 rates a Good Conduct medal.

Answers on page 380

1. _____	11. _____	21. _____
2. _____	12. _____	22. _____
3. _____	13. _____	23. _____
4. _____	14. _____	24. _____
5. _____	15. _____	25. _____
6. _____	16. _____	26. _____
7. _____	17. _____	27. _____
8. _____	18. _____	28. _____
9. _____	19. _____	29. _____
10. _____	20. _____	30. _____

31. _____
32. _____
33. _____
34. _____
35. _____
36. _____
37. _____
38. _____
39. _____
40. _____
41. _____
42. _____
43. _____
44. _____
45. _____
46. _____
47. _____
48. _____
49. _____

50. _____
51. _____
52. _____
53. _____
54. _____
55. _____
56. _____
57. _____
58. _____
59. _____
60. _____
61. _____
62. _____
63. _____
64. _____
65. _____
66. _____
67. _____
68. _____
69. _____

70. _____
71. _____
72. _____
73. _____
74. _____
75. _____
76. _____
77. _____
78. _____
79. _____
80. _____
81. _____
82. _____
83. _____
84. _____
85. _____
86. _____
87. _____
88. _____

DIG THIS

We list 43 words of four or more letters (including the letter P) that may be formed from this diamond. How many can you find?

Give yourself five points for finding the nine-letter word. A score of 25 is pleasing; 32 is delightful; and 40 is enchanting.

Answers on page 381

1. _____	15. _____	30. _____
2. _____	16. _____	31. _____
3. _____	17. _____	32. _____
4. _____	18. _____	33. _____
5. _____	19. _____	34. _____
6. _____	20. _____	35. _____
7. _____	21. _____	36. _____
8. _____	22. _____	37. _____
9. _____	23. _____	38. _____
10. _____	24. _____	39. _____
11. _____	25. _____	40. _____
12. _____	26. _____	41. _____
13. _____	27. _____	42. _____
14. _____	28. _____	43. _____
	29. _____	

FOR A CHANGE

There are at least 26 words of four or more letters (each containing the letter I) that can be formed from the letters in this diamond. How many can you list?

A score of 15 shows promise; 20 is lovely; and 25 should satisfy anyone.

Answers on page 381

1. _____	10. _____	18. _____
2. _____	11. _____	19. _____
3. _____	12. _____	20. _____
4. _____	13. _____	21. _____
5. _____	14. _____	22. _____
6. _____	15. _____	23. _____
7. _____	16. _____	24. _____
8. _____	17. _____	25. _____
9. _____		26. _____

SECURITY

At least 20 words, each containing an R, can be formed from the letters in this diamond. Score five points for getting the nine-letter word.

A score of 12 is safe; 15 is clever; and 18 shows you're a brain trust.

Answers on page 381

1. _____   8. _____   14. _____

2. _____   9. _____   15. _____

3. _____   10. _____   16. _____

4. _____   11. _____   17. _____

5. _____   12. _____   18. _____

6. _____   13. _____   19. _____

7. _____   20. _____

SUPPRESSION

We list 25 words (each including G) that can be formed from the letters in this diamond. How many can you find? Take five extra points for identifying the nine-letter word.

A score of 15 is fair; 19 is praiseworthy; and 24 shows there's no holding you down.

Answers on page 381

1. _____   9. _____   18. _____

2. _____   10. _____   19. _____

3. _____   11. _____   20. _____

4. _____   12. _____   21. _____

5. _____   13. _____   22. _____

6. _____   14. _____   23. _____

7. _____   15. _____   24. _____

8. _____   16. _____   25. _____

                       17. _____

UNDULATION

We found 29 words (each including I) in this diamond. How many can you list?

A score of 17 is not half-bad; 22 is excellent; and 27 gets an ovation.

Answers on page 381

1. _____	11. _____	20. _____
2. _____	12. _____	21. _____
3. _____	13. _____	22. _____
4. _____	14. _____	23. _____
5. _____	15. _____	24. _____
6. _____	16. _____	25. _____
7. _____	17. _____	26. _____
8. _____	18. _____	27. _____
9. _____	19. _____	28. _____
10. _____		29. _____

A TRIFLE

How many words of four letters or more can you make from the letters shown here? Each word must contain the large letter. Find one nine-letter word, and get five additional points.

A score of 13 is passing; 17 is nothing to sneeze at; and 21 is a serious accomplishment.

Answers on page 381

1. _____   8. _____   16. _____

2. _____   9. _____   17. _____

3. _____   10. _____   18. _____

4. _____   11. _____   19. _____

5. _____   12. _____   20. _____

6. _____   13. _____   21. _____

7. _____   14. _____   22. _____

15. _____

NONCHALANCE

We found 41 words of four or more letters (each with an A) in this diamond. How many can you list?

Take five extra points for getting the nine-letter word. If you score 25, that's cool; 32 is pretty sophisticated; and 40 is prodigious.

Answers on page 382

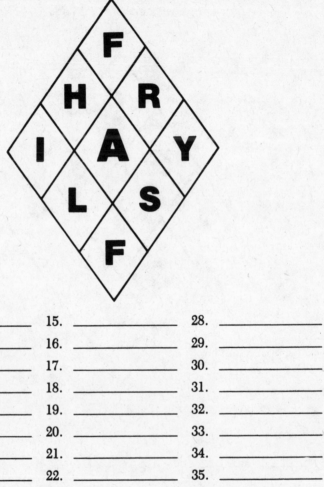

1. _____
2. _____
3. _____
4. _____
5. _____
6. _____
7. _____
8. _____
9. _____
10. _____
11. _____
12. _____
13. _____
14. _____

15. _____
16. _____
17. _____
18. _____
19. _____
20. _____
21. _____
22. _____
23. _____
24. _____
25. _____
26. _____
27. _____

28. _____
29. _____
30. _____
31. _____
32. _____
33. _____
34. _____
35. _____
36. _____
37. _____
38. _____
39. _____
40. _____
41. _____

QUINTESSENTIAL

We list 42 words of four letters or more (each containing E) that can be found from the letters in this diamond. How many can you find?
A score of 24 is fine; 31 is very good; and 40 is unique.

Answers on page 382

1. _____
2. _____
3. _____
4. _____
5. _____
6. _____
7. _____
8. _____
9. _____
10. _____
11. _____
12. _____
13. _____
14. _____

15. _____
16. _____
17. _____
18. _____
19. _____
20. _____
21. _____
22. _____
23. _____
24. _____
25. _____
26. _____
27. _____
28. _____

29. _____
30. _____
31. _____
32. _____
33. _____
34. _____
35. _____
36. _____
37. _____
38. _____
39. _____
40. _____
41. _____
42. _____

RIDDLES

The riddle is perhaps the oldest of all puzzles, and perhaps the most famous of all riddles is the one asked by the Sphinx:

> *What goes on four legs in the morning,*
> *on two at noon, and on three at night?*

Oedipus answered the riddle correctly, and thus became Oedipus Rex.

His solution: "Man. In infancy, he crawls; in his prime, he walks; in old age, he leans on a staff."

Another famous riddle is one that is reputed to have stumped Homer. Someone propounded these two lines to the bard:

> *What we caught we threw away;*
> *What we couldn't catch, we kept.*

The answer to this one is fleas.

It was a long time until the next classic riddle came along:

> *When is a door not a door?*

When it is ajar, naturally. What this riddle loses in classical phrasing it makes up in modern lunacy. Here are some more:

What is worse than a louse, stronger than God, and if you eat it you die?

> *Nothing. What is stronger than God? Nothing. What is worse than a louse? Nothing. And if you eat nothing—you die.*

What's the difference between a bird with one wing and a bird with two wings?

> *A difference of a pinion.*

I am the center of gravity, hold a capital situation in Vienna, and as I am foremost in every victory, am allowed by all to be invaluable. Always out of tune, yet ever in voice; invisible, though clearly seen in the midst of a river. I have three associates in vice, and could name three who are in love with me. Still it is in vain you seek me, for I have long been in heaven, and even now lie embalmed in the grave. Who am I?

> *The letter V.*

Four jolly men sat down to play,
And played all night till break of day;
They played for cash and not for fun,
With a separate score for every one;
Yet when they came to square accounts,
They all had made quite fair amounts!
Can you this paradox explain?
If no one lost, how could all gain?

They were musicians in a dance orchestra.

What has four wheels and flies?

A garbage truck.

What did Cleopatra say when Mark Antony asked if she was true to him?

Omar Khayyam.

What is a crick?

The noise made by a Japanese camera.

Who was Alexander Graham Bell Pulaski?

The first telephone Pole.

What do they call the Englishman who builds ten boats a month?

Sir Launchalot.

What kind of a waiter never accepts a tip?

A dumb waiter.

THE ANSWERS

THE SILVER GAME . . . . page 12

1. Born with a silver spoon in his mouth
2. Silver Springs, Maryland
3. Hi Ho Silver
4. Long John Silver
5. Silver lining
6. Silver standard or free coinage of silver
7. Silver-tongued
8. *Hans Brinker or the Silver Skates*
9. *Silver Threads Among the Gold*
10. *The Silver Cord*
11. The silver screen
12. Silverware
13. Phil Silvers
14. Silversmith
15. *The Silver Tassie*
16. Silver plated
17. *The Silver Box*
18. Silver doctor
19. Silverside
20. Silver Star Medal
21. The Silver State
22. Quicksilver
23. Speech is silver, but silence is gold
24. Silver bells
25. *The Silver Chalice*

NAME THE BEAST . . . . page 13

1. Lone wolf
2. Barfly
3. Eager beaver
4. Loan shark
5. Lounge lizard
6. Gay dog
7. Sourpuss
8. Road hog
9. Early bird
10. Sacred cow
11. Jitterbug
12. Lame duck
13. Shrimp
14. Stool pigeon
15. Slick chick
16. Black sheep
17. Work horse
18. Dumb bunny
19. Night owl
20. Dead duck or dead pigeon
21. News hawk or news hound
22. Grease monkey
23. Social lion
24. Fraidy cat

FAMOUS PAIRS . . . . page 14

1. Eve
2. Juliet
3. Jeff
4. Judy
5. Jill
6. Battery
7. Abel
8. Harriet
9. Whey
10. Pythias
11. Allen
12. Hardy
13. Cressida
14. Omega
15. Gamble
16. Desi
17. Woof
18. Jury
19. Flowers
20. Delilah
21. Chain
22. Half
23. Pocahontas
24. Mary
25. Guinivere
26. Vanzetti

27. Arrow
28. Tweedledee
29. Andy
30. Fauna
31. Olive Oyl
32. Key
33. Cleopatra
34. Pierrette
35. Gaston
36. Fury
37. Isabella
38. Hammerstein
39. Jetsam
40. Psyche
41. Schuster
42. Jerry
43. Sullivan
44. Adonis
45. Chips or tails
46. Abelard
47. Icarus
48. Farewell
49. Remus
50. Myers
51. David
52. Cry
53. Gabriel
54. Gretel
55. McCarthy
56. Pollux
57. Strain
58. Priscilla
59. Eurydice
60. Dale
61. Fletcher
62. Fontanne
63. Board
64. Nicolette
65. Rachel
66. Dixon
67. Columbine
68. Tucker
69. Tell
70. Beatrice
71. Stress
72. Melisande
73. Johnny
74. Costello
75. Bonds
76. Balances
77. Johnson
78. Isolde
79. Thisbe
80. Rustum
81. Bar
82. Soda
83. Verse
84. Chloe
85. Collected
86. Clark
87. Francesca
88. Flow
89. Laura
90. Charybdis
91. Tuck
92. Testament
93. Mehitabel
94. Joliet
95. Circumstance
96. Branch
97. Galatea

TWO OF A KIND . . . . page 17

1. Mice
2. Oxen
3. Echoes
4. Marys
5. Chateaux
6. Altos
7. Embryos
8. Talismans
9. Mosquitoes
10. Taxis
11. They or them
12. Sheaves
13. Emphases
14. Vetoes
15. Embargoes
16. Axes
17. Genera
18. Owls
19. Bison
20. Mesdames
21. Opera
22. Ourselves
23. Larvae
24. Alibis
25. Data
26. Diagnoses
27. Gallowses
28. Residua
29. Battles royal
30. Testatrices
31. Inspectors general
32. Sergeants major
33. Notaries public
34. Ottomans
35. Impetuses
36. Species
37. Valleys
38. Armfuls
39. Lullabies
40. Gross
41. Titmice

THE LITERARY ZOO . . . . page 18

THAT FOREIGN FLAVOR . . . . page 21

abruptly solve a difficulty. (Latin)
Literally, *a god from a machine*
37. Retroactive. (Latin) Literally,
from what is done afterward
38. Object of abhorrence. (French)
Literally, *black beast*
39. O the times! O the manners! (Latin)
40. An economy based on governmental
noninterference. (French) Literally,
let do
41. Evil to him who evil thinks. (French)
42. One out of many. (Latin)
43. A complete meal served at a fixed price.
(French) Literally, *host's table*
44. A small cup in which black coffee is
served. (French) Literally, *a half cup*
45. To your health! (German)
46. Comrade. (Russian)
47. Strong longing for traveling. (German)
48. Readiness in knowing how to act with
propriety. (French) Literally, *to know
how to do*
49. By itself. (Latin)
50. May it do you good! (Latin)
51. Baring the neck and shoulders. (French)
52. Please reply. (French)
53. Tit for tat. (Latin) Literally, *something
for something*
54. An article of artistic worth. (French)
55. An offense against social convention.
(French) Literally, *a false step*
56. Very loud. (Italian)
57. Suicide by disembowelment.
(Japanese) Literally, *belly cutting*
58. There is no disputing about tastes.
(Latin)

BONING UP . . . . page 24

1. Bond
2. Carbon
3. Bonus
4. Bondage
5. Sonny Bono
6. Ribbon
7. Bonnet
8. Debonair
9. Bonn
10. James Bond
11. Bonsai
12. Trombone
13. Bourbon
14. Skull-and-
crossbones
15. Bluebonnet
Bowl
16. Boner
17. Gibbon
18. *Bonanza*
19. Vagabond
20. Make no bones
about
21. Ebony
22. Bubonic plague
23. Bonfire
24. *She Wore a
Yellow Ribbon*
25. Bongo
26. Napoleon
Bonaparte
27. Bona fide
28. Bonbon
29. "Bonnie Blue
Flag"
30. *Pro bono
publico*
31. Sir Edward
Gibbon
32. *Bonhomme
Richard*
33. Gabon
34. "My Bonnie
Lies Over
the Ocean"
35. Bonito (or
bonita)
36. Bon mot
37. Boniface
38. Sorbonne
39. Sawbones
40. Bone of
Contention
41. Rosa Bonheur
42. Bon voyage
43. Dubonnet
44. T-bone steak
45. Di Bondone

MOVING VAN . . . . page 26

1. Vanish
2. Pennsylvania
3. Vandal
4. Relevant
5. Cyrus Vance
6. Weather vane
7. Advantage
8. Dick Van Dyke
9. Martin Van
Buren
10. Vancouver
11. Advance
12. Vanadium
13. Evangelists
14. Vivian Vance
15. Caravan
16. Vanilla
17. *Avanti*
18. Silvanus
19. *Vanity Fair*
20. Van Dyck or
Van Dyke
21. Erevan or
Yerevan
22. Contrivance
23. Vanguard
24. Vanderbilt
25. Dame Edith
Evans
26. Vanquish
27. Sylvania
28. *Evangeline*
29. Transylvania
30. Vanessa
Redgrave
31. Van Johnson
32. Sylvan
33. Divan
34. Ivan the
Terrible
35. Miguel de
Cervantes

FOOT BY FOOT . . . . page 28

1. Footlights
2. Blackfoot
3. To put your best
foot forward
4. Footfault
5. Footnote
6. Tenderfoot
7. Footloose and
fancy free
8. To put your
foot down
9. Footpad
10. To get off on the
wrong foot
11. Foot and mouth
disease
12. Foot-pound
13. Hotfoot
14. Footman
15. Footprint
16. Foothill
17. To have one foot
in the grave
18. Football
19. Footprints on
the sands of time
20. Footwork
21. To open your
mouth and put
your foot in it
22. Foot the bill
23. Footing
24. Underfoot

RAINBOW RIDDLE . . . . page 29

1. Scarlett O'Hara
2. *Yellow
Submarine*
3. Orange Bowl
4. In the red
5. "The Old Gray
Mare"
6. Brownout
7. Purple Onion
8. Yellow peril
9. *The Lavender
Hill Mob*
10. Elizabeth
Barrett
Browning
11. Yellowstone
12. Pink lady
13. Brown study
14. Charles
Brockden Brown

15. Crimson Tide
16. Lt. Pinkerton
17. *A Study in Scarlet*
18. Yellowknife
19. "Flying Purple People-Eater"
20. Good Gray Lady
21. "The Yellow Rose of Texas"
22. Pinkeye
23. "Purple Haze"
24. *Green Grow the Lilacs*
25. *The Scarlet Pimpernel*
26. William of Orange
27. *She Wore a Yellow Ribbon*
28. Brown Derby

Wallace
26. Enthralled
27. Hallmark
28. Maria Callas
29. Allah
30. Fred Allen
31. *All Quiet on the Western Front*
32. Fallacy
33. Valletta
34. Malleable
35. Football
36. Fallow
37. All work and no play
38. Dalliance
39. Morris K. Udall
40. Scallion
41. *All the President's Men*
42. Walla Walla
43. Edgar Allan Poe
44. Ballad

FOWL PLAY .... page 31

1. Owl
2. Nightingale
3. Lark
4. Wren
5. Raven
6. Blackbird
7. Robin
8. Sparrow
9. Orioles
10. Canary
11. Crow
12. Swallows
13. Cuckoo
14. Hawk
15. Eagles
16. Swan
17. Duck
18. Dove
19. Ostrich
20. Goose
21. Parrot
22. Falcons
23. Turkey
24. Chicken

HIM AND HER .... page 35

1. Chimney
2. Therapy
3. Whim
4. Sheriff
5. Sashimi
6. Ether
7. Chimpanzee
8. Thermos
9. Chime
10. Sherwood Forest
11. "A Hymn to Him"
12. Gherkin
13. Thimble
14. *The Shoes of the Fisherman*
15. Himalayas
16. Cherish
17. Chimerical
18. Cherbourg
19. Archimedes
20. Weather
21. Whimper
22. Inherent
23. Hiroshima
24. St. Christopher
25. Shimmer
26. Sherman (William Tecumseh)
27. Mishima
28. Panther
29. Hercules
30. Cherub
31. Whimsy
32. Wither
33. Himmler (Heinrich)
34. Sheraton (Thomas)
35. Shimmy
36. Atmosphere
37. Elohim
38. Cher

AN ALPHABET OF T'S .... page 32

1. Austere
2. Brother
3. Contact
4. Distaff
5. Epitaph
6. Fiction
7. Gesture
8. History
9. Imitate
10. Justice
11. Knotted
12. Lecture
13. Mastiff
14. Nurture
15. Ovation
16. Pretend
17. Quetzal
18. Rupture
19. Sustain
20. Torture
21. Upstart
22. Venture
23. Wistful
24. Xanthus
25. Yatters
26. Zestful

ALL IN ALL .... page 33

1. Gallon
2. Halloween
3. Baseball
4. Stall
5. Valley
6. *All About Eve*
7. Pallor
8. *The Call of the Wild*
9. Wallaby
10. Calliope
11. Rally
12. Dallas
13. *All in the Family*
14. Basketball
15. Gallop
16. *All's Well That Ends Well*
17. Hallowed
18. Tallahassee
19. Sally Rand
20. Gallery
21. "All My Loving"
22. Independence Hall
23. Ballot
24. Stallion
25. Henry A.

THE LONG AND SHORT OF IT .... page 37

1. Shortage
2. Belongings
3. "Short People"
4. Strawberry shortcake
5. The long arm of the law
6. Shorthanded
7. Henry Wadsworth Longfellow
8. Shortstop
9. Long John Silver
10. Short-lived
11. "Long Way to
Tipperary
12. Short story
13. "Long Tall Sally"
14. Short-order cook
15. Longitude
16. Bermuda shorts
17. Crawford W. Long
18. Shortwave
19. Furlong
20. Shortcomings
21. Huey P. Long
22. Short-winded
23. Prolong

24. Make a long story short
25. "Tomorrow Belongs to Me"
26. Longobard
27. Short-circuit
28. Long Kesh
29. Shortening
30. Long shot
31. Jockey shorts
32. Longines
33. Short ribs
34. Long bow
35. Shorthand
36. "The Long and Winding Road"
37. *Short Eyes*
38. Longhair
39. Shortcut
40. *Long Day's Journey into Night*
41. Make short work (or shrift) of
42. Longshoreman
43. Shortsighted
44. *The Longest Day*

9. Quaff
10. Queer
11. Quail
12. Quote
13. Quota
14. Quart
15. Quill
16. Quoth
17. Query
18. Qualm
19. Quilt
20. Quell
21. Quash
22. Quake
23. Queue

ART SMARTS . . . . page 39

1. Mart
2. Tartan
3. Moss Hart
4. Impartial
5. Cartier's
6. Upstart
7. D'Artagnan
8. Partner
9. Arthur Miller
10. Darts
11. Jean Paul Sartre
12. Garter
13. Bartlett's
14. Bret Harte
15. Parthenon
16. Martial arts
17. Spartan
18. Dartmouth
19. Gilbert Stuart
20. Martini

FILTHY LUCRE. . . . . page 40

1. Dime
2. Pennies
3. *Million Dollar*
4. Two bits
5. Nickel
6. Pound
7. Grand
8. Buck
9. Sixpence, six- pence
10. Dimes
11. Penny. . .pound
12. Cent
13. Nickels
14. Penny
15. Five cent
16. Quarter
17. Dollar
18. Penny
19. Million Dollar . . . .Five-and- Ten-Cent
20. Dime
21. Two cents
22. *Penny*
23. Dollars

WE'LL GIVE YOU A CUE. . . . . page 41

1. Quips
2. Queen
3. Quirk
4. Quick
5. Quiet
6. Quest
7. Quite
8. Quasi

PIN YOUR HOPES . . . . page 45

1. Pinup girl
2. Bowling pin
3. So quiet you can hear a pin drop
4. Pinnacle
5. Underpinning
6. Harold Pinter
7. Pincer movement
8. Pinstripe
9. Diaper pin
10. To pin someone
11. Hairpin turn
12. Pin the tail on the donkey
13. Pin the blame
14. Pinball machine
15. Pinocchio
16. Pin seal
17. Pin someone's ears back
18. Kingpin
19. Chaliapin
20. Pinochle
21. On pins and needles
22. Rolling pin
23. Pin-tailed duck
24. Pinafore
25. Hat pin
26. Pink elephants
27. Pince-nez
28. Pin someone down
29. Ping-pong
30. Pinta
31. Pin money
32. Pinwheel
33. Pinky
34. Pinch-hitter
35. Sir Arthur W. Pinero
36. Pinking shears
37. Pinto
38. Pinsetter
39. Pinpoint
40. Pinko
41. Pinkerton (Alan)
42. In the pink
43. To pinch pennies
44. With a pinch of salt
45. Pin curl
46. Pincushion
47. Pinion
48. Pink lady
49. Ezio Pinza
50. Pinata

PULLING YOUR LEG . . . . page 47

1. College
2. Pegleg or wooden leg
3. Legal
4. Legible
5. Allegro
6. American Legion
7. Legend
8. Relegate
9. Bow-legged
10. Legitimate
11. Without a leg to stand on
12. Fernand Leger
13. Alleged
14. Paraplegic
15. Delegate
16. Phlegm
17. Legumes

332

A FAR CRY . . . . page 48

1. A farm
2. James T. Farrell
3. Wells Fargo
4. David Farragut
5. Far-sighted
6. *Rebecca of Sunnybrook Farm*
7. Farina
8. Welfare
9. Mike Farrell
10. Farce
11. *A Farewell to Arms*
12. James Farley
13. Donna Fargo
14. *The Farmer's Almanac*
15. Farrago
16. So far or thus far
17. Farrah Fawcett-Majors
18. Madame Defarge
19. Nefarious
20. *A Bridge Too Far*
21. Thoroughfare
22. *Animal Farm*
23. Michael Faraday
24. *Far from the Madding Crowd*
25. Farthing
26. Farfetched
27. *Dolce far niente*
28. Fannie Farmer
29. "It is a far, far better thing that I do, than I have ever done; it is a far, far better rest that I go to, than I have ever known."
30. "So near and yet so far"
31. Few and far between
32. *The Far Side of Paradise*
33. Farthingale
34. Shofar
35. Eliza Farnham

CALCULATED RISK . . . . page 50

1. Calories
2. Local
3. California
4. Political
5. Calliope
6. Cal Tech
7. Calm
8. Musical
9. Lauren Bacall
10. Decalcomania
11. Caligula
12. Scallion
13. Calf
14. Calvary
15. Escalator
16. Calcium
17. Calvin Coolidge
18. Umbilical cord
19. Critical
20. Calico (or percale)
21. Calendar
22. Calamitous
23. Recalcitrant
24. Scald
25. Caledonia
26. Logical
27. Scalawags
28. *The Little Rascals*
29. Tuscaloosa
30. Catcall
31. Supercalifragilisticexpialidocious
32. Scalp
33. Calumny
34. Mythical
35. Scalpel
36. Calisthenics
37. Mescaline
38. Calculus
39. John Calvin
40. Scallop
41. Calligraphy
42. Optical
43. Baccalaureate
44. Callous
45. Antithetical
46. Caliban
47. Calomine lotion

THE LOW-DOWN . . . . page 52

1. Below
2. Yellow
3. Clown
4. Flow
5. Allow
6. Pillow
7. Odd Fellow
8. Flower
9. Glower (or lower)
10. Slowdown
11. Swallow
12. Henry Wadsworth Longfellow
13. Shallow
14. "Low man on the totem pole"
15. Fellow traveler
16. Weeping willow
17. Low Countries
18. Tallow
19. Plowshares
20. *Mayflower*
21. Mellow
22. Follow
23. Jean Harlow
24. "Flower children"
25. Slow-motion
26. Marshmallows
27. Bellows
28. *The Flowering Peach*
29. Hollow
30. Saul Bellow
31. Juliette Low
32. "Blowin' in the Wind"
33. *Pillow Talk*
34. Gallows
35. Christopher Marlowe
36. "Swing Low Sweet Chariot"
37. Lowbrow
38. Amy Lowell
39. Make allowances for
40. Malcolm Lowry

ARE YOU A PRO? . . . . page 54

1. Prohibition
2. O Promise Me
3. *Pilgrim's Progress*
4. Prosaic
5. Prone
6. Prosciutto
7. Prologue
8. Proverb
9. Promotion
10. Prompt
11. Problem
12. Proxy
13. Prosit
14. Pro forma
15. Prolong
16. Produce
17. Prolix
18. Due process
19. Promissory note
20. *Prometheus Bound*
21. Prodigal
22. Propagate
23. *The Prophet*
24. Provincetown, Mass.

PLACE YOUR BETS . . . . **page 55**

1. Alphabet
2. Hebetude
3. Betwixt and between
4. Sherbet
5. Tibet
6. Bette Davis
7. Beta
8. *Bete noire*
9. Bethlehem
10. Betel
11. Betroth
12. Elizabeth I
13. "Better half"
14. *The Betsy*
15. Bethesda
16. Betty Boop
17. Betray
18. Phi Beta Kappa
19. *Macbeth*

THE SKIN GAME . . . . **page 56**

1. To skin alive
2. Skinflint
3. To jump out of one's skin
4. B.F. Skinner
5. Skinflick
6. By the skin of one's teeth
7. A skinful
8. Skin deep
9. No skin off one's back
10. *I've Got You Under My Skin*
11. To have a thick skin
12. To come out with a whole skin
13. Otis Skinner
14. Cornelia Otis Skinner
15. Skinny
16. Leonard Baskin
17. John Ruskin
18. To get under one's skin
19. To have a thin skin
20. Skin and bones
21. Skin graft
22. Skin tight
23. There are many ways to skin a cat
24. Buskins
25. To skinny dip

STONE UPON STONE . . . . **page 57**

1. Tombstone
2. Gallstone
3. "Stonewall" Jackson
4. Lucy Stone
5. The Stone Age
6. To keep one's nose to the grindstone
7. A rolling stone gathers no moss
8. Stone marten
9. Yellowstone Park
10. Stone deaf
11. Brimstone
12. The Great Stone Face
13. A stone's throw
14. Harlan Fisk Stone
15. To leave no stone unturned
16. Lodestone
17. Blarney Stone
18. Stone broke
19. To get blood out of a stone
20. Rosetta Stone
21. Stonehenge
22. Moonstone
23. Brownstone
24. Cornerstone

HAPPY LANDINGS . . . . **page 58**

1. No man is an island
2. Ireland
3. Michael Landon
4. Colander
5. Bland
6. *Orlando*
7. Land of Opportunity
8. Slander
9. *Babes in Toyland*
10. Ellis Island
11. Portland
12. Martin Landau
13. Switzerland
14. Devil's Island
15. "Sweet land of liberty"
16. Landlord, landlady
17. Land of Enchantment
18. Gland
19. Mainland
20. Garland
21. *Treasure Island*
22. Thailand
23. *Islands in the Stream*
24. Rhode Island
25. Disneyland
26. Blandishment
27. Poland
28. Never Never Land
29. *The Sugarland Express*
30. Grover Cleveland
31. Flanders
32. Land of the free
33. Ray Milland
34. Land of Beulah
35. Michael Bilandic
36. Landslide
37. Howland Owl
38. Clandestine
39. Homeland
40. Holland or The Netherlands
41. "This Land Is Your Land"
42. Swaziland

FOR OLD TIMES' SAKE . . . . **page 60**

1. Holdup
2. Scaffold
3. Old Glory
4. Withhold
5. William Holden
6. Twofold
7. Old-fashioned
8. Soldier
9. Barney Olds
10. Old Testament

11. Scold
12. *Goldfinger*
13. Golda Meir
14. Old maid
15. *Twice Told Tales*
16. Bold
17. "The Old Man and the Sea"
18. Folderol
19. *Arsenic and Old Lace*
20. Doldrums
21. Behold
22. Goldenrod
23. Old Hickory
24. Professor Harold Hill
25. Sold
26. Hermione Gingold
27. Beholden
28. *The Spy Who Came In from the Cold*
29. "Old Folks at Home"
30. The good old days
31. Folding money
32. You can't teach an old dog new tricks
33. "Old Man River"
34. Moldavia
35. *The Gold Rush*
36. Solder
37. Old King Cole
38. *Das Rheingold*
39. Goldie Hawn
40. Old Lady of Threadneedle Street
41. Henrietta Szold
42. Cotswolds
43. Mold

ON THE ROCKS. . . . . page 62

1. Davy Crockett
2. Frock
3. Rocking chair
4. Rock 'n' roll
5. "Rock of Ages"
6. Rock Hudson
7. Rocket
8. *The Rockford Files*
9. Rocky road
10. Black Rock
11. *Rocky*
12. Rock Eagle
13. Rock of Gibraltar
14. "Big Rock Candy Mountain"
15. Crock
16. "Rock around the Clock"
17. Rockefellers
18. Bedrock
19. Rocky the Flying Squirrel
20. *The Hot Rock*
21. Charles Brockden Brown
22. Rockefeller Center
23. Sprocket

24. Rock of Cashel
25. "I Am a Rock"
26. Rockettes
27. Defrock
28. Rocky Graziano
29. *Bad Day at Black Rock*
30. Between the rock and the hard place
31. Knute Rockne
32. *Crock of Gold*
33. Rocky Mountain spotted fever
34. On the rocks
35. Crockery or crockpot cookery
36. Rock bottom
37. Brockton

UP IN ARMS . . . . page 64

1. Alarm clock
2. Farming
3. Swarm
4. Gendarme
5. Charm
6. Varmint
7. No harm in trying
8. *Carmen*
9. Schoolmarm
10. Tarmac
11. *Armies of the Night*
12. Marmoreal
13. Armistice
14. Pharmacy
15. Barmaid
16. Armada
17. Marmalade
18. Garment
19. Carmel
20. Harmony
21. Warm Springs
22. Lukewarm
23. *The Farmer's Daughter*
24. Armadillo
25. Carmine
26. *A Farewell to Arms*
27. Swarmy
28. *The Man With the Golden Arm*
29. Parmesan
30. Army Archard
31. Marmoset
32. *Arms and the Man*
33. Harmless
34. Karma
35. Armegeddon
36. *Animal Farm*
37. Armenia
38. Marmaduke
39. Sergeant-at-arms
40. Disarmament

HERE AND HOW . . . . page 66

1. "Now I lay me down to sleep . . ."
2. The Tomb of the Unknown Soldier
3. Nowhere
4. Minnow
5. *Now, Voyager*
6. Snow White
7. Renown
8. Abominable Snowman
9. "Do You Want to Know a Secret?"
10. "Now is the time for all good men to come to the aid of their party"
11. Now and then
12. "The Snows of Kilimanjaro"

13. Snowmobile
14. "Do You Know the Way to San Jose"
15. Snowbird
16. *The Unknown Soldier and His Wife*
17. Knowledge is power
18. "How now, brown cow?"
19. "Now is the winter of our discontent..."
20. *Heaven Knows, Mr. Allison*
21. *How Now, Dow Jones*

27. Albany
28. Banal
29. "Habanera"
30. *Bananas*
31. Bantam
32. Bandit
33. "American Bandstand"
34. John Banner
35. Shebang

36. Bangs
37. Bandersnatch
38. Albania
39. Banquet
40. Durban
41. Banter
42. Tallulah Bankhead
43. Banshee
44. Bangladesh

BELLRINGERS . . . . page 67

1. Ding dong bell
2. Campbell's
3. Belligerent
4. Liberty Bell
5. Griffin Bell
6. Belle of the ball
7. Bellow
8. Edward Bellamy
9. Clarabelle
10. *For Whom the Bell Tolls*
11. Belladonna
12. Ante-bellum
13. Bellybuster or belly-flop
14. Bellini
15. Bellwether
16. Hubbell Gardner
17. Embellish
18. Bellicose
19. Ma Bell
20. *A Bell for Adano*
21. Belly dancer

22. Boxer Rebellion
23. Bella Abzug
24. Bellerophon
25. Saul Bellow
26. Belle Watling
27. Barbells or dumbbells
28. Bellybutton
29. *Bell, Book and Candle*
30. Hell's bells
31. Whiskey Rebellion
32. *Sunrise at Campobello*
33. Ralph Bellamy
34. *The Bells of St. Mary's*
35. James Branch Cabell
36. Vincenzo Bellini
37. *The Bell Jar*
38. Bell-bottoms
39. Maybelline

BOTTOMS UP. . . . . page 71

1. Upper-classman
2. Supper
3. "Up yours!"
4. Upheaval
5. Ups and downs
6. Give up
7. Seven Up
8. "Why don't you come up and see me sometime?"
9. Upholster
10. John Updike

11. Upper
12. Cupola
13. Muppets
14. Upton Sinclair
15. Frameup
16. "Up, Up, and Away"
17. Live it up
18. Uppity
19. *Once Upon a Mattress*
20. Upset

CAT GOT YOUR TONGUE? . . . . page 72

1. Category
2. Cataract
3. Ducat
4. *Cat's Cradle*
5. Cathedral
6. Catsup
7. Carrie Chapman Catt
8. Cheshire cat
9. Catacombs

10. Catcall
11. Scatter
12. Decathlon
13. *Catch-22*
14. Catskills
15. Catatonia
16. Catullus
17. Catapult
18. Cat-o'-nine-tails

GET ON THE BANDWAGON . . . . page 69

1. Bank
2. Banish
3. "The Star-Spangled Banner"
4. Turban
5. Urban
6. Contraband
7. Banana
8. Bandage
9. Fairbanks
10. Caliban
11. Disband
12. Abandon

13. Urbana
14. Bangles
15. Bannister
16. *Top Banana*
17. Bane
18. Cabana
19. Abba Eban
20. Banjo
21. Lebanon
22. Corybant
23. Bangkok
24. Bandanna
25. Urbane
26. "Ban the bomb"

IN THE CAN. . . . . page 73

1. Canada
2. Pecan
3. Cannibal
4. Incantation
5. Canvas
6. "Oh, say can you see..."
7. Candidate
8. Vatican City
9. Cannon
10. Arcane
11. *Tropic of Cancer*
12. *You Can't Take It With You*

13. Those who can, do; those who can't, teach; those who can't teach, teach teachers.
14. Mendicant
15. Canopy
16. Vacant
17. Canine
18. Mercantilist
19. Canton
20. Toucan
21. Canal
22. Cotton Candy

23. Cannes
24. Decanter
25. Paddle your own canoe
26. Hurricanes
27. Canary Islands
28. Isadora Duncan
29. *The Ugly American*
30. Chicanery
31. Canapes
32. Pemmican
33. "Can't Buy Me Love"
34. Tuscany
35. Canteloupe
36. *Yes, I Can!*
37. Candlestick Park
38. Incandescent
39. *The Canterbury Tales*
40. Pelican
41. Bel canto

SALLY FORTH . . . . page 75

1. Salmon
2. Nasal
3. Salem
4. Salt
5. Salad days
6. Rehearsal
7. Saliva
8. Dr. Jonas Salk
9. Sal Mineo
10. Salient
11. Saloon
12. Psalm
13. Salt Lake City
14. Salambo
15. Salamander
16. Missal
17. A grain of salt
18. Sally Bowles
19. Rosalind Russell
20. Salami
21. Salisbury
22. Salvo
23. Pablo Casals
24. Salad
25. Basalt
26. Salutation
27. Salmonella
28. *Death of a Salesman*
29. Thessaly
30. Vassel
31. El Salvador
32. "Salt of the Earth"
33. Absalom
34. Saluki
35. Dar es Salaam
36. Salome
37. Sally Rand
38. *Pharsalia*
39. Salver
40. Sieur de la Salle
41. Saltimbocca
42. Antonio Salazar
43. Salon

MONTH BY MONTH . . . . page 77

1. Mayan
2. Ides of March
3. Mayerling
4. St. Augustine
5. *March of the Wooden Soldiers*
6. *September 30, 1955*
7. October Revolution
8. Mayflower
9. "April is the cruelest month"
10. Maybe
11. "It's June in January"
12. Augustus Caesar
13. *December Bride*
14. *Born on the Fourth of July*
15. *April Love*
16. June Lockhart
17. Mayo
18. "Marching Through Georgia"
19. *Teahouse of the August Moon*
20. The March King
21. Juneau
22. "September Song"
23. Mayonnaise
24. *The Guns of August*
25. May-December romance
26. *The April Fools*
27. "What is so rare as a day in June?"
28. "The Merry Month of May"
29. Augusta
30. Maynard G. Krebs
31. Jejune
32. Mayor
33. *Seven Days in May*
34. "June Is Busting Out All Over"
35. Mayberry
36. Frederic March
37. Mayhem
38. May Day
39. *The First Monday in October*

TEACHER'S PET . . . . page 79

1. Penn
2. Peter Pan
3. Petulant
4. Petrol
5. *Petrified Forest*
6. Pet peeve
7. Petit four
8. Petty larceny
9. *Petrouchka*
10. Petticoat
11. Petroglyph
12. Petunia
13. Petition
14. Petrarch
15. Petit mal
16. Peter Stuyvesant
17. Petite
18. Pettifoggery
19. Petty cash
20. Hoisted on one's own petard

GETTING MAD . . . . page 80

1. Madrid
2. Madison Avenue
3. Nomad
4. Sierra Madre
5. Madonna
6. Madwoman of Chaillot
7. Ramadan
8. The Mad Hatter
9. James Madison
10. Madder than a wet hen
11. *Madame Butterfly*
12. *The Treasure of the Sierra Madre*
13. "Mademoiselle"
14. Spanish Armada
15. Madagascar
16. Pomade
17. *It's a Mad, Mad, Mad, Mad World*
18. Madras
19. Lester Maddox
20. Mad Anthony Wayne
21. "Lady Madonna"
22. Mad dogs and Englishmen
23. Madrigal
24. Ramada Inns
25. Prima donna
26. Madeira
27. *Madeline*
28. Madam
29. Madame Tussaud's
30. Animadversion
31. Salvador de Madariaga
32. Madame de Stael
33. Madcap

BIG MAC . . . . page 82

1. Stomach
2. Macaw
3. Douglas MacArthur
4. Macramé
5. Ted Mack
6. Machete
7. Macadam (or tarmac)
8. Immaculate
9. Macaroni
10. Sumac
11. *The Time Machine*
12. Macy's
13. Mackerel
14. Grimace
15. Smack
16. *Macbeth*
17. Antimacassar
18. *Danse Macabre*
19. *MacMillan and Wife*
20. James Ramsay MacDonald
21. *Merrimack*
22. Emaciated
23. Macron
24. Niccolo Machiavelli
25. Macedonia
26. Macadamia
27. Mack the Knife
28. Macao
29. Smacker
30. Maccabees
31. Hammacher Shlemmer
32. Macaroon
33. "Mother Machree"
34. Telemachus
35. Macintosh
36. *Andromache*
37. Archibald MacLeish
38. Macduff

22. To accept what one has fought against.
23. The abode of bliss in the world to come.
24. To encounter an opponent who is unexpectedly strong.
25. Something given with a treacherous purpose.
26. To depart this life.
27. Between two dangers, neither of which can be avoided.
28. To cleverly give a dexterous turn to a situation.
29. A burdensome possession.
30. To give alarm without occasion.
31. An illusion of plenty.
32. To admonish with severity and directness.
33. Things affectedly despised because they cannot be possessed.
34. To be rolling in riches.
35. Poignant, delicate wit.
36. To dispose of a difficulty by prompt, arbitrary action.

FOR THE LITERATI . . . . page 84

1. False, affected, hypocritical sorrow.
2. To perform a task without essential material.
3. To make peace.
4. To take things to a place where they already abound.
5. To exhibit cowardice.
6. A stale joke.
7. To take an irrevocable, decisive step.
8. Inextinguishable laughter.
9. A mood of serious or perplexed absorption.
10. The best or largest part.
11. To do a risky deed.
12. A vulnerable point.
13. A private, hidden source of shame or grief.
14. A parting shot.
15. A choice without an alternative.
16. To use artificial, stilted language.
17. The whole.
18. To use artificially beautify something of supreme loveliness.
19. One who maliciously afflicts while ostensibly comforting.
20. To feign ignorance or illness with intent to deceive.
21. An entertainment which causes loss to those providing it.

PLACE NAMES . . . . page 23

1. Irving Berlin
2. Virginia Dare
3. Texas Guinan
4. Stephen Birmingham
5. Jack London
6. India Wilkes
7. Nathan Detroit
8. Georgia O'Keefe
9. Anatole France
10. Robert Indiana
11. Buffalo Bill
12. Virginia Woolf
13. Morey Amsterdam
14. Washington Irving
15. Montgomery Clift

ALL IN SEASON . . . . page 42

1. Bedspring
2. Indian summer
3. Winter-proof
4. Pitfall
5. *Silent Spring*
6. *Winterset*
7. Mainspring
8. Summer school
9. Wintergreen
10. Niagara Falls
11. Offspring
12. Winter melon
13. Handspring
14. Summer stock
15. *The Winter of Our Discontent*
16. Nightfall
17. *Winter's Tales*
18. Jonathan Winters
19. Falling star
20. "Summertime"
21. "Can Spring be far behind?"
22. Fall behind
23. *Suddenly Last Summer*
24. Sioux Falls

25. Wellspring
26. "Winter Wonderland"
27. *After the Fall*
28. *Midsummer Night's Dream*
29. *The Fall of the House of Usher*
30. Springield rifle
31. "Fall in!"
30. Springfield rifle
33. *Summer and Smoke*
34. Downfall
35. Springbod
36. *The Winter's Tale*
37. *The Birds Fall Down*
38. Spring water
39. Springer spaniel
40. *Rise and Fall of the Third Reich*
41. To fall on one's face
42. Spring cleaning
43. "In the Good Old Summer Time"
44. Fall foul of
45. Spring training
46. *The Long Hot Summer*
47. The Winter Garden
48. To fall back on
49. "She's no spring chicken"
50. *A Lion in Winter*

LYMPHOCYTES . . . . page 87

RATTAN RACEWAY . page 90

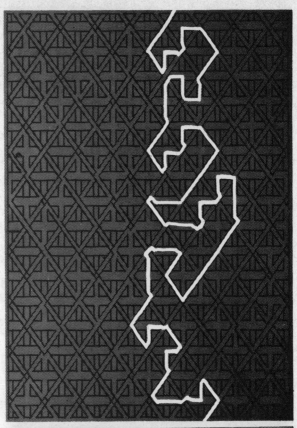

SIX TRICKS . . . . page 91

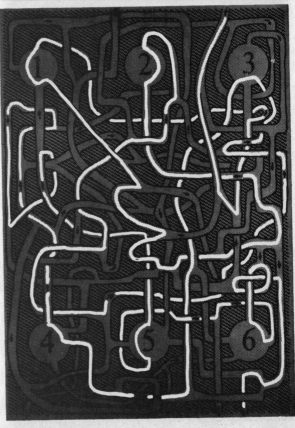

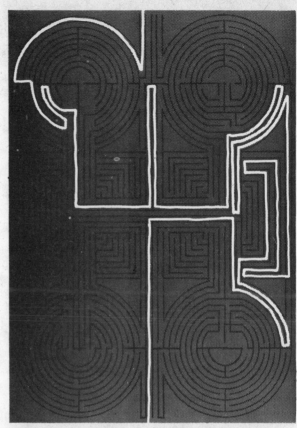

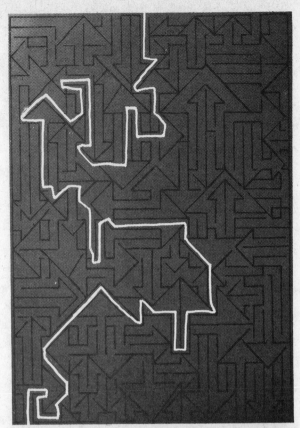

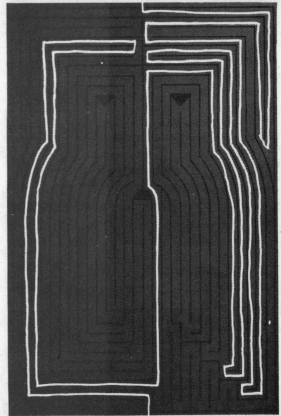

345

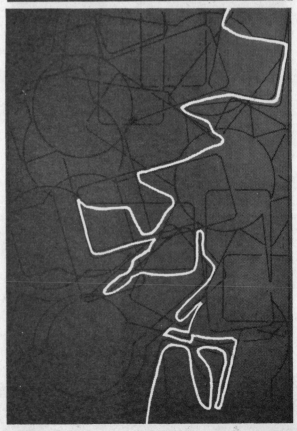

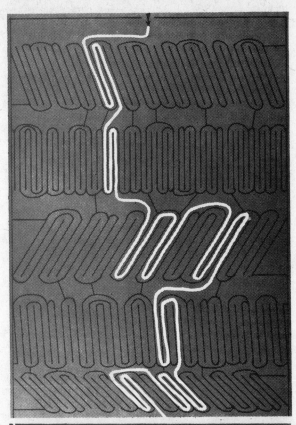

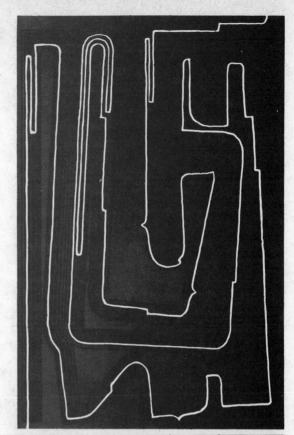

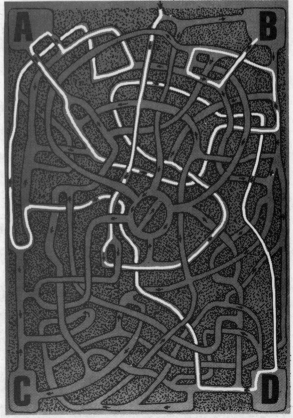

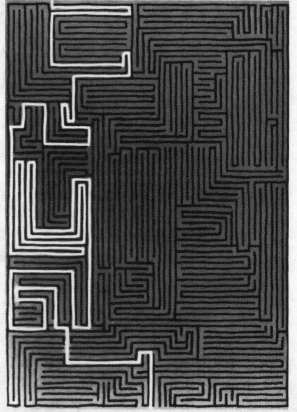

HOW TO HOLD MY OLD MAN . . . . **page 110**

Pa, apt, part, party, pastry.

GUILTY BUT WHITEWASHED . . . . **page 111**

Pet, pert, tripe, pirate, parties, traipses, parasites

IN SHORT ORDER . . . . **page 111**

An, pan, span, pansy, snappy.

GERIATRICS . . . . **page 112**

Pa, nap, span, pains, panics, spinach.

JUST DESSERTS . . . . **page 112**

At, tar, tart, treat, taster, starter, retreats.

THE LITERATI . . . . **page 113**

To, top, spot, poets, poster, riposte.

AT THE SHRINK'S . . . . **page 113**

Id, rid, dire, rides, reside, desires, residents, presidents.

LUM. . . . . **page 118**

1. Alum
2. Aluminum
3. Alumnus
4. Antebellum
5. Asylum
6. Clump
7. Columbine
8. Flummery
9. Glum
10. Illuminate
11. Lumbago
12. Lumber
13. Lumen
14. Luminary
15. Luminous
16. Lummox
17. Lump
18. Lumpen-proletariat
19. Lumpkin
20. Pendulum
21. Plum

22. Plumber
23. Plume
24. Plummet
25. Plump
26. Postbellum
27. Slum
28. Slumber
29. Slump
30. Vellum
31. Volume
32. Voluminous

LTI. . . . . **page 119**

1. Altimeter
2. Altitude
3. Cultivate
4. Ill-timed
5. Kiltie
6. Multiply
7. Saltine
8. Stultify
9. Ultimate
10. Ultimatum

ECH . . . . **page 119**

1. Beech
2. Beseech
3. Echelon
4. Echo
5. Lecher
6. Leech
7. Mechanic
8. Rechannel
9. Recharge
10. Recheck
11. Screech
12. Speech
13. Technical
14. Technique

HOU . . . . **page 119**

1. Although
2. Hour
3. Houri
4. House
5. Should
6. Shoulder
7. Shout
8. Silhouette
9. Thou
10. Though
11. Thought
12. Without

CTU . . . . **page 120**

1. Actual
2. Actuary
3. Actuate
4. Cactus
5. Conflictual
6. Contractual
7. Dictum
8. Effectuate
9. Factual
10. Fluctuate
11. Fructuous
12. Ineffectual
13. Instinctual
14. Intellectual
15. Juncture
16. Lecture
17. Micturate
18. Noctuid
19. Nocturnal
20. Picture
21. Picturesque
22. Punctual
23. Punctuate
24. Puncture

25. Rectum
26. Rectus
27. Sanctuary
28. Sanctum
29. Stricture
30. Structure
31. Tactual
32. Tincture
33. Unctuous
34. Victual
73. Persimmon
74. Philharmonic
75. Promontory
76. Remonstrate
77. Salmon
78. Salmonella
79. Sanctimonious
80. Semimonthly
81. Sermon
82. Simony
83. Testimonial
84. Testimony
85. Thermonuclear
86. Trimonthly

OPA . . . . page 120

1. Copacetic
2. Coparcenary
3. Copartner
4. Dopamine
5. Dopant
6. Jeopardy
7. Leopard
8. Menopause
9. Myopathy
10. Opacity
11. Opah
12. Opal
13. Opalescent
14. Opaque
15. Propaganda
16. Propagate
17. Propane
18. Topaz
19. Zooparasite

VOR . . . . page 122

1. Carnivorous
2. Cavort
3. Endeavor
4. Favor
5. Favorite
6. Flavor
7. Frugivorous
8. Herbivorous
9. Ivory
10. Omnivorous
11. Savor
12. Savory
13. Voracious
14. Vortex

MON . . . . page 121

1. Acrimonious
2. Admonish
3. Alimony
4. Almond
5. Among
6. Antimony
7. Bimonthly
8. Common
9. Demon
10. Demonstrate
11. Diamond
12. Fishmonger
13. Harmonica
14. Harmonics
15. Harmony
16. Hegemony
17. Ironmonger
18. Lemon
19. Matrimony
20. Mnemonic
21. Monad
22. Monandrous
23. Monarch
24. Monastery
25. Monaural
26. Monetary
27. Money
28. Monger
29. Mongolism
30. Mongoose
31. Mongrel
32. Moniker
33. Monism
34. Monitor
35. Monk
36. Monkey
37. Monkshood
38. Monobasic
39. Monochromatic
40. Monocle
41. Monody
42. Monogamy
43. Monogram
44. Monograph
45. Monolith
46. Monologue
47. Monomania
48. Monomial
49. Mononucleosis
50. Monoplane
51. Monopoly
52. Monorail
53. Monosodium
54. Monosyllable
55. Monotheistic
56. Monotone
57. Monotonous
58. Monotype
59. Monoxide
60. Monsieur
61. Monsignor
62. Monsoon
63. Monster
64. Monstrance
65. Montage
66. Monte
67. Month
68. Monument
69. Monumental
70. Pandemonium
71. Parsimonious
72. Patrimony

WED . . . . page 122

1. Allowed
2. Awed
3. Bellowed
4. Billowed
5. Borrowed
6. Bowed
7. Brewed
8. Cawed
9. Crowed
10. Flawed
11. Flowed
12. Followed
13. Furrowed
14. Glowed
15. Gnawed
16. Hallowed
17. Harrowed
18. Hollowed
19. Jawed
20. Mellowed
21. Mewed
22. Mowed
23. Narrowed
24. Plowed
25. Rowed
26. Sawed
27. Sewed
28. Showed
29. Sinewed
30. Snowed
31. Spewed
32. Stewed
33. Stowed
34. Thawed
35. Thewed
36. Towed
37. Wallowed
38. Wedding
39. Wedge
40. Wedlock
41. Yellowed

THU . . . . page 123

1. Ailanthus
2. Enthusiasm
3. Thud
4. Thug
5. Thulium
6. Thumb
7. Thumbnail
8. Thumbscrew
9. Thumbtack
10. Thump
11. Thunder
12. Thunderbird
13. Thunderbolt
14. Thunderhead
15. Thunderous
16. Thunderstruck
17. Thurible
18. Thus

27. Financial
28. Flouncing
29. Glancing
30. Incident
31. Incidental
32. Incinerate
33. Incipient
34. Incision
35. Incisive
36. Incisor
37. Incite
38. Incivility
39. Jouncing
40. Lancing
41. Manciple
42. Mincing
43. Nuncio
44. Oncidium
45. Pencil
46. Pouncing
47. Prancing
48. Principal
49. Principle
50. Pronunciation
51. Provincial
52. Reconcile
53. Renouncing
54. Silencing
55. Stencil
56. Trouncing
57. Uncial
58. Uncinaria
59. Uncivil
60. Uncivilized

NDA. . . . . page 128

1. Agenda
2. Appendage
3. Bandage
4. Bandanna
5. Bondage
6. Commendation
7. Fandango
8. Foundation
9. Fundamental
10. Grandad
11. Mandamus
12. Mandarin
13. Mandate
14. Mandatory
15. Mendacious
16. Mundane
17. Panda
18. Quandary
19. Recommen-
dation
20. Sandal
21. Sandalwood
22. Spondaic
23. Tendance

ARD. . . . . page 128

1. Ardent
2. Ardor
3. Arduous
4. Backward
5. Bard
6. Beard
7. Board
8. Card
9. Cardinal
10. Cardoon
11. Downward
12. Eardrum
13. Fardel
14. Forward
15. Guard
16. Hard
17. Hardly
18. Heard
19. Hoard
20. Inward
21. Lard
22. Leeward
23. Nard
24. Outward
25. Pardner
26. Pardon
27. Poniard
28. Reward
29. Shard
30. Sideward
31. Starboard
32. Stardust
33. Sward
34. Toward
35. Upward
36. Ward
37. Warden
38. Wardrobe
39. Yard

EMI . . . . page 127

1. Abstemious
2. Academic
3. Anemia
4. Effeminate
5. Emigrant
6. Eminent
7. Emir
8. Emissary
9. Emit
10. Endemic
11. Foremilk
12. Hemidemisemi-
quaver
13. Hemihedral
14. Hemiplegia
15. Hemisphere
16. Leukemia
17. Polemic
18. Remind
19. Reminisce
20. Remint
21. Remiss
22. Remission
23. Remit
24. Remittance
25. Semiabstract
26. Semiannual
27. Semiaquatic
28. Semiarboreal
29. Semiautomatic
30. Semiautonomous
31. Semicircle
32. Semicolon
33. Semiconscious-
ness.
34. Semidetached
35. Semidominant
36. Semifinal
37. Semiflexible
38. Semiformal
39. Semi-
independent
40. Semilethal
41. Semiliterate
42. Semimoist
43. Semimonthly
44. Semimystical
45. Seminal
46. Seminar
47. Seminary
48. Seminomad
49. Seminude
50. Semiofficial
51. Semiotic
52. Semiprecious
53. Semiprivate
54. Semipro-
fessional
55. Semipublic
56. Semireligious
57. Semiretired
58. Semirigid
59. Semisecret
60. Semiskilled
61. Semisoft
62. Semisolid
63. Semisweet
64. Semitone
65. Semitropical
66. Semiweekly
67. Semiyearly
68. Uremia

RSI . . . . page 129

1. Adversity
2. Aversion
3. Carsick
4. Conversion
5. Countersign
6. Cursive
7. Discursive
8. Diversified
9. Diversion
10. Excursion
11. Farsighted
12. Immersion
13. Incursion
14. Nearsighted
15. Oversight
16. Oversized
17. Parsimony
18. Persiflage
19. Persimmon
20. Persist
21. Perversion
22. Reversion
23. Torsion
24. Underside
25. Undersigned
26. Undersized
27. University
28. Ursine
29. Varsity
30. Versify
31. Version

MPL page 129

1. Ample
2. Amplify
3. Complacent
4. Complain
5. Complement
6. Complete
7. Complex
8. Complexion
9. Complicate
10. Complicity
11. Compliment
12. Comply
13. Contemplate
14. Crumple
15. Dimple
16. Dumpling
17. Employ
18. Exemplify
19. Implement
20. Implicate
21. Implosion
22. Imply
23. Pimple
24. Rumple
25. Sample
26. Simple
27. Simpleton
28. Simplify
29. Simplistic
30. Templar
31. Template
32. Temple
33. Templet
34. Trample

EMO page 130

1. Bemoan
2. Chemotherapy
3. Democracy
4. Demolish
5. Demon
6. Demonstration
7. Demotion
8. Emoliate
9. Emory
10. Emote
11. Emotion
12. Hegemony
13. Hemoglobin
14. Hemophilia
15. Lemon
16. Lemonade
17. Memo
18. Memoir
19. Memorabilia
20. Memorial
21. Memory
22. Premonition
23. Remonstrate
24. Remorse
25. Remote
26. Remove
27. Semolina
28. Tremor

EPT page 130

1. Accept
2. Adept
3. Concept
4. Crept
5. Deceptive
6. Except
7. Inception
8. Inept
9. Kleptomania
10. Misconception
11. Peptic
12. Peptone
13. Perception
14. Receptacle
15. Reception
16. Receptive
17. Reptile
18. Sceptre
19. Septennial
20. Septic
21. Septuagenarian
22. Septum
23. Skeptical
24. Slept
25. Streptococcus
26. Swept
27. Transept
28. Wept

CLE page 131

1. Article
2. Barnacle
3. Clean
4. Clear
5. Cleat
6. Cleavage
7. Cleaver
8. Cleft
9. Clench
10. Clergy
11. Clerk
12. Clever
13. Inclement
14. Particle

ORS page 131

1. Borscht
2. Corset
3. Corso
4. Doorstep
5. Dorsal
6. Endorse
7. Floorshow
8. Gorse
9. Hors de combat
10. Hors d'oeuvres
11. Horse
12. Morse
13. Morsel
14. Remorse
15. Torsion
16. Torso
17. Worse
18. Worship
19. Worst
20. Worsted

OCH page 131

1. Brooch
2. Epoch
3. Hooch
4. Loch
5. Mocha
6. Mooch
7. Ochlophobia
8. Ochre
9. Parochial
10. Pooch
11. Smooch
12. Trochee

THE BLIND ABBOT page 149

18 monks

1	O	8
O		O
8	O	1

20 monks

4	1	4
1		1
4	1	4

24 monks

3	3	3
3		3
3	3	3

32 monks

1	7	1
7		7
1	7	1

36 monks

O	9	O
9		9
O	9	O

THE COUNTERFEIT COIN .... page 150

Two. The wise man divided the nine coins into three groups of three. First he weighed Group A against Group B. If they balanced, then he knew that each of the coins in these groups were of the same weight, and therefore each of these six coins were made of pure gold.

The counterfeit would then be found in the last group of three. He then took any two of the last three remaining coins, and put one of these two coins on each side of the scale. If these two coins balanced, then the counterfeit coin would have to be the last unweighed coin. If the two coins did not balance, then of course, the lighter coin—the one on the scale that went up—would be the counterfeit coin.

Now suppose that in the first instance, when weighing the two groups of three, one side of the scale went up. It would then be clear that the lighter coin was among this group of three. The sage would then proceed, as stated above, with the three coins among which the lightest one was to be found.

THE LADY AND THE TIGER......... page 151

Before the waiting populace, he plunged his hand into the box, drew forth a paper, and then without reading it, plunged it into his mouth, chewed it, and swallowed it. He then calmly announced that the king's chamberlain would read the remaining piece of paper. Whatever word was written on the remaining piece of paper in the box, the one that he, the candidate, drew forth from the box was clearly the other alternative. Since the paper that was left had the word *Tiger* on it, it was clear to everybody that the young man had indeed won the princess.

THE FIVE OFFICE BOYS .... page 152

	R	W	A	G	H	TOTAL PTS.
Percy	2	3	4	3	0	12
Walter	1	2	3	4	1	11
Fred	4	1	1	2	2	10
Cyril	0	4	2	0	3	9
Foch	3	0	0	1	4	8

THE SOCCER LEAGUE .... page 153

Since the four teams each play the other three teams once, there are six matches in all, and hence a total of 12 points to be awarded. Now we know that United scored five points, Hotspur scored three points, and Villa scored one point, whence it follows that Arsenal scored three points.

THE ADVENTUROUS SNAIL .... page 153

Twenty days.

At the end of 17 days the snail will have climbed 17 feet, and at the end of the 18th day it will be at the top of the wall. It instantly begins slipping while sleeping, and will be two feet down the other side at the end of the 18th night. How long will it take to travel the remaining 18 feet? If it slips two feet at night it clearly overcomes the tendency to slip two feet during the daytime, in climbing up. (In rowing up a river we have the stream against us, but in coming down it is with us and helps us.) If the snail can climb three feet and overcome the tendency to slip two feet in 12 hours' ascent, it could with the same exertion crawl five feet a day on the level. Therefore, in going down, the same exertion carries the snail seven feet in 12 hours; that is, five feet by personal exertion and two feet by slip. This, with the night slip, gives it a descending progress of nine feet in 24 hours. It can therefore do the remaining 18 feet in exactly two days, and the whole journey up and down will take the snail exactly 20 days.

MILITARY SECRETS .... page 154

	Bob	Sam	Tom	Ken
State	Utah	Kansas	Maine	Ohio
Hobby	Dance.	Stamps	Baseb.	Cards
Service	Army	Air F.	Mar.	Navy

Clues 1, 3, 4, and 9 can immediately be filled in. We know from clue 2 that dancing and the Army will go in the same column; Tom's hobby and Ken's service are established, so Bob and Sam are the possibilities for Army and dancing. We know, however, from clue 5 that the Army cannot be in the same column with Kansas, so Bob must be the Army man who likes to dance. Clue 10 says the Marine is from Maine, and Tom is the only serviceman still without service or home state, so he has to be the Marine from Maine. Sam is now the only one without a service branch; thus he has to be the flyer, Ken is now the only one left without a home state, so he has to be from Ohio. Clue 8 can now only mean that Ken is the card player, and we are left with Sam as the stamp collector of clue 6.

THE BAFFLED BUTLER . . . . page 155

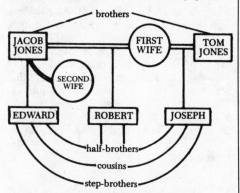

When his brother Tom died, Jacob married his brother's widow. In her first marriage (to Tom), she had had a son, Joseph. As Jacob's wife, she bore another son, Robert. After she died, Jacob married a second time and with his second wife had one more son, Edward.

WHICH MAIL FOR WHICH MALE? . . . . page 156

	1	2	3	4	5
Name	Fred	Tom	Jim	Pat	Mike
Occupa-tion	Plumb.	Farm.	Groc.	Dr.	Law.

The information from clues 2, 4, 6, 8, and 9 can immediately be put into the appropriate boxes. Clue 1 makes Box 5 Mike's. Clue 3 makes Box 1 the plumber's. Clue 7 makes Box 4 the doctor's. Clue 10 makes Box 1 Fred's which leaves Box 4 for Pat (clue 5).

MATCH THEM UP . . . . page 157

Sen.	Claw.	Jones	Henry	Johns.	Rooney	Smith
Bill	Mil. Athl.	Bus-ing	Empl. Handi.	Nat'l. Leaf	St. Pat.	Fed. Lib.
State	Idaho	Ohio	Geo.	Maine	Ind.	Utah
Wife	Jill	Mary	Jane	Kathy	Cor.	Peggy

Fill in the information contained in clues 2, 4, 6, 8, 9, 11, and 13. Now, deduce from the other clues the information to complete the chart. Since the only three remaining states are Indiana, Maine, and Utah, clue 7 tells that Johnson must be from Maine. Therefore, clue 1 indicates that Rooney cannot be from Utah since his wife is Corinne, so Senator Smith is married to Peggy and is from Utah, which means Senator Rooney must be from Indiana and his bill is about St. Patrick's Day (clue 10). Clue 5 shows that Senator Johnson's proposed bill is on the National Leaf. Clue 12 means that Senator Jones' bill is about busing, since this is the only bill left unassigned, and his wife is Mary. Clue 14 makes Kathy Senator Johnson's wife, leaving Jane for Senator Henry.

VACATION VEXATION . . . . page 158

	CC	DD	EE	NN
Hobby	Camp.	Skiing	Fish.	Sail.
Month	July	Dec.	June	Aug-

Clues 3 and 6 can be put in right away. If Charlie is not the fisherman (clue 2), then he doesn't vacation in June (clue 4). Nor does he vacation in August (clue 5), so he must take his vacation in July. This makes his hobby camping (clue 1). Clue 4 can now only refer to Ed. This means that Nick does his sailing in August (clue 5), and the skier has to be Dick.

TYPING TROUBLE . . . . page 159

Letters	BC	DF	GH	JK	LM	NP
Number	77	92	36	5	94	26
Symbol	#	@	$	&	☆	%

Reading through the clues, we see that there are six sets of letters: BC, DF, GH, JK, LM, NP; and six sets of numbers: 5, 26, 36, 77, 92, 94; and six sets of symbols: @, %, ☆, &, $, #. But, which go together with which? Make a grid. Enter into the grid the information given in clues 1, 2, 4, 6, and 10. Now you can deduce the other combinations from the remaining clues. Clue 3 tells that LM cannot be 5; and from clue 7, we know that it is not 92 either. LM must therefore be either 36 or 94; but clue 8 says it is not 36, so it must be 94. Since GH is the only key to which we have not yet assigned a number or a symbol, it is the only key that will fit clue 8; thus, GH must go with 36 and $. Clue 9 tells that since 26 is not #, 77 must be #. And clue 11 establishes, by the same reasoning, that @ must be 92. Which leaves 5 for JK, and % for NP.

THE DORMITORY PUZZLE . . . . **page 160**

1 Kim N.Y.	6 Ruth Cincinnati
2 Lisa Kansas City	5 Mona Cleveland
3 Tina L.A.	4 Rita Chicago

The information from clues 2, 5, 8 and 9 can be charted directly. The rest can be deduced. Lisa must be in room 2 since it's the only non-corner room left (clue 3). Lisa and Mona, the two who live in middle rooms, must come from Kansas City and Cleveland (clues 4 & 6), but which from which? We know that one of Mona's neighbors is Ruth and the other lives in Chicago, so Mona must be the Cleveland girl (clue 1). This means Lisa is the Kansas City girl, and also that Ruth must come from Cincinnati. Lisa's neighbor in room 3 comes from LA, so she must be Tina (clue 4), and Kim from NY (clue 1) must be Lisa's neighbor in room 1. The girl in room 4 has to be Rita.

THE BOYS IN THE LOCKER ROOM . . . . **page 161**

	101	102	103	104	105
Stu.	Jerry	Tom	Gene	Dave	Bob
Sub.	His.	Ger.	Eng.	Math	Shop
Teach.	Jones	Smith	Brown	Green	Bryon

Tackling the lockers first, clues 8 and 10 immediately identify two of the lockers. Since Tom and Jerry's lockers are adjacent (clue 1), and Tom's locker is adjacent to Gene's (clue 11), then Tom must be between Gene and Jerry. So Tom must be in 102 and Jerry in 101; which leaves locker 104 for Dave.

Now for the subjects and teachers. Clues 2, 4, and 12 identify three subjects. This leaves German and English for Tom and Gene. From clues 7, 13, and 3 we can deduce that Tom must take German with Mr. Smith, and Gene takes English with Mr. Brown. From clue 6 we know that Mr. Green teaches math, Dave's subject. This leaves only Bob and Jerry's teachers unidentified. Clue 5 establishes that Mr. Bryon must be the shop teacher, so he must be Bob's teacher, and Jerry's teacher must be Mr. Jones.

GRAB BAG . . . . **page 162**

1. A person of low intelligence
2. Lhasa, Tibet, at an elevation of 12,002 feet
3. Alexander Pope
4. Deer
5. Guinea, Africa, with an average life expectancy of 27 years
6. Musical instrument which resembles a xylophone
7. Timbuktu, Mali, where the average temperature is 84.7°F
8. Reversion to characteristics in one's remote ancestors
9. Bette Davis
10. Gigantic, after Swift's land of giants in *Gulliver's Travels*
11. A quadrilateral rectangle having only two sides parallel
12. Walt Whitman
13. Goldsmith Maid
14. Eatables
15. 29.7 mph
16. The British Museum
17. Giuseppe Verdi
18. Golfer
19. Australia
20. Matthew Webb

21. Bees
22. New Jersey
23. Earth
24. Churchill Downs

À LA MODE . . . . page 164

1. 1960s
2. Coco Chanel
3. Empire
4. 1920s
5. A hoop skirt
6. Mary Quant
7. Silk
8. Culottes
9. Hooded cloak
10. Hat
11. Nineteenth
12. Domino
13. Ermine
14. A farthingale
15. Shawl
16. Garter belts
17. Pillbox
18. Madras
19. Charles Dana Gibson
20. Young girls' pinafores
21. Collar
22. Kimono
23. Cardigan
24. Waist
25. 1970s
26. American
27. 15%

HOOP-LA! . . . . page 166

1. Rhode Island State
2. Wilt Chamberlain, with a total of 31,419 points scored
3. James Naismith
4. Ferdinand Lewis Alcindor
5. Boston Celtics
6. 75,000
7. Mu Tieh-Chu, who is 7'9¾" tall
8. Nat Holman, also known as Mr. Basketball
9. 20,000
10. Canada, in 1893
11. Third
12. New York City College, in 1949-1950
13. The Stilt
14. 1890s
15. 22
16. Oscar Robertson, who sank a total of 7,694 free throws in his career with the Cincinatti Royals and Milwaukee Bucks
17. Interference with the ball on its final arch toward the basket
18. Wesleyan and Yale
19. 12
20. 1936
21. Run with the ball
22. 100, by Wilt Chamberlain.
23. 24 seconds
24. .275
25. United States

FOR BETTE DAVIS FANS . . . . page 168

1. Ruth Elizabeth Davis

2. Lowell, Massachusetts
3. Martha Graham
4. *Beyond the Forest*
5. George Cukor
6. Somerset Maugham
7. Claude Rains
8. 1938
9. *The Catered Affair*
10. Warner Brothers Studios
11. 1931
12. *Dangerous*
13. Elizabeth I of England
14. Joan Crawford
15. Actor Gary Merrill
16. Margot Channing, in *All About Eve*
17. 1941
18. *Sunset Boulevard*. The star was Gloria Swanson
19. Three. Two of the children are adopted
20. *The Man Who Played God*
21. Humphrey Bogart
22. Universal
23. Errol Flynn

BITS AND PIECES . . . . page 170

1. Seven years
2. Salt Lake City
3. Denmark
4. William Howard Taft (In 1910)
5. Mary Mallon
6. Augustus
7. Cleveland's Euclid Avenue
8. Manchester
9. Georgia
10. The *Pieta*
11. Holland
12. Quetzal
13. Six years
14. Coney Island
15. Sears
16. Edward Arlington Robinson
17. Seminoles
18. Four to five billion years old
19. North Dakota
20. James Garfield
21. The swift
22. Birmingham, U.K.
23. Tunisia
24. George Orwell
25. Johnson
26. Hindi
27. Die in a car accident (Sept, 13, 1899, New York City)
28. 180 feet
29. Switzerland
30. Tennessee and Missouri
31. Sturgeon
32. Two (Pyramids at Gizeh, lighthouse at Pharos, Alexandria)
33. 20,000 tons of TNT

34. 21 months
35. Linus
36. Liver
37. New York
38. Pennsylvania
39. Smoked tobacco
40. 1666
41. Four (New Mexico, Wyoming, Colorado, Utah)
42. Amsterdam
43. Shoelace
44. Repealed prohibition
45. Russia
46. Pittsburgh
47. Boston
48. South America
49. James Madison
50. Alaska

NATIVE HABITAT . . . . page 174

1. Australia	15. Canada
2. South America	16. African Congo
3. Africa	17. United States
4. United States	18. India
5. Lapland	19. China
6. Madagascar	20. Africa
7. Africa	21. Africa
8. India	22. Africa
9. South America	23. Australia
10. Indonesia	24. Africa
11. Australia	25. Australia
12. South America	26. Africa
13. Africa	27. Tibet
14. Central Asia	

GAME FOR THE GOURMET . . . . page 176

1. White wine and tomatoes
2. Hollandaise sauce
3. French pancakes with a flaming orange sauce
4. Steak tartare
5. Spaghetti
6. Cake
7. Beef and onions
8. Spicy
9. Apricot jam
10. Scallops
11. Crushed grain
12. Saffron
13. A French roll made with lots of butter
14. Saffron
15. A fresh basil sauce
16. Barbecued in a tomato and molasses sauce
17. Egg yolks, sugar, and wine
18. Green peppers stuffed with meat or cheese
19. Mulligatawny soup
20. A dash
21. Celery, apples, walnuts
22. Mozarella cheese and tomato sauce
23. Ricotta cheese and sometimes ham
24. Cumin, coriander, turmeric, and other pungent spices
25. A choice steak dish, cooked in butter
26. Potatoes

IN YOUR CUPS . . . . page 178

1. Potatoes
2. Apples
3. An apéritif
4. Caraway seed
5. Coffee, whipped cream, and whiskey
6. Plain tomato juice
7. Crème de menthe, crème de cacao, and cream
8. Anisette
9. Very dry
10. Kahlua and vodka
11. Corn
12. Campari
13. Sugar cane or molasses
14. 43 percent
15. Whiskey, sugar, bitters, and club soda
16. Justerini and Brooks
17. Tequila, salt, lime juice, and Triple sec
18. Gin, a dash of vermouth, and a green olive
19. The sap of the Mexican agave plant
20. 8-12 percent
21. Cin cin
22. 1/3 of the population
23. Cointreau, lemon juice, and brandy
24. Dark beer made from malt
25. Pony

THIS AND THAT . . . . page 180

1. The Sugar Bowl
2. The juice of unripe grapes
3. An authority on correct pronunciation
4. A nickname
5. Three
6. Football
7. White wine flavored with aromatic herbs
8. Juniper berries
9. A ram's horn used in Jewish ritual
10. Loo-ward
11. Amelia Earhart
12. Method of criminal identification
13. Edward Everett
14. *Strange Interlude*
15. Galileo

16. A race against time, skiing downhill (between pairs of flags set up on the course)
17. Hamilton
18. A specialist in diseases of the mind
19. Louisiana
20. 50½ miles
21. Edgar Bergen
22. Thomas. Actually, his middle name was Woodrow
23. Ampersand
24. Whitcomb Judson

AN ANTHOLOGY OF OLOGIES . . . . page 182

1. Demonology
2. Cardiology
3. Gerontology
4. Entomology
5. Graphology
6. Meteorology
7. Etymology
8. Ornithology
9. Choreography
10. Astronomy
11. Ontology
12. Cetology
13. Histology
14. Petrology
15. Audiology
16. Otology
17. Dermatology
18. Oenology
19. Epistemology
20. Toxicology
21. Hydrology
22. Sinology
23. Epidemiology
24. Chronology
25. Osteology
26. Araneology
27. Gynecology
28. Paleography
29. Paleontology
30. Ichthyology
31. Geology
32. Myrmecology
33. Pharmacology
34. Oology
35. Papyrology
36. Theology
37. Gemmology
38. Genealogy
39. Cytology
40. Laryngology
41. Penology
42. Anthropology
43. Typology
44. Ecology
45. Herpetology
46. Psychology
47. Coprology
48. Aerology
49. Archaeology

WHO WAS THAT LADY? . . . . page 184

1. Barbara Stanwyck
2. Joan Crawford
3. Katharine Hepburn
4. Bette Davis
5. Natalie Wood
6. Greta Garbo
7. Irene Dunne
8. Gloria Swanson
9. Greta Garbo
10. Ruth Chatterton
11. Vanessa Redgrave
12. Greta Garbo
13. Ruth Chatterton
14. Norma Shearer
15. Joan Fontaine
16. Ginger Rogers
17. Diane Keaton
18. Greer Garson
19. Leslie Caron
20. Greer Garson
21. Ingrid Bergman
22. Rosalind Russell
23. Isabelle Huppert
24. Anne Baxter
25. Shirley MacLaine
26. Giulietta Masina
27. Julie Andrews
28. Debbie Reynolds
29. Lynn Redgrave
30. Faye Dunaway
31. Joanne Woodward
32. Vanessa Redgrave
33. Genvieve Bujold
34. Maggie Smith
35. Ellen Burstyn
36. Raquel Welch
37. Mia Farrow
38. Julie Andrews
39. Ruth Gordon
40. Barbra Streisand
41. Leslie Caron
42. Elizabeth Taylor
43. Cybill Shepherd
44. Pearl White
45. Julie Christie
46. Sissy Spacek
47. Miriam Hopkins
48. Rosalind Russell
49. Bette Davis
50. Sue Lyon

WHERE, OH WHERE? . . . . page 187

1. New York City, U.S.A.
2. Jerusalem, Israel
3. Paris, France
4. Cairo, Egypt
5. Rome, Italy
6. Leningrad, Russia
7. Giza, Egypt
8. Pisa, Italy
9. Rome, Italy
10. New York City, U.S.A.
11. Agra, India
12. Venice, Italy
13. London, England
14. Blarney, Ireland
15. Moscow, Russia
16. Milan, Italy
17. Granada, Spain
18. San Francisco, California, U.S.A.
19. Athens, Greece
20. London, England
21. Mecca, Saudi Arabia
22. Paris, France
23. Madrid, Spain
24. Boston, Massachusetts, U.S.A.

WHO SAID IT? . . . . page 188

1. c) Shakespeare
2. c) Thomas à. Kempis
3. a) Chaucer
4. d) Nikita Krushchev
5. d) Ralph Waldo Emerson
6. a) Jimmy Durante
7. c) Franklin Roosevelt
8. b) Neil Armstrong
9. b) John Heywood
10. d) Exodus, Old Testament
11. c) William Vanderbilt
12. b) Karl Marx

13. c) Cain
14. a) Hamlet
15. c) Victor Hugo
16. b) Aesop
17. d) Winston Churchill
18. c) Elizabeth Barrett Browning
19. c) Richard Nixon
20. d) Mohammed Ali
21. a) Karl Marx
22. b) Harry Truman
23. b) Ebineezer Scrooge
24. c) William Shakespeare
25. a) Admiral Farragut
26. b) Exodus, Old Testament
27. a) Rhett Butler
28. d) Bob Dylan
29. b) Gertrude Stein
30. c) John F. Kennedy
31. c) Marie Antoinette
32. b) Henny Youngman
33. c) Queen Victoria
34. d) Walt Whitman
35. a) John Donne
36. d) Winston Churchill
37. b) Patrick Henry
38. a) Lady Macbeth
39. b) Greta Garbo
40. c) Leonard Cohen
41. a) Alexander Pope
42. d) Herman Melville
43. b) Will Rogers
44. c) Genesis, Old Testament
45. a) Jonathan Swift
46. b) Colonel Sidney Sherman
47. d) Martin Luther King
48. b) Woody Guthrie

SPORTS LEGENDS . . . . page 192

1. Baseball
2. Hockey
3. Golf
4. Football
5. Tennis
6. Golf
7. Swimming
8. Track and field
9. Baseball
10. Hockey
11. Golf, track and field
12. Tennis
13. Boxing
14. Baseball
15. Track and field
16. Swimming
17. Track and field
18. Baseball
19. Football
20. Boxing
21. Horse racing
22. Swimming
23. Skiing
24. Baseball
25. Golf
26. Soccer
27. Baseball
28. Tennis
29. Boxing
30. Track and field
31. Tennis
32. Football
33. Track and field
34. Baseball
35. Golf
36. Football
37. Swimming
38. Track and field
39. Tennis
40. Basketball
41. Baseball
42. Horse racing
43. Football
44. Tennis
45. Boxing
46. Football
47. Track and field
48. Tennis
49. Track and field
50. Baseball

HOW MUCH DO YOU KNOW ABOUT THE AMERICAN REVOLUTION? . . . . . page 194

1. George III
2. Lexington
3. Fort Ticonderoga
4. Thomas Paine
5. Philadelphia
6. Trenton
7. Saratoga
8. Yorktown
9. Francis Marion
10. *Bon Homme Richard*
11. Paris
12. 1781
13. Cornwallis
14. South Carolina
15. John Hancock
16. New York
17. Thirteen
18. 200
19. Patrick Henry
20. Boston
21. John Adams
22. Pennsylvania
23. Alexander Hamilton
24. Delaware
25. John Jay

TUBE TOPICS . . . . page 196

1. Amanda Blake
2. Dentist
3. *Burke's Law*
4. *Alice Doesn't Live Here Anymore*
5. North Carolina
6. Hooterville Cannonball
7. Jim Backus
8. *Hey, Landlord!*
9. Pat Paulsen
10. *The Brady Bunch*
11. Theodore Cleaver
12. *Julia*
13. Jed Clampett
14. *Hawaii Five-O*
15. Albuquerque
16. Ann Sothern
17. *The Monkees*
18. *Love on a Rooftop*
19. Alan Young
20. Oscar Goldman
21. Pernell Roberts
22. Martin Landau and Barbara Bain
23. Gertie

24. *My Living Doll*
25. Jane Wyatt
26. *My World—and Welcome to It*
27. *I Spy*
28. Puerto Rico
29. Fred MacMurray
30. Art Fleming
31. *Green Acres*
32. *Brian's Song*
33. Bill Daly
34. Mel Blanc
35. Georgia Engel
36. Alexander Waverly
37. *He and She*
38. Ed Ames
39. Sada Thompson
40. Red Skelton
41. William Bendix
42. Colonel
43. Kunta Kinte
44. Sebastian Cabot
45. NBC
46. Dr. Smith
47. Michelle Nichols
48. *East Side, West Side*
49. *Saturday Night Live*
50. *Mary Hartman, Mary Hartman*

FAMOUS AMERICAN SLOGANS . . . . . . page 200

1. Patrick Henry
2. Sidney Sherman
3. Franklin Roosevelt
4. Nathan Hale
5. William Prescott
6. John Paul Jones
7. Commodore Perry
8. Horace Greeley
9. Admiral Farragut
10. James Otis
11. Woodrow Wilson
12. Benjamin Franklin
13. Stephen Decatur
14. Charles Pinckney
15. Henry Clay
16. William J. Bryan
17. Thomas Paine
18. Douglas MacArthur
19. Franklin Roosevelt
20. William Allen

THE LADY IN THE CASE . . . . page 202

1. Waitress
2. Mistress
3. Masseuse
4. Tigress
5. Marchioness
6. Hen
7. Queen
8. Stewardess
9. Duck
10. Countess
11. Heifer
12. Couturière
13. Matriarch
14. Vixen
15. Testatrix
16. Bride
17. Usherette
18. Doe
19. Lady
20. Abbess

21. Bitch
22. Barmaid
23. Peahen
24. Nun
25. Madame or mademoiselle
26. Aviatrix
27. Dam
28. Ewe
29. Sultana
30. Duchess
31. Filly
32. Maharanee
33. Blonde
34. Sow
35. Lass
36. Kaiserin
37. Mare
38. Tsarina
39. Fiancée
40. Maid of honor
41. Swan
42. Heroine
43. Hind
44. Señora or señorita
45. Pierrette
46. Nanny goat
47. Dame
48. Goose
49. Squaw
50. Cow

IN THE BEGINNING . . . . page 204

1. *The Way of All Flesh*, Samuel Butler
2. *The Picture of Dorian Gray*, Oscar Wilde
3. *Twelfth Night*, William Shakespeare
4. *Uncle Tom's Cabin*, Harriet Beecher Stowe
5. *The Three Musketeers*, Alexandre Dumas
6. *Spoon River Anthology*, Edgar Lee Masters
7. *The Waste Land*, T.S. Eliot
8. *The Great Gatsby*, F. Scott Fitzgerald
9. *Moby Dick*, Herman Melville
10. *Anna Karenina*, Leo Tolstoy
11. *The Scarlet Letter*, Nathaniel Hawthorne
12. *The Canterbury Tales*, Geoffrey Chaucer
13. *Ben-Hur*, Lewis Wallace
14. *Pride and Prejudice*, Jane Austen
15. *A Tale of Two Cities*, Charles Dickens
16. *Ivanhoe*, Sir Walter Scott
17. *Richard III*, William Shakespeare
18. *The Communist Manifesto*, Karl Marx and Friedrich Engels
19. *Catch-22*, Joseph Heller
20. *The Aeneid*, Virgil
21. *Salambo*, Gustave Flaubert
22. *Gone with the Wind*, Margaret Mitchell
23. *Through the Looking Glass*, Lewis Carroll
24. *Fathers and Sons*, Ivan Turgenev
25. *The Monkey's Paw*, W.W. Jacobs

POT-AU-FEU . . . . page 208

1. Angola, Africa, with a rate of 30.2 deaths per thousand of population
2. Beginner

3. *A Bill of Divorcement*
4. 1947
5. A tortoise; the giant tortoise lives as long as 300 years
6. The cormorant
7. Feud
8. List of books published previously
9. The Sahara
10. 1895
11. A cave-dweller
12. Ostrich
13. The Battle of the Marne
14. Bright lights used in the theater
15. Taft
16. Children's apron
17. 1889, between Kilrain and Sullivan
18. $200 per pound
19. In the Great Lakes
20. Camel
21. Slingshot
22. Michelangelo
23. Manuscript in which later writing is superimposed on earlier
24. Feasting and rejoicing
25. Wandering knight
26. Coypu
27. Dover
28. Emily Bronte

PASSIONATE PAIRS . . . . page 210

1. Cleopatra
2. Ruth
3. Ulysses
4. Juliet
5. Marion Davies
6. Isolde
7. Scarlett O'Hara
8. Louis XV
9. Abelard
10. Helen of Troy
11. Dashiell Hammett
12. Maid Marian
13. Beatrice
14. Orpheus
15. Wally Simpson
16. Guinevere
17. Osiris
18. Jean Paul Sartre
19. Galatea
20. Elizabeth Barrett
21. Roberto Rossellini
22. Clark Gable
23. Josephine
24. Lauren Bacall
25. Ellen Terry
26. Charles II
27. Cathy Linton
28. Priscilla
29. Lord Nelson
30. Edith Bolling
31. Spencer Tracy
32. Zelda Fitzgerald
33. John Lennon
34. Queen Victoria
35. Estella
36. Ingmar Bergman
37. Benedick
38. George Henry Lewes
39. Tatiana
40. Daisy Mae
41. Anais Nin
42. Stanley Kowalski
43. Sophia Loren
44. Olive Oyl
45. Bianca Jagger
46. Petruchio
47. Thisbe

48. Daisy Buchanan
49. Theodora
50. Rebecca

EMPORIA OF IMPORT . . . . page 212

1. Dallas
2. New York
3. London
4. Hartford
5. Boston
6. Moscow
7. Paris
8. Copenhagen
9. Paris
10. Oslo
11. New York
12. New York
13. Boston
14. Paris
15. London
16. London
17. Madrid
18. New York
19. London
20. San Francisco
21. Chicago
22. Mexico City
23. New York
24. New York
25. Rome

WHO'S THE POET? . . . . page 213

1. Ben Jonson
2. Thomas Brown
3. Lord Byron
4. Edgar Allan Poe
5. Richard Lovelace
6. Emily Dickinson
7. Alexander Pope
8. John Howard Payne
9. William Butler Yeats
10. William Shakespeare
11. Edward Arlington Robinson
12. T.S. Eliot
13. Elizabeth Barrett Browning
14. William Blake
15. Alfred Lord Tennyson
16. Robert Burns
17. A.E. Housman
18. Leigh Hunt
19. Emma Lazarus
20. Dorothy Parker

FOR CHAPLIN FANS . . . . page 216

1. The Little Tramp
2. 1889
3. Four
4. D.W. Griffith
5. Edna Purviance
6. *A Night Out*, made in 1915
7. Hitler
8. London
9. Mary Pickford
10. Eugene O'Neill
11. *The Kid*

12. *The Gold Rush*
13. The Lone Prospector
14. Two years
15. Paulette Goddard
16. *A Countess from Hong Kong.* Incidentally, this movie starred Sophia Loren
17. Five
18. Paulette Goddard
19. Switzerland
20. 1972
21. Joan Barry
22. Scraps
23. Geraldine
24. Orson Welles
25. 1977

MOVIE MONIKERS . . . . page 218

1. *Star Wars*, Mark Hamill
2. *A Funny Thing Happened on the Way to the Forum*, Zero Mostel
3. *The Maltese Falcon*, Humphrey Bogart
4. *Cabaret*, Liza Minnelli
5. *Psycho*, Anthony Perkins
6. *The Sting*, Robert Redford
7. *Equus*, Sir Richard Burton
8. *Gone with the Wind*, Olivia de Havilland
9. *The Robe*, Jay Robinson
10. *The Grapes of Wrath*, Henry Fonda
11. *The Graduate*, Dustin Hoffman
12. *All About Eve*, Bette Davis
13. *The Wizard of Oz*, Frank Morgan
14. *The Exorcist*, Jason Miller
15. *You Can't Cheat an Honest Man*, W.C. Fields
16. *The Pink Panther*, Peter Sellers
17. *The Miracle Worker*, Anne Bancroft
18. *Long Day's Journey into Night*, Jason Robards
19. *Annie Hall*, Woody Allen
20. *My Fair Lady*, Audrey Hepburn
21. *Bird Man of Alcatraz*, Burt Lancaster
22. *Julia*, Jason Robards
23. *Mutiny on the Bounty*, Clark Gable, Marlon Brando
24. *M*A*S*H**, Donald Sutherland
25. *Sunset Boulevard*, Gloria Swanson
26. *Harvey*, James Stewart
27. *The Producers*, Zero Mostel
28. *Mister Roberts*, Jack Lemmon
29. *The Music Man*, Robert Preston
30. *A Streetcar Named Desire*, Marlon Brando
31. *Around the World in Eighty Days*, David Niven
32. *Duck Soup*, Groucho Marx
33. *Twenty Thousand Leagues Under the Sea*, James Mason

34. *The Way We Were*, Robert Redford
35. *Bananas*, Woody Allen
36. *My Little Chickadee*, W.C. Fields
37. *Arsenic and Old Lace*, Cary Grant
38. *The Treasure of the Sierra Madre*, Humphrey Bogart
39. *Blazing Saddles*, Harvey Korman
40. *The Bank Dick*, Franklin Pangborn

NOMENCLATURE . . . . page 222

1. Acorn	48. Enema
2. Actor	49. Enlace
3. Acumen	50. Enter
4. Alone	51. Entrance
5. Alter	52. Lacer
6. Ameer	53. Lament
7. Anemone	54. Lance
8. Anent	55. Lancer
9. Anneal	56. Lancet
10. Annul	57. Later
11. Antler	58. Leaner
12. Cameo	59. Learn
13. Canner	60. Lecture
14. Cannot	61. Lemon
15. Canter	62. Lemur
16. Cantor	63. Loaner
17. Careen	64. Locate
18. Carom	65. Lumen
19. Center	66. Manner
20. Clamor	67. Manor
21. Clarence	68. Mantel
22. Claret	69. Mantle
23. Clean	70. Marten
24. Cleaner	71. Mater
25. Clear	72. Mature
26. Cleat	73. Meant
27. Clone	74. Melon
28. Cloture	75. Mental
29. Clout	76. Mentor
30. Column	77. Meter
31. Count	78. Molten
32. Counter	79. Moral
33. Cream	80. Morale
34. Create	81. Mortal
35. Crane	82. Moult
36. Crone	83. Mount
37. Cruel	84. Mourn
38. Cruet	85. Namer
39. Eater	86. Nature
40. Eclat	87. Neaten
41. Elate	88. Neater
42. Elater	89. Neuron
43. Electron	90. Noter
44. Enamel	91. Ocular
45. Enamor	92. Oracle
46. Encore	93. Orate
47. Encounter	94. Ornate

111. Romance
112. Route
113. Talcum
114. Talent
115. Talon
116. Tamer
117. Tanner
118. Tenace
119. Tenor
120. Tenure
121. Toluene
122. Trace
123. Trance
124. Treacle
125. Trounce
126. Truce
127. Tuner
128. Ulcer
129. Ulcerate
130. Ultra
131. Uncle
132. Unclear
133. Unlace

95. Ounce
96. Outer
97. Outran
98. Outré
99. React
100. Reactor
101. Recant
102. Recent
103. Recount
104. Relace
105. Relate
106. Remnant
107. Remount
108. Rennet
109. Rental
110. Retune
134. Unlearn
135. Unman
136. Unmeant
137. Unmeet
138. Unmoral
139. Unreal
140. Unreel

INSTITUTIONAL . . . . page 224

1. Anion
2. Annul
3. Anoint
4. Initial
5. Instal
6. Instant
7. Instil
8. Institution
9. Insult
10. Lotus
11. Lunation
12. Lutanist
13. Nation
14. Nonsuit
15. Saint
16. Situation
17. Slant
18. Sonant
19. Stain
20. Station

21. Stilt
22. Stint
23. Stoat
24. Stout
25. Stunt
26. Taint
27. Talon
28. Talus
29. Taunt
30. Titan
31. Titian
32. Tonal
33. Tonsil
34. Tonus
35. Total
36. Tuition
37. Union
38. Unison
39. Until

APHRODITE . . . . page 225

1. Adept
2. Adopt
3. Adore
4. Adroit
5. Aider
6. Aired
7. Aphid

8. Atrophied
9. Darted
10. Dater
11. Death
12. Dearth
13. Depart
14. Deport

15. Depot
16. Diaper
17. Dither
18. Dopier
19. Doter
20. Drape
21. Earth
22. Editor
23. Ephod
24. Ephor
25. Hated
26. Heard
27. Heart
28. Hired
29. Hoard
30. Hoped
31. Irate
32. Oared
33. Opera
34. Opted
35. Orate
36. Oread
37. Other
38. Paired
39. Pared
40. Parted
41. Partied
42. Pater
43. Patio
44. Period
45. Pirate

46. Pored
47. Prated
48. Pride
49. Pried
50. Radio
51. Raped
52. Rated
53. Ratio
54. Repaid
55. Report
56. Repot
57. Rioted
58. Roped
59. Taped
60. Taper
61. Tapir
62. Tepid
63. Their
64. Third
65. Thread
66. Tirade
67. Tired
68. Toper
69. Trade
70. Tread
71. Trepid
72. Triad
73. Tried
74. Tripe
75. Trope

DELIGHTFUL . . . . page 226

1. Delight
2. Delft
3. Dight
4. Dilute
5. Eight
6. Fetid
7. Fidget
8. Field
9. Fight
10. Filed
11. Filet
12. Filled
13. Fillet
14. Filth
15. Flight
16. Fluid
17. Flute
18. Fluted
19. Fudge
20. Futile
21. Gelid

22. Gifted
23. Gilled
24. Glide
25. Glued
26. Guide
27. Guild
28. Guile
29. Guilt
30. Gulfed
31. Gullet
32. Hulled
33. Legit
34. Lifted
35. Light
36. Lithe
37. Tilde
38. Tiled
39. Tilled
40. Tuille
41. Tulle
42. Utile

TRIBULATION . . . . page 226

1. Ablution
2. About
3. Abort
4. Albino
5. Alibi
6. Bailor
7. Blain
8. Bloat
9. Blunt
10. Blurt
11. Brain
12. Broil
13. Bruin
14. Brunt
15. Built
16. Burial
17. Burin
18. Butanol
19. Button
20. Introit
21. Intuit
22. Labor
23. Libation
24. Lunar
25. Oration
26. Orbit
27. Outran
28. Ratio
29. Ration
30. Riant
31. Ritual
32. Robin
33. Tailor
34. Taint
35. Talon
36. Tibia
37. Titan
38. Titian
39. Titular
40. Tonal
41. Total
42. Trail
43. Train
44. Tribunal
45. Trout
46. Truant
47. Tuition
48. Turban
49. Turbinal
50. Turbot
51. Unlit
52. Until
53. Urban

ESCALATED . . . . page 228

1. Acted
2. Alate
3. Atlas
4. Cadet
5. Cased
6. Caste
7. Castle
8. Cease
9. Cleat
10. Dealt
11. Decal
12. Delta
13. Eased
14. Easel
15. Elated
16. Eldest
17. Laced
18. Lease
19. Least
20. Sated
21. Scald
22. Scale
23. Sealed
24. Sedate
25. Slate
26. Sleet
27. Stale
28. Stead
29. Steal
30. Steed
31. Steel
32. Tease
33. Teasel

CHAMPIONSHIP . . . . page 228

1. Amino
2. Apish
3. Aspic
4. Camion
5. Campion
6. Capon
7. Chain
8. Champ
9. Champion
10. Chaos
11. Chasm
12. Chimp
13. Chino
14. Chomp
15. Hippo
16. Impish
17. Macho
18. Manic
19. Mason
20. Mishap
21. Mocha
22. Panic
23. Phonic
24. Piano
25. Pinch
26. Scampi
27. Scion
28. Simian
29. Sonic
30. Spinach

WATCHMAKER . . . . page 227

1. Awake
2. Aware
3. Caret
4. Cater
5. Charm
6. Chart
7. Cheat
8. Crate
9. Cream
10. Earth
11. Hacker
12. Hawker
13. Heart
14. Ketch
15. Maker
16. March
17. Market
18. Match
19. Mater
20. Rachet
21. Racket
22. Ramate
23. Ramet
24. Reach
25. Retch
26. Tacker
27. Taker
28. Tamer
29. Teach
30. Trace
31. Track
32. Waker
33. Warmer
34. Warmth
35. Watch
36. Watcher
37. Water
38. Whack
39. Wheat
40. Wrath
41. Wreak
42. Wreath
43. Wreck
44. Wretch

COMPOUNDED . . . . page 229

1. Coded
2. Comedo
3. Compound
4. Coned
5. Cooped
6. Coped
7. Coupe
8. Coupon
9. Demon
10. Domed
11. Doped
12. Dumped
13. Dunce
14. Mooned
15. Moped
16. Mound
17. Ounce
18. Pounce
19. Pound
20. Pounded
21. Upend

ANTICIPATION . . . . page 229

1. Action
2. Anion
3. Anoint
4. Antic
5. Cannot
6. Canon
7. Cantina
8. Canto
9. Canton
10. Capon
11. Captain
12. Caption
13. Catnip
14. Citation
15. Contain
16. Inaction
17. Inapt
18. Intact
19. Nation
20. Nicotiana
21. Ontic
22. Optic
23. Paint
24. Panic
25. Patina
26. Pinion
27. Pinta
28. Pinto
29. Piton
30. Point
31. Tacit
32. Taction
33. Tannic
34. Tinct
35. Titan
36. Titanic
37. Titian
38. Tonic
39. Topic

INTROVERT . . . . page 230

1. Inert
2. Inter
3. Ironer
4. Niter
5. Noter
6. Orient
7. Otter
8. Overt
9. Ovine
10. Retin
11. Retort
12. Riven
13. River
14. Rivet
15. Rotten
16. Rotter
17. Rover
18. Tenor
19. Torrent
20. Toter
21. Trite
22. Trivet
23. Trove
24. Trover
25. Voter

DIMINUTIVE . . . . page 230

1. Demit
2. Dunite
3. Invite
4. Invited
5. Mined
6. Minted
7. Minute
8. Muted
9. Nitid
10. Tedium
11. Timed
12. Tined
13. Tumid
14. Tuned
15. Undie
16. Unite
17. United
18. Untie
19. Untied
20. Vined

GEOMETRY . . . . page 231

1. Egret
2. Emery
3. Emote
4. Ergot
5. Greet
6. Merge
7. Meter
8. Remote

LACHRYMOSE . . . . page 231

1. Archly
2. Arose
3. Calmer
4. Camel
5. Cameo
6. Carol
7. Charm
8. Chary
9. Chase
10. Choler
11. Cholera
12. Choral
13. Chorale
14. Chore
15. Chorea
16. Chose
17. Chrome
18. Clamor
19. Clear
20. Close
21. Coral
22. Early
23. Hoarse
24. Holey
25. Homer
26. Hoary
27. Horse
28. Larch
29. Leary
30. Loach
31. Loamy
32. Macho
33. March
34. Mealy
35. Mocha
36. Molar
37. Moral
38. Morale
39. Morsel
40. Mosey
41. Reach
42. Roach
43. Shale
44. Shame
45. Share
46. Shear
47. Shoal
48. Shore
49. Slayer
50. Slyer
51. Smear
52. Solar

PSYCHOLOGICAL . . . . page 232

1. Alcohol
2. Alloy
3. Aspic
4. Caliph
5. Calypso
6. Chill
7. Choosy
8. Clash
9. Clasp
10. Coach
11. Cocoa
12. Colic
13. Collop
14. Coolly
15. Gallop
16. Gipsy
17. Glyph
18. Golly
19. Hilly
20. Holly
21. Lilac
22. Loach
23. Local
24. Logic
25. Logical
26. Pally
27. Palsy
28. Poach
29. Polly
30. Pooch
31. Psych
32. Psycho
33. Sally
34. Scalp
35. School
36. Shall
37. Shill
38. Shoal
39. Sloop
40. Soapy
41. Spall
42. Spill
43. Spoil
44. Spool
45. Yahoo

CONVENTIONAL . . . . page 233

1. Action
2. Alcove
3. Alien
4. Aline
5. Alive
6. Alone
7. Ancient
8. Anent
9. Anion
10. Anoint
11. Antic
12. Anvil
13. Atone
14. Cannon
15. Cannot
16. Canoe
17. Canon
18. Canto
19. Canton
20. Cavil
21. Civet
22. Clean
23. Cleat
24. Clone
25. Clove
26. Cloven
27. Colon
28. Connive
29. Contain
30. Convent
31. Convention
32. Coven
33. Covet
34. Elation
35. Entail
36. Evict
37. Innate
38. Innovate
39. Intone
40. Invent
41. Lactone
42. Lance
43. Lento
44. Linen
45. Liven
46. Locate
47. Lotion
48. Nation
49. Navel
50. Notice
51. Notion
52. Novel
53. Oaten
54. Ocean
55. Onion
56. Ontic
57. Ovate
58. Ovation
59. Ovine
60. Talon
61. Tannic
62. Tonal
63. Tonic
64. Valet
65. Venal
66. Venial
67. Venin
68. Ventail
69. Vinca
70. Vineal
71. Viola
72. Violate
73. Violent
74. Violet
75. Vital
76. Vocal
77. Voice
78. Voile
79. Volant
80. Voltaic

FRATERNITY . . . . page 234

1. Afire
2. After
3. Artery
4. Attire
5. Entry
6. Errant
7. Faint
8. Fairer
9. Fairy
10. Fatten
11. Fatter
12. Fatty
13. Feint
14. Fiery
15. Finery
16. Friar
17. Fritter
18. Fryer
19. Inert
20. Infer
21. Inter
22. Irate
23. Iterant
24. Natty
25. Nifty
26. Niter
27. Rafter
28. Rainy
29. Ranter
30. Rater
31. Ratite
32. Ratty
33. Refit
34. Refrain
35. Retain
36. Retin
37. Retina
38. Retrain
39. Riant
40. Taint
41. Tarry
42. Teary
43. Terry
44. Tinea
45. Train
46. Trainer
47. Trait
48. Treat
49. Treaty
50. Trier
51. Trite
52. Yearn

EMBARRASS . . . . page 235

1. Abase
2. Abeam
3. Amass
4. Amber
5. Arras
6. Barer
7. Baser
8. Brass
9. Bream
10. Massa
11. Masse
12. Rearm
13. Saber
14. Sabra
15. Samba
16. Smear

MENDACIOUS . . . . page 236

1. Acumen
2. Adieu
3. Adios
4. Admen
5. Aimed
6. Amend
7. Amino
8. Amuse
9. Anemic
10. Animus
11. Anosmic
12. Ascend
13. Aside
14. Audio
15. Cameo
16. Camion
17. Candies
18. Caned
19. Cased
20. Casein
21. Cause
22. Caused
23. Coned
24. Cosine
25. Cousin
26. Dance
27. Deacon
28. Deism
29. Demon
30. Denim
31. Domain
32. Douse
33. Dunce
34. Iceman
35. Income
36. Induce
37. Maiden
38. Maned
39. Manic
40. Manse
41. Mason
42. Media
43. Median
44. Medico
45. Meson
46. Minced
47. Mined
48. Minus
49. Moaned
50. Monad
51. Mound
52. Mouse
53. Named
54. Nomad
55. Noise
56. Nosed
57. Ocean
58. Odeum

59. Odium
60. Onside
61. Ounce
62. Scion
63. Scone
64. Sedan
65. Snide
66. Sound
67. Sumac
68. Undies
69. Unmade
70. Unsaid

FURNITURE .... page 237

1. Finer
2. Fruit
3. Future
4. Inert
5. Infer
6. Inter
7. Niter
8. Nurture
9. Refit
10. Retin
11. Ruiner
12. Return
13. Trier
14. Trine
15. Truer
16. Triune
17. Tuner
18. Turner
19. Unite
20. Untie

MEDIOCRITY .... page 237

1. Cider
2. Cited
3. Citied
4. Coder
5. Comedy
6. Comer
7. Comet
8. Comity
9. Cored
10. Credit
11. Cried
12. Crime
13. Decoy
14. Deity
15. Dicer
16. Dimity
17. Direct
18. Dirty
19. Doter
20. Editor
21. Idiom
22. Idiot
23. Medic
24. Merit
25. Mired
26. Moire
27. Remit
28. Rimed
29. Rioted
30. Tired
31. Torii
32. Trice
33. Tried

PREVARICATION AS AN ART........ page 239

Any fool can tell the truth, but it requires a man of some sense to know how to lie well.

Samuel Butler

BRAT AT A BALL .... page 240

Pretty pampered Polly peevishly pouted, prissily put on her purple pom-pom, and pettishly perambulated at a plodding pace.

ABSOLUTELY! .... page 241

The only thing that the artist cannot see is the obvious. The only thing that the public can see is the obvious.

Oscar Wilde

THE POWER OF MUSIC .... page 242

Into an inn entered an innocent nun. Ennui imminent, she intoned an air.

ERSE PHILOSOPHY .... page 243

I don't think there's any point in being Irish if you don't know that the world is going to break your heart eventually.

Daniel Patrick Moynihan

THE CULT OF INCOHERENCE............... page 244

Many a writer seems to think he is not profound unless he himself can't understand what he has put down on paper.

TALISMAN .... page 245

A fool there was and he made his prayer to a rag and a bone and a hank of hair.

Rudyard Kipling

RUBBING IT IN .... page 246

Of all the horrid, hideous notes of woe, sadder than owl-songs or the midnight blast, is that portentous phrase "I told you so."

Lord Byron

ONE-TRACK MIND............... page 247

The plump cook broke the back of the bookkeeper who nevertheless kept asking for coffee.

SOUND PERCEPTION .... page 248

Not many sounds in life, and I include all urban and all rural sounds, exceed in interest a knock at the door.

Charles Lamb

I can not give you the formula for success, but I can give you the formula for failure—which is "Try to please everybody."

Herbert Bayard Swope

Try praising your wife, even if it does frighten her at first.

Billy Sunday

I sneezed a sneeze into the air,
And no one knew from whence or where;
But long and hard were the looks of those,
In whose vicinity I snoze!

The judge should not be young; he should have learned to know evil, not from his own soul, but from long observation. Knowledge should be his guide, not personal experience.

Plato

Not in the clamor of the crowded street,
Not in the shouts and plaudits of the
    throng,
But in ourselves are triumph and defeat.

NATURE, *Henry Wadsworth Longfellow*

An appeal is when you ask one court to show its contempt for another court.

Finley Peter Dunne

Mark how my fame rings out from zone to
    zone;
A thousand critics shouting: "He's
    unknown!"

Ambrose Bierce

Sing me not in mournful dirges, "I am broke! Too many splurges!"

Then, drawing on my fine command of language, I said nothing.

Robert Benchley

He looked at me as if I was a side dish he hadn't ordered.

Ring Lardner

If you cannot catch a bird of paradise, better take a wet hen.

Nikita Khrushchev

(DAVID) VISCOTT
THE LANGUAGE OF FEELINGS

A free person accepts responsibility for the good and. . . . bad in his life. A free person doesn't waste time and energy getting involved in things that can't be changed, but instead focuses on the areas he can affect. . . . He simply defines what his goals are.

A   V EDIC
B   I SSUS
C   S HELLEY WINTERS
D   C HACO CANYON
E   O PHIDIAN
F   T HE BAND WAGON
G   T ARGHEE
H   T ACONITE
I   H AGGARD
J   E STATES
K   L EVEE
L   A PPOSITE
M   N ORMAND
N   G IFFORD PINCHOT
O   U NHITCHED
P   A MBIT

Q	**G** RIFTER
R	**E** DDA
S	**O** SPREY
T	**F** ALSTAFF
U	**F** IFE
V	**E** THANES
W	**E** RSE
X	**L** ASSEN
Y	**I** NTENT
Z	**N** ONES
Z¹	**G** IBBET
Z²	**S** ENSE

ACROSS-TIC No. 2 . . . . page 262

ARTHUR MARX
GOLDWYN: A BIOGRAPHY

The Goldwyn touch was not. . . . sheer brilliance or even good box office. . . . It was an ineffable something that had to do with quality, good taste, and honest and intelligent workmanship. It could be compared to a suit. . . . fashioned from an expensive bolt of material.

A	**A** LICE ADAMS
B	**R** AFFISH
C	**T** AFFETA
D	**H** OOFED
E	**U** LITHI
F	**R** OWED
G	**M** ISPRISION
H	**A** DAMANT
I	**R** IBBED
J	**X** ENON
K	**G** AVOTTE
L	**O** BEAH
M	**L** EXICON
N	**D** AS RHEINGOLD
O	**W** HITLOW
P	**Y** EVTUSHENKO
Q	**N** ETTED
R	**A** CCENTING
S	**B** ALLOTTEMENT
T	**I** NQUEST
U	**O** FFSHOOT
V	**G** ATLING
W	**R** EHOBOAM
X	**A** TTUNE
Y	**P** ONTOON
Z	**H** IS COWARD LIPS
Z¹	**Y** OWLED

ACROSS-TIC No. 3 . . . . page 264

MICHI WEGLYN
YEARS OF INFAMY

I believed, as did most Japanese Amer-

icans, that somehow the stain of dishonor we collectively felt for. . . . Pearl Harbor must be eradicated, however great the sacrifice, however little we were responsible for it. In our immaturity,. . . . many of us believed this was the only way.

A	**M** ARY MARTIN
B	**I** NCISIVE
C	**C** ORDED
D	**H** ORSE FEATHERS
E	**I** MPERATIVE
F	**W** HITE WITH SNOW
G	**E** THER
H	**G** IBBOUS
I	**L** EAVE IT TO ME
J	**Y** EDO
K	**N** OOSE
L	**Y** ESHIVA
M	**E** RECHTHEUM
N	**A** LLOCATE
O	**R** UMORED
P	**S** WALLOWWORT
Q	**O** BJECTED
R	**F** EDERALIST
S	**I** NFILTRATE
T	**N** ACELLE
U	**F** ROSTS AND FASTS
V	**A** PPREHENSIVE
W	**M** OBILE BAY
X	**Y** OUR WIFE WITHAL

ACROSS-TIC No. 4 . . . . page 266

BOB CONSIDINE
IT'S ALL NEWS TO ME

China was America's problem child, exasperating but tolerated, expensive but endured. If any American, in or out of public office at that time, suspected that one day China would be considered a major menace to the welfare of the United States, he held his tongue.

A	**B** ATTEN
B	**O** TTER
C	**B** ALL OF FIRE
D	**C** ACODEMON
E	**O** UT OF FAULTS
F	**N** IDE
G	**S** TADIA
H	**I** VIEW IN THEE
I	**D** IFFUSE
J	**I** MPART
K	**N** OLAN RYAN
L	**E** CCRINE
M	**I** MPEDED
N	**T** HE HAPPY TIME
O	**S** EXTET

P	ADJUNCT
Q	LOUISE BROUGH
R	LEXINGTON
S	NESTED
T	ECBATANA
U	WHEELHOUSE
V	SACCHARIDE
W	TEETER
X	OPHIUCHUS
Y	MACABRE
Z	EDWARD THOMAS

ACROSS-TIC No. 5 . . . . page 268

IVAN ILLICH
MEDICAL NEMESIS

By joining together, consumers do have power to get more for their money; changes in licensing and in modes of financing can protect the population not only against non-professional quacks but also, in some cases, against professional abuse. . . .

A	IATRIC
B	VAGRANT
C	ANYTHING GOES
D	NEPENTHE
E	INTRO
F	LOFOTENS
G	LOOKOUT
H	INJUNCTION
I	CONSONANT
J	HIPPOGRIFF
K	MACCABEES
L	EAGER
M	DON BUDGE
N	ICHTHYOSIS
O	COCONINO
P	AFFORDS NO LAW
Q	LINGUINE
R	NOISELESS TENOR
S	EPERGNE
T	MARSALA
U	EMBASSY
V	SQUAMATE
W	IMPOST
X	SPONSON

ACROSS-TIC No. 6 . . . . page 270

WILLIE SUTTON
WHERE THE MONEY WAS

The thing that really had the police so confused was that I was using so many different disguises. I would dye my hair different colors. I had sideburns which I could paste on. I could make my eyebrows very heavy by intertwining separate little patches of hair.

A	WITTICISM
B	IDLY
C	LHASA
D	LITHOGRAPHY
E	INSIST
F	ELICIT
G	SYMPATHY
H	UNTO THE BREACH
I	TAFFY
J	TANGY
K	OPPRESSIVE
L	NADIR
M	WHITTIER
N	HEDGEROWS
O	EASTON
P	RIDDLED
Q	EURIDICE
R	THE CAINE MUTINY
S	HULL HOUSE
T	EBRO
U	MAKE BELIEVE
V	OFFHAND
W	NOSES
X	EDDA
Y	YOUNGSTOWN
Z	WHIRLAWAY
Z¹	AFFORD
Z²	SUCCESS

HOW SELF-ASSERTIVE
ARE YOU? . . . . page 272

Count the number of A answers you have chosen, the number of B's and of C's. The A's represent introvert reactions, the B's, ambivert or "middling" reactions, while the C's are decidedly extrovert.

If you have six or more A's you probably avoid asserting yourself; six or more B's, you will assert yourself sometimes and at other times, avoid situations that make you come out front; six or more C's, you are a decided extrovert, and achieve your rights and goals.

Now add your A's and B's, and your B's and C's. If your total of A's plus B's is larger than the total of your B's plus C's, you have a rather "middling" temperament with a leaning toward introversion. A larger total of B's plus C's indicates a leaning toward extroversion.

WOULD YOU MAKE A GOOD COUNTER-SPY?............... page 274

1. HASTE MAKES WASTE. Solution: Read the letters backwards. 10 points.

2. THEY SHALL NOT PREVAIL AGAINST THEE. Solution: Reverse the letters of the alphabet. A = Z, B = Y, C = X, etc. 10 points.

3. IN GOD WE TRUST. Solution: Substitute a sequential number for each letter of the alphabet. A = 1; B = 2, C = 3, etc. 10 points.

4. PUT ONLY AMERICANS ON GUARD TONIGHT. Solution: Find the junction of the two numbers on the vertical and horizontal scale to get each letter. 15 points.

5. AMERICA THE BEAUTIFUL. Solution: Each letter of the message is two *back* from the one given in the code. C = A; D = B; G = E, etc. 15 points.

6. MAKE HASTE SLOWLY. Solution: Each letter is represented by the configuration of the "pen" in which it appears. If there is no dot in the code configuration, it indicates the top letter in the designated "pen." The middle and bottom letters in each "pen" are indicated by one and two dots respectively in the code configuration. 30 points.

IF YOU SCORED BETWEEN:

80-90: A brilliant score, showing the mind of a super cryptographer. The maximum score is 90.

60-75: This is above average. You have a natural aptitude for this kind of thinking.

40-55: You are in the average bracket. Very likely, if you had worked longer on these problems you would have scored higher.

20-35: This is not a world-shaking score, but maybe you caught on now and will do better in the future.

0-15: Even if you are on the bottom of the heap on this test, don't worry. Your talents probably lie in other directions.

OBSERVATION TEST............. page 276

1. 10
2. c and e
3. a and e
4. b and f
5. a and e
6. 8
7. d
8. a

9. a
10. c
11. 3
12. 2
13. 2
14. 2
15. 1

ARE YOU VAIN?................ page 279

1. a-10; b-0; c-0. In controlled research, it was found that those who themselves tended to be vain, saw vanity in the picture. Those who were more modest, saw the drawing either as a symbol of friendship or as having no special meaning.
2. Yes-10; No-0.
3. Yes-10; No-0.
4. Yes-10; No-0.
5. Yes-0; No-10.
6. Yes-10; No-0.
7. Yes-0; No-10.
8. Yes-10; No-0.
9. Yes-10; No-0.
10. Yes-10; No-0.

IF YOU SCORED BETWEEN:

80-100: This indicates you use vanity as a shield against your own insecurities. You may primp and preen, name-drop, and flaunt money in an effort to build up your own frail ego and be liked by others. "Vanity keeps persons in favor with themselves who are out of favor with others." (Shakespeare). If you would try concentrating on the other person instead of on yourself, you would begin to find people responding favorably to you.

40-70: This is quite a normal, human score. Most people keep up their self-respect with a certain degree of vanity. "Virtue would not go far if vanity did not keep it company." (Francois Rochefoucauld, French moralist).

0-30: This score sometimes indicates an "I don't care" attitude. However, it suggests you are usually liked because you are not vain. You probably view those who act like "big wheels" with a critical eye.

HOW SOCIABLE ARE YOU?........ page 280

Give yourself points for your answers as follows:

1. If you placed your initials on: the large front block, 8 points; a block in the first bottom row, 4 points; a block in the middle row, 0 points; center block in the

back row, 7 points; any other block in the back row, 6 points.

2. a-6; b-8; c-1; d-5.
3. a-6; b-3.
4. a-2; b-5; c-4.
5. Yes-2; No-1.
6. Yes-4; No-2.
7. Yes-0; No-1.
8. Yes-3; No-2.
9. Yes-2; No-1.
10. Yes-4; No-1.
11. Yes-0; No-2.
12. Yes-2; No-1.
13. Yes-2; No-3.
14. Yes-0; No-1.

IF YOU SCORED BETWEEN:

40-51: You are extremely sociable. Just be careful that in your casual, happy-go-lucky way, you don't spend too much time talking, and not enough time listening.

30-39: This score indicates a gregarious personality, but you can listen if you want to.

23-29: You often prefer to be alone than in the company of others. But you do speak when you have something to say. Words, to you, are a precious commodity.

16-22: You tend to be the silent type, prone to brood. Try to get out and mix more.

HOW DETERMINED ARE YOU? . . . . page 282

1. a-5; b-10; c-0. In studies that were done, testees who evidenced the greatest amount of determination chose the strong bricklike pattern b. A was the choice of those who were well-organized, and enjoyed their own personal growth, but were not as strong-willed as b. C was the choice of those who tended to bend with the "winds of fortune" rather than to buck up against life.
2. a-0; b-10; c-5.
3. a-10; b-5; c-0.
4. a-3; b-0; c-10.
5. a-0; b-5; c-10.
6. a-0; b-3; c-10.
7. a-5; b-0; c-10.
8. a-0; b-5; c-10.
9. a-5; b-0; c-10.
10. a-0; b-10; c-0.

IF YOU SCORED BETWEEN:

80-100: Testees in this bracket showed de-termined traits in their living patterns. They were not always easy to work or to live with, because, to their less deter-mined associates, they sometimes seemed obstinate and bull-headed. "I like a person who knows his own mind and sticks to it; one who sees at once what, in given cir-cumstances, is to be done and does it." (William Hazlitt, English critic).

40-78: This score shows a practical person who knows her abilities and limitations. "I hate to see things done by halves.—If it be right, do it boldly,—if it be wrong, leave it undone." (Bernard Gilpin, English cler-gyman)

0-38: This is the mark of those who usual-ly have little ambition, are easily discour-aged and have no strong motives for their daily actions. "Men must be decided on what they will not do, and then they are able to act with vigor in that which they ought to do." (Mencius, Chinese sage).

HOW WELL-LIKED ARE YOU? . . . . page 284

Give yourself 3 points for each A answer; 1 point for each B answer; 2 points for each C answer. Highest possible score: 42.

IF YOU SCORED BETWEEN:

30-42: People like you very much. You ob-viously have the quality of winning friend-ship and respect. It could be that you sometimes weary of so much attention and applause, of being asked to do everything at all times. For your own sake, you must occasionally relax and let your host of friends take over.

20-29: You are probably thought of as re-liable and likeable. This is a high score and one which is earned by good members of a community with a wholesome family life. You have very few friendship prob-lems.

10-19: You have a few very good friends. "The friends thou hast, grapple to thy soul with hooks of steel." (Shakespeare). It might also be wise to try to expand your list of friends.

0-9: The score of a lonely person. The ap-proval of others can only be gained by your trust in them. You must make the first step, give the handshake. You will be surprised at what will happen!

1. If either line was drawn to hole 3, give yourself 50 points, but no points for the second line. If both lines were drawn to hole 2, give yourself 25 points. All other lines 0 points.

2. A: a-0; b-10; c-4.
   B: a-0; b-10; c-4.
   C: a-10; b-0; c-7.
   D: a-0; b-4; c-10.
   E: a-0; b-10; c-3.
   F: a-5; b-10; c-0.

3. If you initialed block A, give yourself 20 points.

IF YOU SCORED BETWEEN:

100-130: This score indicates that you can be as silent as the Sphinx. You are trustworthy as far as secrets are concerned. People may complain that you are tight-mouthed, but they respect your ability to keep secrets.

60-99: This is an average score. Very probably when someone confides in you, you share a secret with someone else who is close to you, with the admonishment NOT TO TELL.

40-59: You are not a good risk with a secret. You must learn to think before you speak. Those around you know more about you and your friends than they probably want to know because you keep spilling the beans.

0-39: A very low score, which indicates that you are unable to keep a secret. You may even use your own imagination to embellish the facts. See if you can't make an effort to restrain yourself. You may find you enjoy knowing something almost no one else knows.

HOW WELL DO YOU CONCENTRATE?.. page 288

1. 10. The number at the top is subtracted from the number at the left to arrive at the number at the right. 25 points.
2. The letters of the alphabet are sequentially numbered: A = 1; B = 2, C = 3, etc. a. Spain (19-16-1-9-14); b. Italy (9-20-1-12-25). 10 points each.
3. e (November). 5 points.
4. u (Sunday). 5 points.
5. n. 5 points.
6. Blind:did. In the other examples, the

first letter of the first word is the same as the last letter of the last word, and the last letter of the first word is the same as the first letter of the second word. 25 points.

7. A N S W R T U K Z X M L F. 15 points.

8. Form a triangle as illustrated below. 25 points.

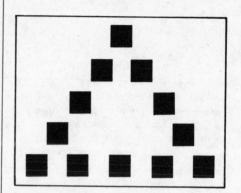

This test requires patient application. If you scored above 60, your powers of concentration are excellent and you are well disciplined. A perfect score is 125.

30-55: A score in this range indicates average ability to concentrate.

0-25: A score below 25 indicates a tendency to stare out the window and fidget at work. It also suggests poor concentration on the problem at hand.

DO YOU FEEL INFERIOR? .... page 290

1. If you chose c or d, you generally wake up feeling it will be another hard day—give yourself 20 points; if you chose d, you're anticipating having to cope with problems— give yourself 7 points; if you chose b, you're not sure what awaits you—give yourself 2 points; if you chose a, you feel things will mesh for you—give yourself 0 points.

2. If you chose a, you clearly don't feel up to it—give yourself 20 points; if you chose b, you're not sure of your ability to do it—15 points; if you chose c or d, you feel grim, but determined—5 points; and if you chose e, you love the challenge, 0 points.

3. a-20; b-5; c-0   5. a-20; b-0; c-10
4. a-20; b-0; c-10   6. a-0; b-10; c-20

7. a-0; b-20; c-8
8. a-20; b-0; c-7
9. a-15; b-8; c-5
10. a-20; b-0; c-0

IF YOU SCORE BETWEEN:

100-195 points: You have the strength of a bowl of jelly. You punish yourself unmercifully with your feelings of inferiority. Make a list of the things you can do. You will be surprised how many items you can name.

60-99 points: You feel secure in some of your activities—but not as much as you might. Probably you sometimes have fearful dreams and an occasional sleepless night. Concentrate on your abilities instead of your shortcomings.

40-59 points: This is an average score. Being human and honest with yourself, you have moments when you feel inadequate. This is healthy, because complete self-satisfaction can stunt personal growth.

0-39 points: Little or no feeling of inferiority in this score, but watch out that you do not appear too cocky.

ARE YOU A PLEASURE TO BE WITH? . . page 292

Give yourself 2 points for each No answer. The questions fall under three separate headings:

1 through 6 are bad habits which you can break with thought and awareness of your actions.

7 through 12 may indicate thoughtlessness, nervousness, fatigue, or self-consciousness. By becoming aware of the cause, you may be able to develop the self-control to change these behaviors.

13 through 18 are concerned with characteristics which are more difficult to control because they stem from the inner you, your basic personality and needs.

IF YOU SCORED BETWEEN:

30-36: You have the appearance of being calm and self-assured, even if you don't always feel that way inside. People like you, in all probability, and you have many close friends and many more acquaintances because you have hardly any annoying habits.

20-28: Since we are all human and imperfect, this is an average rating. However, personal growth keeps us alive, so keep working to eliminate the flaws which annoy others.

10-18: You are very likely a highly nervous person with many things on your mind which disturb you. Why not relax a bit and study the mannerisms of some very calm person whose traits you admire?

0-8: This score falls into the danger zone. Probably you annoy people and they annoy you, thus creating a vicious cycle. To break this cycle, you might seek the help of your mate, close friend, or a counselor.

CROSSWORD PUZZLE NO. 1 . . . . page 294

CROSSWORD PUZZLE NO. 2 . . . . page 295

```
BEVEL SODA  OPAL
ALIVE PRIM  MACE
SATAN IAGO  EIRE
ETA DENT ROLLER
SELL REE OWE
    OAR  VULTURE
PEDAL SPAS    NOD
EVADE HAS  TRIPE
LET  CUTE  WATER
TREASON    GOT
    SUM  AMA ERAL
EMBLEM DASH  ELI
GALE  ETON ALLOT
GLUE  NERO SEINE
STEP  DEER PACER
```

```
TEND SAND  ROAR
HAIR TIER ELVER
ISLE ARROW DATA
STEADY OMAR  LIT
    MISS EYE  ORE
CHASM HAD  DUNES
OUR EMANATES
PETS ADORE  EPIC
    PARODIES ORA
FLOAT WEE  OTTER
LOP ORB  SILO
ICE MOOD REWARD
TANK EXILE  ELIA
STEEP EVEN  ROOM
    EDNA SAGE SETS
```

```
PACE AMID  OWLS
AWAY CONE TREAT
NAPE CONFLUENCE
ERR SOS TAN DEW
LEISURE    SIP
    POND RESCINDS
PLANK FADE  TORO
ION RUNGS  MAR
PATH URGE RIDGE
ENSEMBLE SOME
    WEB  STOPPLE
SHE TEA EAT  LAX
PEPPERMINT  TUBE
AREAS ERSE  AMOR
NEED  SEES  PERT
```

```
CART  MUG  STEP
RATIO TORO  CORE
ATOM PIANO  EARN
ZEN WARN  DENS
EREMITE TWEETER
    ASH PAIRS  LO
BROTH TALLY  PAD
RIPE BETEL  LATE
ANT DANES  VIREO
IS DICES  BIN
DETRACT PANTHER
    HULA RILO  ADO
ARID ROUTE  TRIM
RING ANDY  CRETE
CAKE  TEE  AIMS
```

```
KIT MACAW SCAMP
IDA ADORE LABOR
DEDUCED AFAR  LI
    PEN CREW  LAC
PECOS CASE  FARE
ALAN LOG  TRAM
RIB WAVES AMASS
IT CAPE NAPE  LO
SEWER SCANT  BAD
    IDEA AFT  COMO
PALE PERU CHASM
ABE TENT  LOO
GI AIDA AIRWAYS
ADAGE TENSE  RIA
NEWER EXITS  APT
```

```
CRAM ALAS DEMOS
AUTO MALI EVADE
SLOPE WAN VALOR
TEMPLE NERO  ERG
    EDGY WITS  SE
WANDERED  GETS
ALE REARS SATAN
ITEM TROTS BORE
TODAY SPANS  NEW
    SPED STILLEST
PA SAYS  EPEE
OLA READ SEVERS
SALON FIG  PERIL
EMILE EVER  RITA
DOTED SAME  SEEM
```

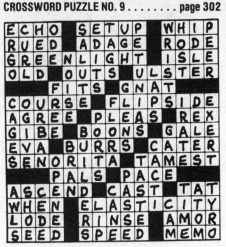

ECHO SETUP WHIP
RUED ADAGE RODE
GREENLIGHT ISLE
OLD OUTS ULSTER
FITS GNAT
COURSE FLIPSIDE
AGREE PLEAS REX
GIBE BOONS GALE
EVA BURRS CATER
SENORITA TAMEST
PALS PACE
ASCEND CAST TAT
WHEN ELASTICITY
LODE RINSE AMOR
SEED SPEED MEMO

GEM FOLIO GRABS
AWE ABASH LATIN
BEND EST HAY SO
RASH GOD YOU
GREASE LAW SENT
RISKS SAY NIL
OGEE HUG COPPER
PO AIM LUG MI
ERRAND YET WEPT
ODD TAD MATTE
SOLO ARM DELAYS
ALL PSI METE
VI AUK BUT SAGE
OVERT EASED ROB
RESTS THERE CAB

VALOR MANE SHOW
ABIDE EVIL CAPE
SLEEP TITFORTAT
TEN LEAD FEELS
FILL SAFE
ATTACK SERENADE
DRAMA DARER WAN
MAKE BRIGS WANT
ICE ALONE FARSE
TENEMENT CAREER
LUBE SAND
ATLAS DINT ROB
PROPELLER ALIVE
SIRS YALE SEDAN
EPEE EDEN YIELD

ARGO BOAR EACH
COOP URGE ARROW
MORE REED STATE
EMENDS DRY VEE
EAT SEA HELD
WORDY SINGLE
EGO CAR LONDON
ERA TAP RAT EVE
PERSON BUN LEE
UNISON BLEND
FILM NEW TOO
ACE PEA HAILED
TIARA RATE TIDE
ENVOY CHAR EVEN
GETS HARE RENT

HAFT MILL OBESE
AGAR IDOL RANEE
RAVE NOVA ORDER
SPOKEN EMU TONY
HER TOT ANTE
POWER DORMER
ALIEN PAPER IRE
PUTT SEVER OMIT
ETE SHEET TRESS
SERAPE NABOB
TALC LEO SSW
SCAT LAS CLAMOR
PANIC RINK BIDE
AGORA OLEO ELAN
TENET MOON LESS

EVEN OGRES CHOP
SINE SLANT HALE
SNOOP ERSE ALEE
EEL ALAE PASTOR
SPIN STIES
HASTEN SPURS GT
ASTER STARS MER
SPEW STAIN WINE
PEP STERN RETIA
SN SAREE DIETED
SEVER WISP
ELEVEN DANE ABA
RAVE GOOD RAVEL
AVER TWEED LIDA
SANE HESSE EDEN

THIS HAS PULL . . . . page 313

1. Agar
2. Agate
3. Agave
4. Agitate
5. Area
6. Aria
7. Attar
8. Attire
9. Aver
10. Avert
11. Aviate
12. Gait
13. Gaiter
14. Gate
15. Gave
16. Gear
17. Grate
18. Grave
19. GRAVITATE
20. Great
21. Irate
22. Rage
23. Rate
24. Ratite
25. Ravage
26. Rave
27. Regatta
28. Riata
29. Tare
30. Target
31. Tart
32. Tear
33. Teat
34. Terai
35. Tiara
36. Trait
37. Treat
38. Triage
39. Vara
40. Variate
41. Virgate
42. Vita
43. Vitta

WAY-OUT . . . . page 314

1. Emir
2. Emit
3. Emmer
4. Emmet
5. Emmets
6. EXTREMISM
7. Immerse
8. Item
9. Items
10. Meet
11. Meets
12. Mere
13. Merit
14. Merits
15. Mete
16. Metes
17. Meter
18. Meters
19. Metier
20. Metis
21. Mime
22. Mimes
23. Mire
24. Miser
25. Mist
26. Mister
27. Mite
28. Mitre
29. Mixer
30. Mixes
31. Remise
32. Remit
33. Remits
34. Rime
35. Seem
36. Simmer
37. Smite
38. Stem
39. Teem
40. Teems
41. Term
42. Terms
43. Time
44. Times
45. Timer
46. Timers
47. Trim
48. Trims

ENCHANTÉ . . . . page 315

1. Admiring
2. Aiding
3. Aiming
4. Airing
5. Arising
6. Arming
7. Daring
8. DISARMING
9. Drag
10. Drags
11. Gain
12. Gains
13. Gird
14. Girds
15. Gradin
16. Grain
17. Grains
18. Gram
19. Grams
20. Grand
21. Grid
22. Grids
23. Grim
24. Grin
25. Grins
26. Grind
27. Grinds
28. Margin
29. Margins
30. Miring
31. Raiding
32. Raising
33. Rang
34. Rasing
35. Riding
36. Rigid
37. Riming
38. Ring
39. Rings
40. Rising
41. Sang
42. Siding
43. Sign
44. Sing
45. Siring
46. Snag

MORAL UPLIFT . . . . page 316

1. Egoist
2. Eight
3. Ergot
4. Ethos
5. Ghost
6. Girt
7. Girth
8. Gist
9. Goiter
10. Gout
11. Grist
12. Grit
13. Grits
14. Grout
15. Guest
16. Gust
17. Guts
18. Hirsute
19. Hoist
20. Hoister
21. Host
22. Hurt
23. Hurts
24. Iter
25. Other
26. Others
27. Ought
28. Oust
29. Ouster
30. Outer
31. Reshot
32. Resit
33. Rest
34. Right
35. RIGHTEOUS
36. Riot
37. Rite
38. Rites
39. Rote
40. Roust
41. Rout
42. Route
43. Routes
44. Rust
45. Ruth
46. Ruts
47. Shirt
48. Short
49. Shot
50. Shout
51. Shut
52. Sight
53. Site
54. Sort
55. Sortie
56. Sought
57. South
58. Stir
59. Stogie
60. Store
61. Suit
62. Suite
63. Suitor
64. Their
65. This
66. Those
67. Thou
68. Throe

69. Throes
70. Thug
71. Thugs
72. Thus
73. Ties
74. Tiger
75. Tire
76. Tires
77. Tiro
78. Toes
79. Togs
80. Tore
81. Torus
82. Tough
83. Tour
84. Tours
85. Tries
86. Trough
87. True
88. Tugs

SECURITY . . . . page 320

1. Aorta
2. Arow
3. Arrant
4. Arrow
5. Narrator
6. Narrow
7. Rant
8. Roan
9. Roar
10. Rota
11. Rowan
12. Tarn
13. Torn
14. Torr
15. Warn
16. Warrant
17. WARRANTOR
18. Wart
19. Worn
20. Wort

DIG THIS . . . . page 318

1. Grip
2. Group
3. Inpour
4. Input
5. Opting
6. Option
7. Pignut
8. Ping
9. Pint
10. Pinto
11. Pion
12. Piton
13. Pogo
14. Point
15. Pong
16. Pongo
17. Poor
18. Poring
19. Port
20. Portion
21. Potion
22. Pour
23. Pouring
24. Pout
25. Pouting
26. Prig
27. Print
28. Prong
29. Pronto
30. Proton
31. Punt
32. Roping
33. Roup
34. Ruption
35. Toping
36. Trip
37. Troop
38. Trooping
39. Turnip
40. Unrip
41. Upon
42. Uproot
43. UPROOTING

SUPPRESSION . . . . page 321

1. Aguish
2. Anguish
3. Assign
4. Gain
5. Gash
6. Gauss
7. Gnash
8. Guan
9. Gush
10. Hang
11. Hung
12. Nigh
13. Quag
14. Quashing
15. Sang
16. Shag
17. Sigh
18. Sign
19. Sing
20. Snag
21. Snug
22. SQUASHING
23. Suing
24. Sung
25. Using

UNDULATION . . . . page 322

1. Cling
2. Clink
3. Clinking
4. CRINKLING
5. Girl
6. Grin
7. Icing
8. Inking
9. Inkling
10. Irking
11. Kiln
12. Kilning
13. King
14. Kinin
15. Lick
16. Licking
17. Lignin
18. Liking
19. Ling
20. Lining
21. Link
22. Linking
23. Nick
24. Nicking
25. Rick
26. Ricking
27. Riling
28. Ring
29. Rink

FOR A CHANGE . . . . page 319

1. Anti
2. Aria
3. Avian
4. Aviation
5. Aviator
6. Into
7. Iota
8. Iron
9. Naira
10. Nitro
11. Ovarian
12. Rain
13. Ratio
14. Ration
15. Ravin
16. Riant
17. Riata
18. Riot
19. Tiara
20. Tiro
21. Train
22. Trio
23. Trivia
24. Vain
25. Variant
26. VARIATION

A TRIFLE . . . . page 323

1. Fitly
2. Flirt
3. Flirty
4. Flit
5. Foil
6. Frit
7. Frivol
8. FRIVOLITY
9. Ivory
10. Lift

11. Oily
12. Rift
13. Rifty
14. Riot
15. Roil
16. Tiro

17. Toil
18. Trio
19. Vilify
20. Viol
21. Vitrify
22. Vitriol

37. Rash
38. Rashly
39. Sail

40. Shaly
41. Slay

NONCHALANCE . . . . page 324

1. Ails
2. Airs
3. Airy
4. Aril
5. Aryl
6. Ashy
7. Fail
8. Fails
9. Fair
10. Fairly
11. Fairs
12. Fairy
13. Falsify
14. Flair
15. Flash
16. Flashy
17. Flay
18. Flays

19. Frail
20. Fray
21. Frays
22. Hail
23. Hails
24. Hair
25. Hairs
26. Hairy
27. Half
28. Lair
29. Lairs
30. Lash
31. Liar
32. Liars
33. Raffish
34. RAFFISHLY
35. Rail
36. Rails

QUINTESSENTIAL . . . . page 325

1. Esquire
2. Ester
3. Queer
4. Querist
5. Quest
6. Quiet
7. Quire
8. Quite
9. Request
10. REQUISITE
11. Requite
12. Requites
13. Reset
14. Resit
15. Rest
16. Retuse
17. Reuse
18. Rise
19. Risque
20. Rite
21. Rites

22. Ruse
23. Seer
24. Sere
25. Sire
26. Site
27. Squire
28. Steer
29. Stere
30. Suer
31. Suet
32. Suite
33. Sure
34. Terse
35. Tier
36. Tiers
37. Tire
38. Tires
39. Tree
40. Trees
41. True
42. User

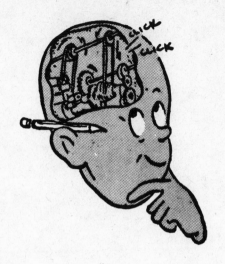